**Illustrator:**
Howard Chaney

**Editor:**
Marsha Kearns

**Editorial Project Manager:**
Ina Massler Levin, M.A.

**Editor in Chief:**
Sharon Coan, M.S. Ed.

**Art Director:**
Elayne Roberts

**Associate Designer:**
Denise Bauer

**Cover Artist:**
Sue Fullam

**Product Manager:**
Phil Garcia

**Imaging:**
Alfred Lau
Ralph Olmedo, Jr.

**Publishers:**
Rachelle Cracchiolo, M.S. Ed.
Mary Dupuy Smith, M.S. Ed.

# Interdisciplinary Unit

# Ancient Egypt

## CHALLENGING

**Author:**

*Michelle Breyer, M.A.*

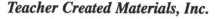

*Teacher Created Materials, Inc.*
P.O. Box 1040
Huntington Beach, CA   92647
**ISBN-1-55734-574-0**

©*1996 Teacher Created Materials, Inc.*         Made in U.S.A.

# Table of Contents

# Table of Contents *(cont.)*

# Introduction

*Ancient Egypt* is an exciting, whole-language, interdisciplinary unit. Its pages are filled with a wide variety of lesson ideas as well as reproducible pages for use with intermediate and middle school students. The ancient Egypt theme is connected to the curriculum with individual, classroom, and cooperative learning activities in reading, language arts (written and oral), science, social studies, math, art, music, and life skills.

This unit is divided into the following sections to allow for easy thematic planning: Geography; Economy, Trade, and Transportation; Science and Achievement; Education and the Arts; Religion; Government; Society and Family; and Literature Connection: *The Golden Goblet*. The lessons are designed so that they can be used in conjunction with social studies and science textbooks.

This interdisciplinary unit includes the following:

- Bulletin Board and Transparency Ideas—provide motivational, interactive, and informative ideas

- Curriculum Connections—incorporate skills in math, science, language arts, fine arts, and social studies

- Visual and Performing Arts—create opportunities for students in the areas of art, architecture, construction, drama, and music

- Whole-Language Experiences—offer a wide variety of reading techniques, ideas for writing passages and poetry, and oral language activities

- Group Projects and Activities—foster cooperative learning strategies and critical thinking skills

- Moments in Time—transport students back in time through reading selections, readers theater, and reenactments

- Living History—A Day in Ancient Egypt—provides research ideas, activities, and suggestions for re-creating a day in the life of the Ancient Egyptians

- Literature Connection: *The Golden Goblet*—a book and activities related to the theme

- Technology—suggests uses of technology that can be integrated throughout the unit and correlated with the theme

- Bibliography—lists additional materials related to the theme

## Moments in Time—Readers Theater Center

Each section has an informative and enjoyable read-aloud play or narrative about Ancient Egypt. Through reenactment, students will experience "going back in time." Reproduce a script for each student so they can participate and/or read along as the plays or narratives are presented orally to the class. Use the scripts as a springboard for introducing and discussing how the Ancient Egyptians lived. Vocabulary and comprehension activities further understanding and knowledge of this important civilization.

# Historical Developments in Ancient Egypt

In order for students to grasp the significance and magnitude of the span of time Ancient Egypt encompasses and how long ago it existed, this lesson provides an overview of the historical developments within broad time periods.

## Preparing for the lesson:

1. Students will work in cooperative groups. Reproduce the Chart of Ancient Egypt's History (pages 6–8) for each group.

2. Gather five pieces of 12" x 18" (30 cm x 46 cm) white construction paper, crayons or colored pencils, scissors, a black marker, and tape for each group.

## Teaching the lesson:

1. Elicit from students how long the United States as a country has lasted. (From the first English settlement in 1607 at Jamestown through today is almost 400 years.) Brainstorm with the class cultural and technological advances that have occurred in that time and some of the famous people they know about. Also elicit that many of the basic elements in our life, such as mathematics, medicine, government, education, and religion, actually began with other civilizations.

2. Tell students that Ancient Egypt began 5,000 years ago and lasted for nearly 4,000 years—ten times longer than civilization in what is now the United States has existed. Ask them to imagine how many changes could have occurred in that span of time. Have students generate a list of people and things they know about Egypt. Write it on the chalkboard.

3. Tell students that Ancient Egypt is one of the earliest civilizations and elicit that these people must have had to invent or refine many of the things that we take for granted, such as tools, building, measuring, medicine, etc. Tell students that in this unit they will learn more about the people, events, and achievements of this important ancient culture and civilization.

4. Tell the class that they will create a time line showing the major people and developments in each Ancient Egyptian period.

5. Divide the class into cooperative groups and distribute the materials. Have the groups divide up tasks so everyone is working. Tell students to follow the directions at the top of page six of the chart to create their time lines.

6. Be sure you read and understand the directions on the six so you can circulate around the room and help as needed. Hang the completed time lines on a wall or bulletin board, and label them "Ancient Egypt."

# Chart of Ancient Egypt's History

**Directions:** Divide the tasks among students in your group so you can all work at the same time. Use the materials your teacher provides.

1. Starting at a short end of a piece of construction paper, fold it into 8 equal horizontal bars or pleate. Each pleat will be about 2" (5 cm) long.

2. Make an Ancient Egypt time line by labeling the pleats in 100-year spans. Label the first pleat 3000 B.C., the second one 2900 B.C., etc., until you get to A.D. 700. (Remember that B.C. dates move back in time and A.D. dates move forward.)

3. Tape the pleated papers together to form a complete time line.

4. Cut apart the period blocks on the chart (pages 6–8) and color each one a different color.

5. On the time line, color the span of time each period covered in the same color as the period chart. Estimate where one period ends and another begins within a 100-year span (pleat).

6. Glue the period blocks onto the time line in the appropriate place. Display the time line in your classroom.

## The Archaic Period
## Ruler of Two Lands—3000 B.C.–2700 B.C.

- King Menes (Narmer) unifies Upper (white crown) and Lower (red crown) Egypt.
- Memphis becomes the capital of Egypt.
- People begin using hieroglyphics to write.
- The earliest known textbook about surgery is written.
- Achievements include using stone masonry in burial chambers, using baking pots and bricks in kilns, and building irrigation and drainage ditches.

## Old Kingdom
## Age of the Pyramid Builders—2700 B.C.–2180 B.C.

- The first pyramid, the step pyramid, is built for King Zoser (Djoser) near Memphis by his chief advisor, Imhotep.
- The Great Pyramid of Giza and the Sphinx are built for King Khufu (Cheops).
- Egyptians travel into and settle Nubia.
- The god Re becomes important.
- King (pharaoh) is believed to enjoy eternal life.
- Achievements include adoption of the 365-day calendar, boat building, wood and stone sculpture, art, literature, and embalming.

## First Intermediate Period
## 2180 B.C.–2133 B.C.

- Government breaks down. Egypt is divided into many small, warring kingdoms, each with a different ruler.
- Pyramids, tombs, statues, and temples are looted and destroyed.

# Chart of Ancient Egypt's History *(cont.)*

## The Middle Kingdom
## Two Lands Reunited—2133 B.C.–1633 B.C.

- Egypt is reunified by Theban rulers. The empire moves farther into Nubia.
- Trade increases with Syria and Mesopotamia.
- Cataracts are built along the Nile to provide trading posts and fortresses.
- A canal is built connecting the Nile River to the Red Sea.
- The gods Amon and Osiris are worshiped by many.
- The earliest schools are established.

## Second Intermediate Period
## 1633 B.C.–1567 B.C.

- Egypt is conquered by Hysksos and Asiatic people, whose overthrow creates many different rulers.
- The Hysksos introduce the horse drawn chariot, the use of bronze, new weapons, and improved spinning and weaving techniques.

## The New Kingdom
## Age of a Powerful Empire—1567 B.C.–1085 B.C.

- Egypt dominates the Ancient World. Thebes becomes the capital of Egypt.
- Thutmose I–IV rule, expanding Egypt's domination south throughout Nubia and Kush.
- Gold, slaves, and other African commodities such as ivory, ebony, ostrich feathers, and perfumes become key elements of Egyptian economy.
- Queen Hapshepsut reigns as the first female pharaoh. During her rule Egyptians create the famous obelisks and other beautification projects.
- King Amenhotep IV introduces the worship of only one god, Aten. He moves the capital to Akhetaton (Tell-el-Amarna) and changes his name to Akhenaten. He marries the famous and beautiful Queen Nefertiti.
- Prince Tutankhaton marries one of Akhenaten's daughters. Once Akhenaten dies, Tutankhaton becomes king and changes his name to Tutankhamen. He abandons the worship of only one god and restores Egypt to polytheism. He moves the capital back to Thebes.
- Kings Ramses I–XII rule Egypt, but their power is declining. Ramses II builds Abu Simbel and other great temples in Nubia.

# Chart of Ancient Egypt's History *(cont.)*

## The Late Period
## A Time of Foreign Rulers—1085 B.C.–332 B.C.

- Egypt's power declines. Kush becomes strong and conquers Egypt. Egyptian religion and government deteriorate.

- The Assyrians invade Egypt. Greece helps Egypt regain independence.

- The Greeks explore and trade with Egypt.

- Crafts, especially metalwork, flourish.

- The Persians invade and conquer Egypt. The Greeks help liberate Egypt again.

## The Graeco-Roman Period (Ptolemaic Period)
## The End of Egyptian Culture—332 B.C.– A.D. 641

- Alexander the Great from Greece conquers Egypt and establishes Alexandria as the capital and learning center.

- Ptolemy Soter, one of Alexander's generals, founds the Ptolemaic line of 15 rulers that ends with Cleopatra.

- Cleopatra, the last Egyptian queen, attempts to gain power for Egypt with the help of Julius Caesar of Rome. Caesar is killed by Romans who fear he is giving Roman power to Egypt.

- The Roman Provenances are divided between Caesar's friend Mark Antony (who some believe was Caesar's son) and Caesar's nephew Octavian.

- Mark Antony falls in love with Cleopatra and takes control of land to the east, including Egypt. He and Cleopatra marry and live in Egypt.

- Octavian, now known as Augustus Caesar, wants all of the Roman territories. He defeats and kills Mark Antony. In love and grief, Cleopatra kills herself with a poisonous snake.

- Egypt comes under Roman rule. Christianity becomes the main religion.

- Egypt becomes a Muslim nation under the rule of Arabs and the Islam religion.

# Comparison Chart

Make a chart out of two pieces of tagboard to use throughout this unit and with future units on ancient civilizations. Use a black marker and index cards to write down the information for each category. Tape the card onto the chart when studying the category. Use a different color of index cards for each civilization.

## Comparison Chart

|  | Middle East | Egypt | Greece | Rome |
|---|---|---|---|---|
| Geography |  |  |  |  |
| Science/Achievements |  |  |  |  |
| The Arts |  |  |  |  |
| Education |  |  |  |  |
| Religion |  |  |  |  |
| Government |  |  |  |  |
| Economy/Trade/Transportation |  |  |  |  |
| Society/Family |  |  |  |  |

## Picture Dictionary

When you start the unit, give each student a large resealable plastic bag and large blank white index cards. Tell students that they will create a picture dictionary of words they learn as you work through the unit. Explain that you will write the words on the chalkboard, and they will copy each word onto a card. They will research the words and write a definition. Then they will draw a picture. At the end of the unit, they will put the cards in alphabetical order, punch holes in the left margin, create a cover, and bind their dictionary with metal rings or yarn. You may wish to ask students to provide index cards, since they will need a large number of them. You might wish to encourage students to be thorough, by telling them they will be able to use their dictionaries on the unit test.

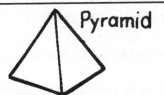

Pyramid—huge structure with square base and four triangular sides that meet in a point at the top and built from limestone. Pyramids were used as tombs for the burial of pharaohs during the Old Kingdom. The largest pyramid is at Giza.

## Using Videos

Motivate students and enhance their awareness by showing videos about Egypt. Check your local library for video tapes about the Nile, mummies, pyramids, Egyptian mythology, and other relevant topics. Note: Old movies such as Elizabeth Taylor in *Cleopatra* may be too long and tedious for students. You should preview and show only appropriate sections to your students. Remind students that these movies are Hollywood's version of history and, therefore, probably are not very accurate or authentic.

# Saba the Farmer

| **Narrators 1–8** | **Saba,** the farmer | **Mara,** his wife | **Setu,** his friend |
|---|---|---|---|
| **Nebu,** his son | **Hada,** his friend | **Tika,** his daughter | **Ptah,** a peasant |

**Narrator 1:** Ancient Egyptian life centered around the life-giving waters of the **Nile,** the longest river in the world. Many other African rivers and marshlands feed into it on its 4,150-mile journey northward to the **Mediterranean Sea.** As the river approaches the sea, it comes to a head, where it divides into many small channels and streams that form a triangle of marshy land called a **delta.**

**Narrator 2:** In ancient times, the delta contained seven mouths, or flows, that emptied into the sea. Today there are two main mouths—the Rosetta on the west and the Demietta on the east. Cairo, the capital city of modern Egypt, sits at the head of the delta. Listen now, as we go back in time to Ancient Egypt to hear the story of one farmer who lives and works along the banks of this great river.

**Saba:** Hello. My name is Saba, and I am a humble farmer who works the land to provide for my family. I live in a small village north of Thebes, the capital of Egypt. My village is very near the Nile, in the area known as the **fertile valley.** All of us who live in Egypt, from the poorest peasant to our wealthy king, the pharaoh, depend upon the Nile. My friends Setu and Hada will help explain why the river is so important to us.

**Setu:** If you look at a map of Egypt, you can see that most of the land is desert. The Arabian Desert to the east and the Libyan Desert to the west are both part of the Sahara, a vast desert that covers much of northern Africa. Few people live in these desert regions because crops will not grow. Indeed, the only land with soil able to grow crops lies along the banks of the Nile. This narrow strip of land is what Saba referred to as the fertile valley.

**Hada:** The fertile valley replenishes its rich soil each year when the Nile floods. We consider the flooding an annual miracle. Without it, we would be unable to farm, for the land would be barren desert like the rest of Egypt. In gratitude we worship H'apy, the god of the Nile, who provides us with food and is the creator of all good.

**Saba:** Some years there are "high Niles." During these years, crops grow well and there is plenty to eat. In other years, the flood waters are low. The fields are baked by the sun, dry out, and are worthless for planting. If several years of low water occur in a row, we cannot grow enough food, and people starve.

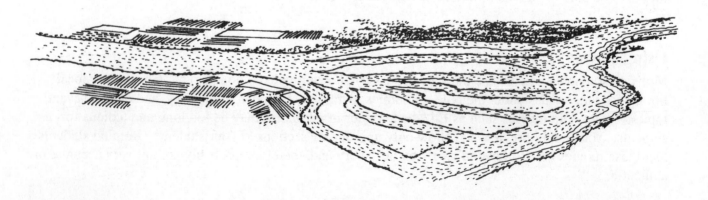

# Saba the Farmer *(cont.)*

**Setu:** When Egypt was suffering through seven years of famine because of low flooding, King Zoser from the Old Kingdom turned to his advisor Imhotep for help. Imhotep said they needed to learn the name of the Nile god who controlled the floodgates so they could ask him to send more water to Egypt. It was believed that the god of the Nile slept in two caverns below a temple at the southern tip of Egypt. Then the Nile god, H'apy, came to King Zoser in a dream and said he would flood the land if the people would worship him. King Zoser made it so, and a high Nile ended the famine. Later, Imhotep furthers the fame of King Zoser by building the first pyramid in Egypt for him.

**Narrator 3:** Egypt gets almost no rain. The myth of King Zoser was a way for people to feel they could influence their fate. We now know that the right weather conditions must occur in other parts of Africa for the Nile to flow and flood. At the end of winter, snow on the mountains of central Africa melts and runs into the small tributaries that feed the Nile. Spring rains are followed by summer monsoons, swelling the Nile and its tributaries. Join us as we walk through the farmlands before the flooding begins in early August.

**Nebu:** Hello, Father and friends! I am working hard to finish the harvest and repair the farming equipment and irrigation canals. As you know, we cannot predict when the flooding will begin. I am hoping the yearly inundation will not be too little or too great. If the waters do not rise high enough, some farm land will remain barren. If the flooding is too great, our **irrigation system**, our home, and other buildings may be damaged.

**Saba:** We were fortunate to have a high Nile last year, and our crops were bountiful, as you can see. The floodwaters carried great amounts of alluvium, or silt, which greatly enriched our soil when the flooding receded. We can only hope it is the same this year. We will keep an eye on the Nilometer.

**Narrator 4:** A **Nilometer** is a measuring device used to help predict the height of the coming flood waters. Notches are made along the stone walls of the Nile channels to mark previous flood levels. Priests read the water level at the beginning of the year and compare it to an average year. This comparison allows people along the banks to decide whether or not they need to move their houses and livestock to higher ground and to better prepare for the planting season.

**Nebu:** Father, your workers are preparing the land for the flooding. Please check that they correctly dig the **channels** from the river that form our irrigation system. I will then make sure that they are cleaned out properly so water can run through them with ease. I believe Ptah is helping build an earthen **dike**.

**Saba:** Hello, Ptah. How is the work progressing under this hot sun?

# Saba the Farmer *(cont.)*

**Ptah:** Greetings, Saba! The work is difficult, but if you are prepared and have a good growing season, it benefits us all. The many dikes or dams we build will hold the water when the floods start receding. They must be in good working order. It will be too late to repair or rebuild them once the inundation has begun. During the flooding, the channels are opened. They are closed once the river has reached its maximum height. The checkerboard of fields can then be drained or irrigated as needed during the rest of the year. This is a very complicated system in which every member of the village community plays a role. I am doing my part.

**Narrator 5:** Like Ptah, most of the men who work for Saba are peasants. However, he also has a few male slaves who help on the farm and some female slaves who work in their house with his wife. They are treated well in exchange for hard work, loyalty, and honesty. Slaves who have worked diligently for a long time are sometimes given their freedom.

**Saba:** Let us go to my house. I believe Mara is working with the slaves to weave some of the **flax** from the harvest. Tika is also there, sorting the grains to preserve seeds for planting and to store those we will use for food.

**Narrator 6:** Saba and his friends head toward his house, a structure of sun-dried bricks. The walled courtyard contains silos of grain. They pass some herds of animals and enter the courtyard where Tika is sorting grains at the silos. Geese and goats roam freely and eat grain that slaves provide. On the upper deck under a thatched roof, Mara weaves on a loom. She comes down to greet her husband and guests and sends a slave girl for refreshments.

**Mara:** Greetings, husband and honored guests. How are things in the fields?

**Saba:** It is hot and laborious work preparing for the inundation. But we had a bountiful harvest.

**Mara:** Yes. We grew a variety of crops this year. Wheat and barley are being ground to make the bread and beer you enjoy with your meals. The flax harvest was abundant. Even after discarding the older plants whose fibers are too tough to weave, we had plenty of young plants to provide us supple fibers for cloth and sitting mats. We will soon make ropes and heavier fabric to use in the fields.

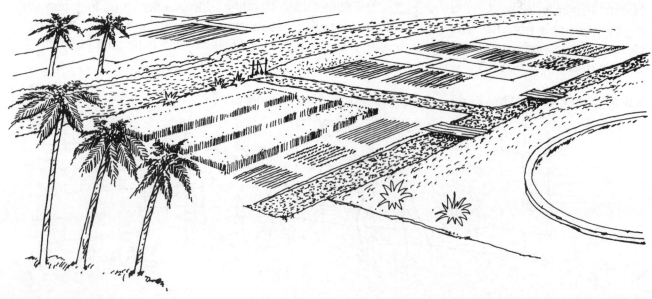

# Saba the Farmer *(cont.)*

**Saba:** Ah, here are the refreshments. Tika, come join us. Mara, send someone to fetch Nebu. It isn't often we have guests in the middle of the day.

**Setu:** I understand you also have a garden near your home.

**Mara:** Yes. Our house has been built far enough away from the river to be out of reach of the flooding, but irrigation channels have been dug so that there is a supply of water to the house and garden. We grow different fruits and vegetables in the garden, and I am especially proud of our vineyard. Most of the grapes are used for making wine, although we pick some for the table. You are eating some that have been dried into raisins. We also grew the figs and dates you are enjoying.

**Tika:** It is so pleasant sitting here overlooking the fields. Every season brings something new and exciting. I like the way we divide the seasons so that they are not based on climate but on the flooding of the Nile.

**Narrator 7:** The Ancient Egyptian year begins in June, and there are three seasons. The first season is known as **shait, or the season of inundation**. From the middle of July through October the waters of the Nile rise, bringing with them the precious silt that makes the soil fertile.

**Tika:** Shait is my favorite time of the year. There is not much work on the farm when our fields are flooded. I like to go to the banks of the Nile and watch as the farmers float blocks of limestone across the swollen river to use for pyramids for the pharaoh. It seems like hard and dangerous work.

**Saba:** I, too, enjoy the season of inundation and look forward to the months ahead. During these months I travel by boat to check my fields and arrange other work. Sometimes the tops of the dikes remind me of a well-traveled roadway running through the water and leading me to a new adventure in trading, bartering, and meeting new people. I may even be commissioned to help with one of the pharaoh's special building projects.

**Nebu:** I prefer the time of the year when the water starts to recede. During **piruit, the season of emergence**, the soil is ready for planting. This brings much work but also many new possibilities. The channels will be filled with water, and we will plant a new series of crops.

# Saba the Farmer *(cont.)*

**Narrator 8:** The planting is not easy work. First, the soil must be broken up. They used a plow called a mattock. The soil can be very heavy after the flooding, and the plowman must be strong to keep the blade down as it cuts. Then the farmers scatter barley or wheat seeds over the field, and they are plowed under. Finally, a herd of goats or sheep will be driven over the field so that their hooves can firmly embed the seed into the ground.

**Nebu:** Once the crops are sown, we move on to land farther away from the river. This is the first soil to dry out, and so we must make sure that the channels and ditches that carry water to this land later in the year are clear of any debris, such as trees or branches.

**Narrator 9:** Sometimes farmers use a **shaduf** to raise the water over the Nile's bank to the higher level of the channels. A shaduf is a type of lever made from a pole on a pivot. There is a clay weight on one end that balances a bucket on the other end. It makes it easier for farmers to collect water from the river to pour into the irrigation channels.

**Nebu:** From October through February we will care for our plants as they grow. This is an exciting time of the year when we see whether new irrigation and planting techniques have been successful.

**Hada:** Nebu will make a fine proprietor of your lands, Saba, once the great gods carry your body off to the afterworld. Although there is great satisfaction in watching crops grow, there can also be problems. Birds and insects are a continual hazard. In my own fields I often have small boys make noises to frighten the winged beasts away. Sometimes we try to catch birds with a flaxen net. We then kill them for food. Insects are a different matter. What can you do?

**Setu:** Nebu and Tika were too young to remember the devastation caused by the plague of **locusts**. The whole sky was blackened by the insects, and they ate everything in their path.

**Saba:** And storms and gales can also damage a crop beyond repair. However, despite all of these difficulties, it is rare that my land doesn't provide more than enough for my family to eat—and even provide a surplus that I can sell. The land of Egypt truly is the gift of the Nile.

**Hada:** That is why I like **shemu, the season of harvest**, when the crops are gathered by all members of the family and great feasts are planned. Watching the ripe grain being cut by the reapers swinging their curved wooden sickles with flint teeth is almost like watching a dance.

# Saba the Farmer *(cont.)*

**Narrator 10:** Harvested grain is taken to the threshing floor where oxen trample the stalks, leaving chaff and grain that workers will winnow, using wooden trays. As the workers throw the grain and chaff into the air, the chaff blows away and leaves the precious grain behind. Donkeys carry it to the granaries and family silos. From February until the end of May, everyone is busy harvesting and selling their wares. This is the time of the year when the Nile is at its lowest.

**Saba:** Yes, and the time for getting another visit from the tax assessors, eh? I always make sure that my land is well marked with clear boundaries. This is an urgent task once the flooding has receded. Later the tax assessors will come to estimate the yield of my crop so they can calculate the taxes that have to be paid. Then, during the harvest, they return to collect my tax payment. Many is the time that I have seen disputes as landowners argued over the boundary or title of the land once the tax assessor arrived. Sometimes I pity the assessors, for they are often harassed and their lives made difficult. No one likes to give away part of their crops as a tax payment.

**Mara:** I feel truly thankful for all of the gifts the Nile brings to our family. Not only does it provide rich soil for growing crops but it also gives us fish and fowl for our table. The Nile nurtures **papyrus**, the long, thin reed that grows wild along the riverbanks. Saba and Nebu use it to build boats. I use papyrus to make baskets, sandals, and lightweight paper. How fortunate Egypt is to be the sole provider of this valuable and sought-after writing medium.

**Tika:** And don't forget how useful the Nile is for transportation and trading. The Nile is Egypt's main highway. In six places cataracts have been built to fill the river full of rocks. This creates ports for trade since it slows down the boats and makes it difficult to travel.

**Saba:** Yes, and the Nile also provides us transportation to the afterworld. During the funeral processions to the Valley of the Kings, the deceased and his possessions are floated across the Nile to be buried in a secret tomb. It is truly amazing, the number of ways our lives depend upon and benefit from this marvelous river.

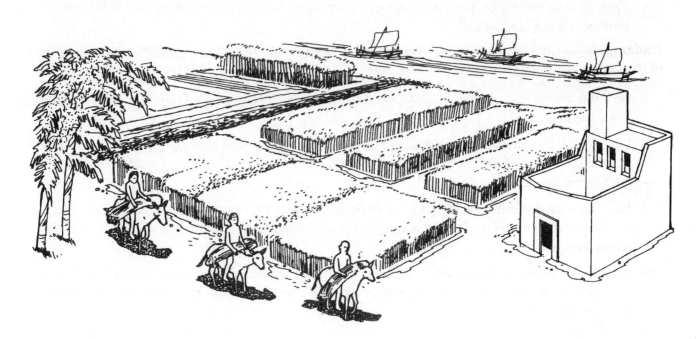

# Saba the Farmer—Vocabulary and Comprehension

Write the following words on the chalkboard for students to copy on index cards for their picture dictionary. Remind them to research and write a complete definition, explanation, or example and draw a picture.

| | | |
|---|---|---|
| Nile | delta | flax |
| irrigation system—channels, dikes | Nilometer | papyrus |
| shait, the season of inundation | piruit, the season of emergence | fertile valley |
| shemu, the season of harvest | Mediterranean Sea | locusts |
| cataracts | shaduf | |

Use some or all of the following questions for whole-class discussion, small-group work, or individual written assessment. Allow students to refer to *Saba the Farmer* to answer them.

1. Why does Egypt have so much fertile soil? *(from the annual flooding of the Nile)* What is inundation? *(flooding)*

3. Why does the Nile flood, and how does the flooding affect all aspects of Egyptian life? *(The Nile floods because of rain and snowmelt in other parts of Africa. When the flooding occurs, farmers can no longer work their fields. Instead they work on building projects for the pharaoh and use the swollen river for transportation and trading expeditions. The floods deposit fertile silt that revitalizes the soil.)*

4. How did the Egyptians divide the year? How is this different from our seasons? *(They divided it into the three phases of the Nile—shait, the season of inundation or flooding; piruit, the season of emergence or time for planting; and shemu, the season of harvest when the Nile is at its lowest level and crops are ready to pick. Our four seasons are based on the sun and climate changes.)*

5. Name at least three tools used in farming or irrigation. *(any three—plow, shovel, Nilometer, mattock, shaduf, and sickle)*

6. What were some of the dangers to crops? *(too much or too little water, birds, locusts and other insects, and storms)*

7. How did the cataracts affect the transportation of goods? *(They created ports for trade by slowing down the boats.)*

8. Describe an Egyptian irrigation system. *(It is a series of channels that run from the river onto the farmland. Shadufs raise water into the channels. Dikes control the flow of water to different portions of the fields.)*

9. Name at least three gifts of the Nile. *(any three—fertile soil, water, papyrus, food crops, flax for clothing and other items, fish and water fowl to eat, transportation, trade, and help for building the pyramids)*

10. Why was papyrus so significant to the Egyptians? *(Egypt was the only area able to produce and provide it to others, which meant it provided a good income because it was much in demand by many people.)*

16

# Make a Map

Refer to a map of Egypt to color and label the map on this page, using the guidelines given. Make a map key to show what the colors and symbols represent.

## Color and label these geographical features:

Mediterranean Sea (blue)

Red Sea (blue)

Nile River (blue)

Nile Delta (brown)

Arabian Desert (yellow)

Libyan Desert (yellow)

Fertile Valley (green)

cataracts (red)

## Label these regions:

Upper Egypt

Lower Egypt

Nubia

## Locate these cities with a star and label them:

Cairo

Heliopolis

Giza

Memphis

Akhetaton (Tell el Amarna)

Abydos

Thebes

Luxor

Valley of the Kings

Aswan

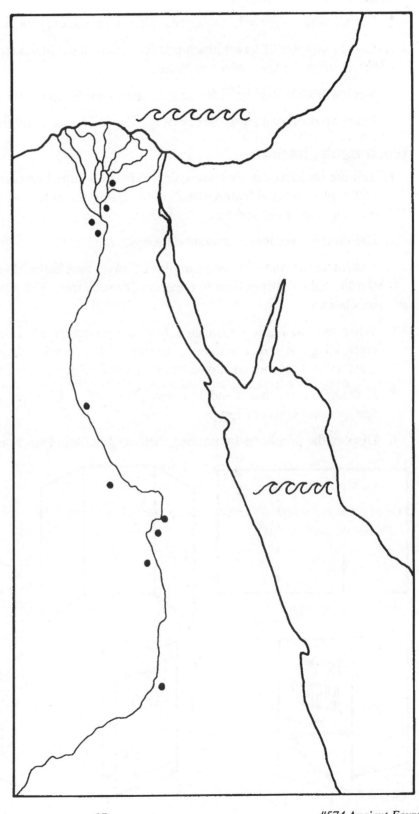

# Make a Travel Brochure and Commercial

After students have made their maps of Egypt on page 17, divide the class into cooperative groups to create travel brochures and commercials for Egypt.

## Preparing for the lesson:

1. Gather white tagboard, magazines, glue, scissors, crayons, and markers for each group.

2. Gather samples of travel brochures for different countries from a local travel agency for students to get ideas for their own brochures.

3. Review how to use the video camera and recorder to videotape the commercials.

4. Make an overhead transparency of the Egyptian cities and their descriptions (page 19).

## Teaching the lesson:

1. Tell the students that they are going to make a large tagboard travel brochure that highlights some of Egypt's physical features and cities. Using the overhead transparency, review the Egyptian cities and their desciptions.

2. Divide the class into cooperative groups.

3. Distribute the materials and samples of travel brochures. Direct students to fold the tagboard into thirds. Allow groups time to create their brochures. Tell students to decorate all six sides of the brochure.

4. When the brochures are finished, have the groups create a one- to three-minute commercial convincing the audience to come to Egypt. If desired, videotape the commercials. Students may need a day to gather costumes and props before performing their commercials for the class.

5. Evaluate the brochures and commercials based on how well the students conveyed the physical features and sights of Egypt.

6. Display the brochures by pinning them to a bulletin board or standing them on a table.

# The Ancient Cities of Egypt

| City | Description |
|---|---|
| **Cairo** | The modern capital of The United Arab Republic, in Egypt, on the Nile. The national museum here contains the most expansive collection of Egyptian antiquities. |
| **Heliopolis** | Known as the City of the Sun, this city also came to be known for the many obelisks flanking its temple doors. There are only three obelisks still standing in Egypt today. One is in Heliopolis. |
| **Giza** | A city famous for its pyramids and the Sphinx. The largest pyramid ever built was for King Khufu (Cheops) and covers 13 acres. Archaeologists believe it took over 100,000 men to build this pyramid, and the work may have lasted for over 20 years. Pyramids were built in this region only during the Old Kingdom. |
| **Memphis** | The capital of Ancient Egypt during the Old Kingdom. It was always an important city, even after the capital was moved to Thebes. This city was sacred to the god Ptah. |
| **Akhetaton (Tell el Amarna)** | Built by King Akhenaten when he moved the Egyptian capital here from Thebes during the New Kingdom. It is the home of a magnificent temple honoring his god, Aten, who looked like a sun with many extended arms. The famous statue of Queen Nefertiti, Akhenaten's wife, was found here. |
| **Abydos** | A place in Middle Egypt, the mythical tomb of Osiris was located here. Since Osiris is the god of the Dead and rules over the afterworld, thousands of people came here to worship in hopes of assuring themselves eternal life. |
| **Thebes** | The capital of Ancient Egypt and center of the great Egyptian Empire during the height of its power in the time of the New Kingdom. Two obelisks still stand in Thebes. One of the obelisks was built by Queen Hapshepsut to honor the god Amon-Re. It is made of Aswan granite, and its pyramid-shaped top was once covered with precious metals to reflect the sun's rays. |
| **Luxor** | This modern city sits on the ancient site of Thebes. Luxor boasts the famous temple of Karnak—huge because for centuries each pharaoh would add buildings to the temple as a tribute to the gods. |
| **Valley of the Kings** | Located west of Thebes, this is where many pharaohs were secretly buried in tombs carved into rock. King Tut's tomb was discovered here by Carter and Carnarvon. Although the young pharaoh was not a significant ruler, his tomb was the first discovered that was virtually untouched by tomb robbers. |
| **Aswan** | Here, 600 miles from Cairo, modern Egyptians have built a large dam to control the Nile. |

# News on the Nile

Have students write newspaper articles and create news programs to report on the conditions and activities during the three Egyptian seasons.

## Preparing for the lesson:

1. Gather other resources, such as books and encyclopedias, that describe the seasons and the cultural activities special to each.

2. Provide samples of newspaper articles for students to use for ideas about format, writing style, headings, quotations, etc.

## Teaching the lesson:

1. Divide the class into three groups and assign each group a season. Have each student write an individual article but work with others as a group to create a news broadcast. Tell students to imagine that they are reporters with the local newspaper. The editor has asked them to tour the land and each write a short news article regarding the local conditions and activities.

2. Have student groups research the season they have chosen. On the chalkboard, write the following as guidelines for information students are to include in their articles:

   - the weather conditions
   - the state of the fertile valley
   - the irrigation system conditions
   - workers' activities

   - a heading and a picture with a caption
   - quotes from local inhabitants
   - information on water wildlife

3. Distribute sample newspaper articles and have students write rough drafts of their article. Have students proofread their drafts. Then, assign writing the final draft as homework. Have students design and write their articles in the newspaper style—columns, heads, pictures, captions. Allow them to refer to *Saba the Farmer* as they write.

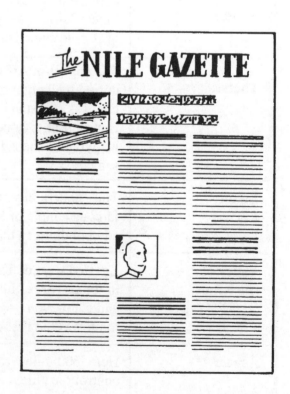

4. The next day, have groups meet and share their articles. Have each group prepare a news broadcast about their season to perform for the class. The broadcast may have anchor people, reporters on location, interviews with local inhabitants, etc. They may wish to insert a commercial promoting the season.

5. Allow time for students to organize their broadcast, practice, and gather costumes and props.

6. Have students perform their new broadcasts for the class. Evaluate how effectively students are able to convey the conditions and activities for their season.

# Farming the Land

Read the passage below, written by a farmer who lived 3,500 years ago. He tells his sons how to farm their fields. The passage was found in Nippur in 1950 on a stone tablet only three inches wide (7.5 cm) and four and one-half inches long (11.25 cm).

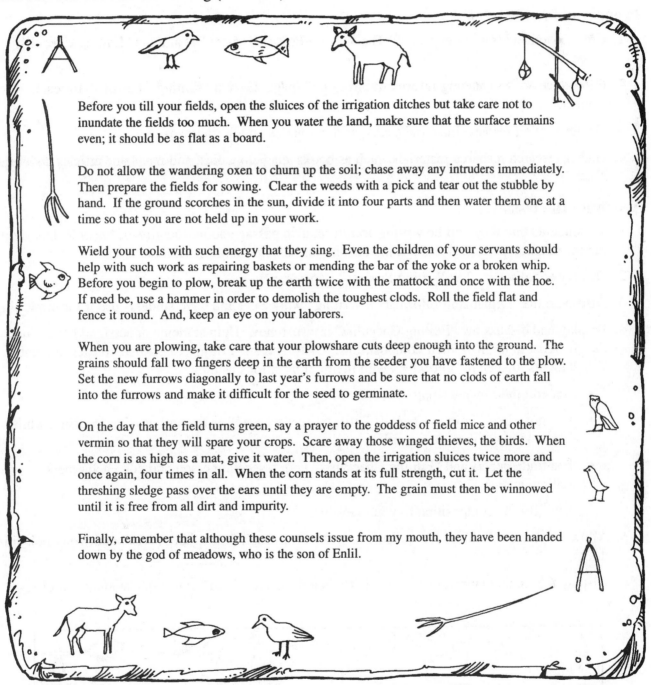

Before you till your fields, open the sluices of the irrigation ditches but take care not to inundate the fields too much. When you water the land, make sure that the surface remains even; it should be as flat as a board.

Do not allow the wandering oxen to churn up the soil; chase away any intruders immediately. Then prepare the fields for sowing. Clear the weeds with a pick and tear out the stubble by hand. If the ground scorches in the sun, divide it into four parts and then water them one at a time so that you are not held up in your work.

Wield your tools with such energy that they sing. Even the children of your servants should help with such work as repairing baskets or mending the bar of the yoke or a broken whip. Before you begin to plow, break up the earth twice with the mattock and once with the hoe. If need be, use a hammer in order to demolish the toughest clods. Roll the field flat and fence it round. And, keep an eye on your laborers.

When you are plowing, take care that your plowshare cuts deep enough into the ground. The grains should fall two fingers deep in the earth from the seeder you have fastened to the plow. Set the new furrows diagonally to last year's furrows and be sure that no clods of earth fall into the furrows and make it difficult for the seed to germinate.

On the day that the field turns green, say a prayer to the goddess of field mice and other vermin so that they will spare your crops. Scare away those winged thieves, the birds. When the corn is as high as a mat, give it water. Then, open the irrigation sluices twice more and once again, four times in all. When the corn stands at its full strength, cut it. Let the threshing sledge pass over the ears until they are empty. The grain must then be winnowed until it is free from all dirt and impurity.

Finally, remember that although these counsels issue from my mouth, they have been handed down by the god of meadows, who is the son of Enlil.

## Choose one of the following activities to show your understanding of the passage:

1. Make a poster that shows the many steps needed to farm the land. Label the activities in the picture.
2. Make a cartoon strip that shows the different steps to farming the land.
3. Write a diary as if you were one of the sons. Each day describe your feelings and activities on the farm.

# Informative Writing

Assess your students' understanding of the Nile's role in Ancient Egypt by having them write an informative passage about the gifts of the Nile.

## Preparing for the lesson:

1. Create overhead transparencies of "The Writing Process" (page 24) and the "Editing Checklist" (page 25).

2. Reproduce an "Organizing Informative Writing" (page 23) and "Editing Checklist" for each student.

3. Gather writing resource materials, such as dictionaries and thesauruses.

4. Gather research resource materials, such as books, encyclopedias, and magazine articles about the Nile.

## Teaching the lesson:

1. Tell students that they will be writing an informative passage about the gifts of the Nile, based on the information presented in *Saba the Farmer* and other resource materials.

2. Display and discuss "The Writing Process" transparency.

3. Distribute the "Organizing Informative Writing" worksheet and have students use it for prewriting.

4. Display and discuss the "Editing Checklist" transparency. Help students understand how to use the checklist to improve their compositions. Distribute an "Editing Checklist" to each student. Tell students to keep the checklists with their compositions as they

   - first edit their own writing,

   - next give their "Editing Checklist" to a partner who will listen and provide feedback while they read aloud their composition,

   - then trade papers and "Editing Checklists" with a second person and edit each others' writing, and

   - then give the composition to you to evaluate.

5. Allow plenty of class time for students to write their rough drafts, edit, revise, and write their final drafts.

6. Display the final compositions on a bulletin board, or save them for use in a student anthology.

# Organizing Informative Writing

**Prompt:** Life in Ancient Egypt revolved around the Nile River. The Greek historian Herodotus, who visited Egypt in 450 B.C., said, "Egypt is the gift of the Nile." Describe in detail the many gifts the Nile brought to the people of Ancient Egypt.

**Introduction:** State the main idea and give interesting background information.

_____

_____

_____

**Body:** Provide points specific information and many supporting details. Elaborate with figurative language (adjectives, vivid descriptions) and examples.

Point             Supporting Details
_____

         _____

         _____

_____

         _____

         _____

_____

         _____

         _____

**Conclusion:** Summarize the main idea and write a strong closing statement.

_____

_____

_____

# The Writing Process

## PREWRITING

Cluster, outline, brainstorm, draw, and discuss your ideas. Then, make a plan to organize your ideas.

↓

## WRITING A FIRST DRAFT

Write down your ideas, skipping every other line. Use the information you recorded on your prewriting plan to organize your ideas in a logical manner. Do not worry about spelling, capitalization, punctuation, or grammar. Read over and evaluate your first draft at this point to make sure it makes sense.

↓

## GETTING A RESPONSE

Read your composition to a partner and ask for feedback to help clarify ideas, recognize strengths, and improve weaknesses in your writing.

↓

## REVISING

Add details and descriptive words or phrases. If necessary, change the sentence sequence to clarify ideas.

↓

## EDITING AND REWRITING

Have a second partner read your composition and help you make grammatical and mechanical (spelling, capitalization, punctuation) corrections. Note any other suggestions this editor makes and incorporate them if they will improve your writing.

↓

## EVALUATING

Make sure your partners and your teacher use your Editing Checklist to document their evaluation of your writing.

↓

## PUBLISHING

Type or use your best handwriting to write a final draft. Check it over carefully before turning it in to your teacher for final evaluation.

# Editing Checklist

Name_____

Composition Title _____

**X** = No changes needed.   ✔ = Okay, but could improve.   ✱ = Problem.  Editor will help make corrections.

| | Editor 1 Listen and revise. | Editor 2 Read and revise. | Teacher |
|---|---|---|---|
| Proper format? (introduction, supporting details, conclusion) | | | |
| Details and descriptions? (figurative language, examples) | | | |
| Correct sentence structure, grammar, and word use? | | | |
| Correct spelling? | ✕ | | |
| Correct punctuation? (periods, commas, quotation marks) | ✕ | | |
| Correct capitalization? (proper nouns, beginnings of sentences) | ✕ | | |
| Strengths of composition? | | | |
| Weaknesses of composition? (editor helps correct) | | | |
| Name of editor? | | | |

Teacher Evaluation:    Expression _____

Mechanics _____

# Make Paper from Papyrus

One of the most important gifts of the Nile was papyrus, a reed that could be made into rope, mats, sandals, and paper.  Follow the steps below to make your own papyrus paper.  If papyrus does not grow locally, check with a nursery or gardening store.

**Materials:** (makes one sheet of papyrus paper 5" x 5" [13 cm x 13 cm])

- papyrus reed cut into 5" (13 cm) pieces
- liquid bleach
- large, covered mixing bowl
- wheat flour paste and water mixed together to make a thin gruel
- two 7" x 7" x 1" (18 cm x 18 cm x 2.5 cm) pieces of wood covered with aluminum foil
- mallet
- sharp knife or razor
- clamps or heavy objects to press the paper
- several rags
- iron

**Directions:**

1. Peel off the outer green skin to expose the inner pith of the papyrus reed.
2. Slice the pith into very thin strips.  You will need enough pith slices to make two 5" x 5" (13 cm x 13 cm) layers.
3. Put the slices into the mixing bowl with a couple of tablespoons (30 mL) of bleach.  Cover the bowl and let the mixture stand overnight.
4. Lay a rag on one of the 7" x 7" (18 cm x 18 cm) foil-covered boards.
5. Make a layer of papyrus strips by dipping each strip in the flour/water gruel and overlapping them on the rag until you have a 5" x 5" (13 cm x 13 cm) square.
6. Make a second layer of strips on top of the first, using the same procedure but overlapping the strips perpendicular to the first strips.
7. Place another rag over the two layers and pound them gently with the mallet.  This squeezes out the water and eventually merges the two layers into a single sheet of paper.
8. Carefully replace the damp rags with dry rags.
9. Sandwich the pounded papyrus between the pieces of foil-covered wood.  Clamp them together tightly or place heavy objects on top of them to press.
10. Check the rags and replace them with dry ones daily.
11. When the papyrus paper is still barely damp, sandwich it between dry rags and use the iron to press it dry.
12. Make sure the paper is completely dry (approximately three days) before you use it, or it will curl.  Use the sheet of papyrus paper to write hieroglyphics or to make your own cartouche (page 96) .

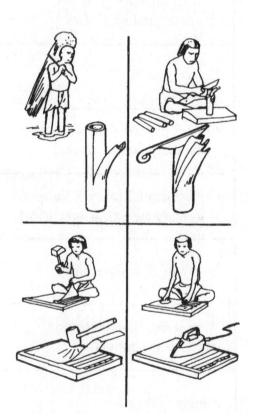

# Make Paper from Other Paper

Here is another recipe for making paper much like the Chinese did. For other papermaking ideas, consult *Paper by Kids* by Arnold E. Grummer (Dillon Press, Inc., 1990) or *50 Simple Things Kids Can Do to Save the Earth* by the Earthworks Group (Andrews and McMeel, 1990).

## Materials:

- blender
- construction paper, tissue paper, or newspaper torn into 1" (2.5 cm) squares
- several rags
- papermaking screen (wire screen securely sandwiched between two wooden frames)
- large tub
- flat, heavy objects to press the paper
- large sponge

## Directions:

1. Blend the paper pieces with enough water to make thin pulp.

2. Hold the screen over the tub. Carefully pour the pulp evenly onto the screen, making an even layer of pulp and letting the water drain through. The drained pulp should have the consistency of cooked oatmeal.

3. Place the screen on top of a dry rag. Place another rag on top of the screen. Using the sponge, gently compress the pulp fibers and press the remaining water from the pulp. Squeeze out the sponge frequently.

4. Flip the screen over onto another dry rag. Using the sponge, repeat the compressing process.

5. Carefully lift off the screen and place a dry rag on top of the paper. Using a heavy object, press the paper firmly.

6. Carefully lift out the piece of paper and sandwich it between dry rags. Put a flat, heavy object on top.

7. Replace the damp rags with dry ones each day until the paper is completely dry in about three days.

8. Use the paper.

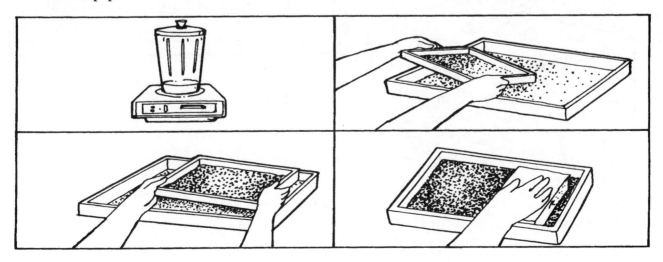

*Geography*

# Gifts of the Nile

Ask the class to brainstorm a list of the many gifts the Nile brought to the people of Ancient Egypt. Write the gifts on the chalkboard.

1. Provide shoe boxes and construction paper and have each student or group of students create a diorama about one of the Nile's gifts.

2. Wrap box with bows before doing diorama.

3. Create a display entitled "Gifts of the Nile" by thumbtacking or stapling the gift boxes onto a bulletin board.

4. Have students prepare cards labeling and describing their gifts.

# Misa the Merchant

| **Narrators 1–6** | **Misa,** the merchant | **Marta,** his wife | **Chempa,** a friend |
| **Kempa,** the captain | **Sabu,** the sailor | **Iba,** the trader | **Bast,** a friend |

**Narrator 1:** Prior to Egypt's New Kingdom period, merchants sailed their ships up and down the Nile River and traded in the villages along its banks. As Egypt grew and developed, trade within the country stayed relatively limited because each section of the country was more or less self-supporting. Foreign trade flourished, however, and helped Egypt become rich and powerful.

**Narrator 2:** Egypt was rich in many resources because of the fertile soil brought by the annual flooding of the Nile. But Egypt also needed to **import** building materials and luxury items. **Bartering** was the means to sell and acquire goods. Join us along the banks of the Nilie when King Ramses rules, and Misa will lead us on a tour of the trading business in Ancient Egypt.

**Misa:** Greetings. May H'apy, the god of the Nile, smile upon us today as we walk along the banks of our beloved river. Ahead is my merchant stall where I sell paper scrolls, ropes, mats, and sandals made from papyrus. My wife minds the goods while I am out trading. I am fortunate to be one of the chosen suppliers to the pharaoh himself. It is the time of collecting taxes for the bountiful harvest we had this season, and the royal scribes are kept quite busy recording the transactions.

**Narrator 3:** Because there was no use of coins in Egypt until 380 B.C., farmers paid their annual taxes to the pharaoh in honey, grain, oil, leather, flax, and other goods. These were collected by temple officials or the pharaoh's people and used to pay for other goods or services. Sailors, soldiers, priests, scribes, and craftsmen all worked for the pharaoh or for the temples.

**Narrator 4:** Since the same kinds of objects were usually swapped every day by traders, people had a good idea of what things were worth. Everything had a value that could be stated in weights of copper or silver. The smallest measure was a *kite*. Ten kites equaled one *deben*, which was about three ounces. Silver was more valuable than copper, so about ten debens of copper was worth one kite of silver. Goods changed hands, but the metals themselves usually did not.

**Misa:** How is the trading this morning, my lovely wife?

# Misa the Merchant *(cont.)*

**Marta:** Slow but steady. It is still early, and many boats have not yet arrived. I saw Duru the carpenter trade an unpainted coffin to one of King Ramses scribes for a calf. He must be preparing for his wife's funeral. She must have been a fine lady, for he has paid bread, ox flesh, wine, sweet oil, olive oil, fat, honey, figs, fish, and vegetables for her funeral items throughout the week.

**Misa:** Aren't we lucky to have such keen eyes watching over our open-air **market**? It is as if Horus, the hawk god himself, were perched in our stall.

**Bast:** You may jest, but you are lucky to have such an observant wife. It is important to keep a watchful eye with so many foreign sailors and traders roaming about the docks. The bustle of crowds attracts thieves, and you do not have a faithful baboon trained to bite culprits like so many tradesmen do. Recently, a merchant vessel supposedly laden with grain, glass jars, and fans from the East came ashore. After bartering for our local cattle, fruit, and vegetables, the captain left, and it was discovered that some of his cargo boxes were filled with rocks.

**Chempa:** We have many desired exports and must be diligent in our trading if we are to keep up with supply and demand. You sell our most precious resource, papyrus, which grows only along the banks of the Nile. We also trade items made from flax; building stones from the desert used in making the fine temples; copper and gold from our mines to make tools, jewelry, and cups; semiprecious stones for jewelry and ornaments; and, of course, livestock and agriculture crops. Here comes a Lebanese trader now.

**Iba:** Greetings. Word around the dock is that your stall has the finest sandals. I am in great need of a new pair.

**Misa:** I am honored. My wife will help fit you with what you need. What brings you to our port today?

**Iba:** I am with the ship *Byblos Trader,* which just returned from Phoenicia. I joined them there and am now overseeing the cargo of cedar from Lebanon to be shaped into strong masts for the pharaoh's new ships. Although you have lumber here in Egypt adequate for making ship hulls, you must **import** wood suitable for masts. Ah, these are fine sandals. May they last to walk many a deck. Come with me back to my ship and see the latest design.

# Misa the Merchant *(cont.)*

**Misa:** Thank you. I will leave negotiations to my capable wife, the shrewd trader in our family.

**Narrator 5:** The three men follow Iba to his ship and are met by the captain and one of his sailors.

**Kempa:** I see you found the sandals you were seeking. They seem to be of excellent craftsmanship. Whom do you bring with you, Iba?

**Iba:** This is Misa and his friends. I was telling them of our new ship.

**Kempa:** Ah, yes! The pharaoh's new ships will be of this design. Sabu, take the men below and show them the hull.

**Sabu:** As you can see, the hull is constructed of planks about three feet long fitted together like bricks and held firmly by long spikes. The seams between the planks are caulked from the inside with papyrus. In heavy seas, the planks are secured by great ropes that prevent them from bending.

**Bast:** A superior design, to be sure. Shall we join the captain back on the deck?

**Sabu:** Of course. Watch your step around the barrel of olive oil from Crete. I do not want to think of what the captain would do if it were to spill. It was a difficult journey across the Mediterranean, a voyage I do not wish to repeat soon. As you know, Egypt trades with the Nubians to the south, the Lybians to the west, with Phoenicia and Syria to the East, and with many other exotic places.

**Narrator 5:** Because the Egyptians believed the pharaoh ruled everywhere that the sun shone, their paintings depicted everything that came from abroad as being a tribute to the god-king. Some Egyptologists interpret this "tribute" as trade goods.

**Kempa:** Over the years, the king has planned hundreds of **expeditions** for trading and mining. I have been to the mines of Sinai for copper and turquoise, to Palestine for silver and horses, and down to the Red Sea for ivory, gold, and spices. Still, my favorite journey is down the length of the Nile into Nubia and Kush. There they have the most interesting animals and wares for importation—ivory, ebony, gold, precious stones, ostrich feathers, and monkeys, panthers, and giraffes for the royal zoo.

# Misa the Merchant *(cont.)*

**Iba:** One of the most famous expeditions was commissioned by Queen Hapshepsut to the land of Punt below the southern tip of the Red Sea. Although it happened long before our time, my great-great-grandfather was a sailor and trader who joined some other men who had made the journey. They claimed that the men dismantled their ships and carried them across by donkey to the Red Sea, reassembling them on the coast to sail southeast. I still enjoy visiting the temple near Thebes to admire the pictures of this marvelous adventure.

**Narrator 6:** Although the actual location of Punt has never been determined, it is thought to have been located in what is now Somaliland. The Egyptians knew it so well that they didn't think it necessary to locate it for anyone. Fortunately, they did leave us such fascinating information as the type of vessels used, the exports they brought to Punt, the reception they received from the Puntites, and even the words used by the chief of Punt in greeting them. Records show that the Egyptians returned with the imports of myrrh trees, ebony, ivory, gold, cinnamon wood, cosmetics, apes, dogs, and panther skins.

**Misa:** I'm afraid we must head back to the market. I see more boats and ships arriving, and I have left my wife tending the stall alone for too long. We wish you a pleasant and prosperous stay in our port. Farewell, my new friends.

32

# Misa the Merchant—Vocabulary and Comprehension

Write the following words on the chalkboard for students to copy on index cards for their picture dictionary. Remind them to research and write a complete definition, explanation, or example and draw a picture.

**barter   exports of Egypt   imports of Egypt   expeditions   market**

Use some or all of the following questions for whole-class discussion, small-group work, or individual written assessment. Allow students to refer to *Misa the Merchant* to answer them.

1. How did the Ancient Egyptians purchase their goods? *(The Egyptians used bartering, or trading goods, in order to purchase things. They also purchased goods by using a deben, equal to a weight of copper or silver.)*

2. Where did they go to do their shopping? *(They shopped at an open-air market, usually located near the docks or entrance to the city.)*

3. What is a deben? *(A deben is a weight of silver or copper used like money. Ten kite equaled one deben.)*

4. Who were some of the Egyptians' foreign trade partners? *(Lebanon, Crete, Greece, Nubia and Kush, Libya, Phoenicia, and Syria)*

5. List at least five items imported into Egypt and where they came from. *(any five— cedar wood from Lebanon; olive oil from Crete; copper and turquoise from Sinai; silver and horses from Palestine; ivory, gold, and spices from Punt; ivory, ebony, gold, precious stones, ostrich feathers, monkeys, panthers, and giraffes from Nubia and Kush)*

6. List at least three of Egypt's leading exports. *(any three— items made from papyrus, items made from flax, building stones, copper, gold, semiprecious stones, crops, and livestock)*

# Travel Log

Ancient Egyptian ships sailed to many parts of the civilized world. They traveled in all directions to trade for goods they needed. Two famous destinations included expeditions south into the Nubia and Kush region and also to the land of Punt.

Imagine that you have been transported back in time and are aboard one of these Egyptian vessels. Write in the travel log below describing your voyage. Include your destination, the sailing conditions, the geography you see, the items imported and exported for trade, and any other noteworthy events.

**Bonus Work:** Research the many different types of boats used by the Egyptians for trading and traveling. Then, use construction paper to design a model of an authentic Egyptian boat or ship.

34

# Create a Barter Market

Have your class simulate an open-air market like those in Ancient Egypt. Plan a lunch period in the classroom during which students barter for lunch items. Students will come to understand the pressures of selling, the joy of striking a good bargain, and the role of supply and demand in the marketplace.

## Preparing for the lesson:

1. Choose a date for your lunch barter.

2. Write and reproduce a letter to parents, describing the lunch barter, its purpose, the item their child has chosen, and the date of the barter.

3. Gather construction paper for product signs.

4. One week before the lunch barter, send the parent letter home with students.

5. One day before the lunch barter, remind students that they need to bring their products the following day.

## Teaching the lesson:

1. Tell students that they are going to simulate an open-market. They will barter for goods—their ability will determine what they eat for lunch that day.

2. Brainstorm with students a list of healthful luncheon products that they could supply (mini-sandwiches, fruit, carrot or celery sticks, etc.) Let students be creative, but limit sugar or junk food items.

3. Have students each choose one healthful lunch item as their product to barter with. Tell each they will need to bring 15–20 of the item they have chosen. Also tell them to supply their own beverages and napkins.

4. On lunch barter day, arrange the desks (stalls) in a large circle. Have each student make a construction paper sign for his/her stall describing his/her product.

5. Open the market by allowing five to ten students to take their products around to the different stalls and barter for other goods. After ten minutes, allow a different group to get up and "shop." Tell students that whatever they have they can trade. They might trade a sandwich for an orange, only to trade the orange later for a hunk of cheese. Continue until all students have had a turn.

6. Have students go to their "stalls" and discuss whether or not they are happy with what they ended up with for lunch. Discuss the advantages and disadvantages of using the barter system to acquire goods.

7. Discuss supply and demand. What product was most in demand? Least in demand? Who felt they made the best bargains and why?

8. If someone ends up with a seriously unbalanced meal, encourage students to voluntarily share so everyone gets enough to eat.

# Trace the Trade Routes

Use the map below to answer these questions.

1. Name at least five places one could travel for precious metals.

2. Name at least three places one could travel for exotic animals or skins.

3. What spices can be found in Punt?

4. Where could one go for wood supplies?

5. What island would you reach if you sailed north up the Nile and northwest across the Mediterranean Sea?

6. If you started at the Egyptian delta, then traveled east on the Mediterranean Sea,

what direction would you need to go to get to the Hittite Empire?

7. Using specific directions, describe one way to get from Egypt to India.

8. Using specific directions, describe one way to get from Egypt to Assyria.

9. Name four places Egyptians could travel to using only waterways.

10. Name three places to which Egyptians would need to travel by land on at least part of their journey.

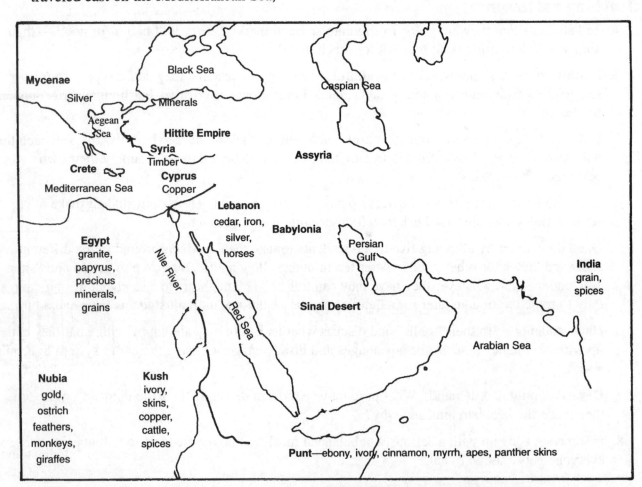

-------------------------------------------------------------------

**\*Fold up answers before reproducing for students.**

Answers: 1. Mycenae, Cyprus, Nubia, Lebanon, Kush; 2. Any three—Nubia, Punt, Lebanon, Kush; 3. cinnamon and myrrh; 4. Syria, Punt, Lebanon; 5. Crete; 6. north; 7. any reasonable answer; 8. any reasonable answer; 9. Any four—Mycenae, Crete, Cyprus, Lebanon, Nubia, Kush; 10. Any three—Hittite Empire, Syria, Punt, India, Assyria, Babylonia, Sinai Desert

# Egyptian Math and Medicine

Many written and pictorial discoveries tell us that the Egyptians were very advanced in their scientific knowledge of math, astronomy, and medicine. Along with hieroglyphics for words, the Egyptians developed a symbol system for writing numbers, including fractions. There were seven basic signs for numbers, each representing a place value from one to one million. Although this system was superior to making tally marks, writing large numbers was still slow business.

There was no concept of zero and no multiplication or division. Instead, the Egyptians added the number to itself as many times as needed for multiplication or subtracted repeatedly to divide. Many papyrus scrolls exist that are filled with mathematics problems involving everyday situations. They describe examples of how to divide rations among workers, how to calculate the area of a field, and even how to calculate the area of a circle. Keeping accurate records and computations were important to all Egyptian farmers, merchants, tradesmen, and scribes.

Egyptians also made advances using astronomy. From their study of the heavens and their sense of arithmetic, the Egyptians were able to measure time and develop an extremely accurate calendar. They divided the 24 hours of day and night into equal segments, 12 hours measured from sunrise to sunset and 12 hours from sunset to sunrise.

In addition to the 24-hour day, we can also attribute our yearly calendar to the Egyptians. The Babylonians had developed a lunar calendar based on the phases of the moon. The Egyptians based their farmers' calendar on both the moon and the star Sirius. They had observed that Sirius, the brightest star in the sky, appeared at the same time each year, and this corresponded to the time of the year that the Nile flooded. This calendar was more accurate than the lunar calendar because it corresponded almost exactly to their seasons.

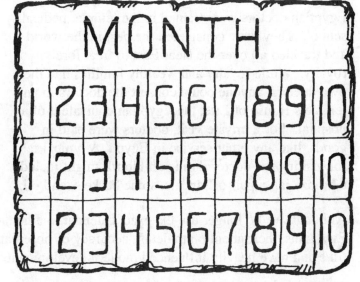

Egyptians also developed a "civil" calendar of 365 days, in which the year was divided into 12 months, each with three 10-day weeks, or 30 days. There were four months in each of the three annual Egyptian seasons. The five days left over were used as holy festival days at the end of the year. Because the Egyptians did not provide for a leap year, the civil calendar became more and more out of step with the farmers' calendar as time passed.

Other discoveries show the Egyptians to be highly skilled doctors and surgeons. Papyrus medical texts tell us that the Egyptians believed the heart had vital control throughout the body and that it "spoke" through the pulse. They knew the heart circulated blood, but they also believed it distributed air, water, nerves, and food to the body. They regarded the brain as being of little or no consequence to the functions of the body. In fact, the brain was so unimportant to Egyptians that it was discarded during the mummification process. Other organs were preserved in containers called canopic jars, which were buried with the dead.

# Egyptian Math and Medicine *(cont.)*

Ancient medical writings are divided into sections listing medicines and giving advice to doctors on how to treat such ailments as burns, head injuries, tumors, eye diseases, and stomach problems. The writings stress the importance of careful observation and gentle treatment, including rest and soothing herbal remedies. One treatment recommends wrapping a slice of raw meat over a wound. After a day, the patient removes the meat and applies grease, honey, and lint until the wound heals. Willow leaves, which contain salicylic acid, or aspirin, were applied to wounds to reduce inflammation. Copper and sodium salts were applied to help dry a wound. Cream and flour were mixed to make a cast for a broken limb. Faced with more difficult diseases for which they did not understand the cause, doctors might mix potions with magic spells or prayers. Then, even if the medicine failed, the patient would be comforted by the prayers.

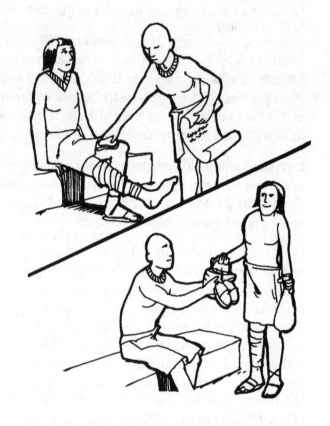

Egyptian doctors were trained in the temple medical school. They were considered the best in the world and traveled all over the Near East to treat foreign royalty. While royalty and wealthy families had their own doctors, anyone could consult the doctors in any temple's House of Life, the Egyptian equivalent of a hospital. For a private visit, doctors were paid in goods, like any other service in Egypt. A typical fee for visiting the doctor during childbirth might include a bronze jar, a pair of sandals, some baskets, and oil.

Although we no longer use the exact calendar, mathematics, or medicine developed by the Ancient Egyptians, their attention to detail, accuracy of observations, and use of logic were remarkable for that time and have heavily influenced modern developments.

## Choose one of the following activities to show your understanding of the passage:

1. Write a diary entry describing your day as a doctor in Ancient Egypt.

2. Draw and label a picture of a House of Life. Be sure to include items for treatment and payment.

3. Make an Egyptian calendar. Label the months, weeks, and days. Include the three seasons and the five festival days.

# Count Like an Egyptian

The Egyptians used seven basic symbols to write their numbers.

1  a staff  |

10  an arch  ∩

100  a coiled rope  ⌒

1,000  a flower  ⚘

10,000  a bent finger  ◁

100,000  a tadpole  ⌔

1,000,000  an astonished man  ⚲

A particular number was written by writing the number of ones, then tens, then hundreds, etc. For example, the number 14 would be written ____|||| ∩____ and the number 345 would be written ||||| ∩∩∩∩ ⌒⌒ .

## Use Egyptian symbols to write the following numbers:

1. _____ 73
2. _____ 139
3. _____ 470
4. _____ 3,471
5. _____ 2,506

6. _____ 13,592
7. _____ 231,861
8. _____ 450,900
9. _____ 2,130,135
10. _____ 6,003,004

## Write the numbers these Egyptian symbols represent:

11. ||| ∩∩ ⌒⌒  _____

12. || ⚘⚘ ◁ ⚲  _____

13. ∩∩∩∩ ⚘ ⌒⌒⌒⌒ ⌔⌔  _____

14. ||||||| ⌒⌒⌒⌒⌒ ⚘ ⚲  _____

15. ||| ⚘⚘⚘⚘ ◁◁ ⌔⌔⌔⌔  _____

16. ∩∩∩∩∩∩∩∩ ⚘⚘⚘ ⌔⌔ ⚲  _____

# Egyptian Computation

**Use > or < to compare these Egyptian numbers:**

1. |||∩∩∩ ◯ |||||||||∩∩ ?

2. |||||∩∩∩∩∩∩∩∩ ??? ◯ |||? ⚚

3. ||∩ ??? ◯ ||| ⚚

4. ∩∩∩ ⚚⚚⚚ ⟨ ◯ ⟩ ⚘

5. | ⟨⟨⟨⟨ ⟟⟟ ◯ ∩∩∩∩ ⟟⟟⟟

**Add and subtract to solve the problems. You may need to regroup.**

6. ??? ∩∩∩∩∩ ||||||
   + ?∩∩∩∩∩ ||||
   _____

7. ??? ∩∩∩∩ |||
   − ? ∩∩ ||||||
   _____

8. ?????? ∩∩ |||||||
   + ????? ∩∩ |||||||
   _____

9. ??? ∩∩∩∩∩ ||
   − ?? ∩∩∩ ||||
   _____

10. ⚚⚚ ?? |||
    + ?? |||||||||||
    _____

11. ⚚ ∩∩ |||
    − ∩∩∩ |||||
    _____

12. How many symbols are used to write 57,895?

13. How many symbols are used to write 9,999,999?

14. Even though it takes a lot of symbols, it's still better than making tally marks. How many tally marks are needed to write 9,999,999?

# Egyptian Mathematics—Answer Key

## Count like an Egyptian (page 39)

1. (hieroglyphic numeral)
2. (hieroglyphic numeral)
3. (hieroglyphic numeral)
4. (hieroglyphic numeral)
5. (hieroglyphic numeral)
6. (hieroglyphic numeral)
7. (hieroglyphic numeral)
8. (hieroglyphic numeral)
9. (hieroglyphic numeral)
10. (hieroglyphic numeral)
11. 233
12. 1,012,002
13. 231,040
14. 1,001,507
15. 524,003
16. 1,303,080

## Egyptian Computation (page 40)

1. <
2. <
3. <
4. <
5. <
6. 490 or (hieroglyphic numeral)
7. 217 or (hieroglyphic numeral)
8. 1,064 or (hieroglyphic numeral)
9. 108 or (hieroglyphic numeral)
10. 2503 or (hieroglyphic numeral)
11. 989 or (hieroglyphic numeral)
12. 34
13. 63
14. 9,999,999

# Make a Water Clock

The Ancient Egyptians used a water clock to measure time. A stone bowl was notched in circular rows around the inside, and a hole was made in the bottom. People could tell how much time had passed by watching the level of water as it dropped past the notches. With a partner, make a model of an Egyptian water clock.

## Materials:

- 2 small, disposable white paper cups the same size
- extra-thick sewing needle
- 2–4 heavy books
- wax paper, aluminum foil, or plastic bags
- digital watch (or analog watch with a second hand)
- colored pencils or crayons
- 2 strong rubber bands
- strong ruler
- pencil

## Directions:

1. Using colored pencils or crayons, decorate the outsides of the cups with Egyptian designs.

2. With the needle, poke a small hole in the center of the bottom of one cup.

3. Use rubber bands to attach that cup to the top of the ruler.

4. Protect the books by covering them with wax paper or aluminum foil or by putting them in plastic bags.

5. Stand the ruler up by bracing it between the heavy books.

6. Hold on to the top cup and ruler as you cover the hole with your finger. Have your partner fill the top cup with water to about ¹/₂" (1.25 cm) from the top. Put the other cup under the cup with the hole to catch the water as it drips.

7. With a pencil, mark the water level inside the cup.

8. Remove your finger and start timing the water as it drips through the hole. After one minute has passed, mark the level of water inside the cup. Continue marking the water level at one-minute intervals until the cup is empty. (Hang on to the ruler and cup so that they do not tip over accidentally.)

9. Double-check how accurate your water clock is by filling the top cup to the first water line and timing it again. Was it the same the second time? Why or why not?

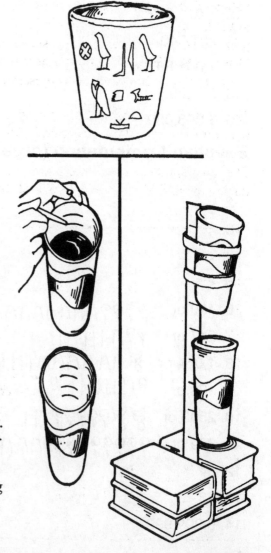

42

# Building the Pyramids

Narrators 1–12          **Imhotep,** the vizier          **Factah,** the foreman

**Sadah,** the stonemason          **King Khufu** (Cheops)          **Asashti,** the architect

**King Zoser**          **King Menes**          **King Khafre**

**Cabal,** the surveyor          **King Tutankhamen** (Tut)

**Wasat,** the engineer

**Narrator 1:** The Egyptians were an advanced civilization of people highly knowledgeable in math, science, and the arts. Some of their most astounding skills can be seen in their magnificent architecture. Their most famous buildings include royal palaces, vast temples, and, of course, the pyramids. These stone giants were not conceived overnight. Many stages and years transpired before the first pyramid was ever built. Join us now for a walk through time as we visit some leaders and builders of Ancient Egypt. We begin with the first pharaoh of unified Egypt, King Menes.

**Menes:** We Egyptians go to a great deal of trouble to see that we pass on to the next world as easily as possible. One of the most important aspects leading to a happy afterlife is the tomb we are buried in. This is especially true for the pharaoh, or king, since he is also regarded as a living god. Egyptians believe that when the pharaoh dies, he joins the immortal gods. Some believe that his spirit, or ba, flies to the horizon in the shape of the hawk god Horus to be joined with the sun. Others believe his spirit joins those of his ancestors as a star in the sky or descends into the Underworld to rule as the god Osiris. Therefore, we believe that if we can keep his body safe for all eternity, his ba will be able to return to it, and his power will preserve Egypt.

**Narrator 2:** Starting with the first dynasty during the Archaic Period, the pharaoh, King Menes, was buried in a tomb called a **mastaba,** which in Arabic means bench. The mastaba was like a house with rooms. Later mastabas became grand structures containing a chapel and other rooms for ceremonies. The development of building these grand tombs for the pharaoh was taken a step further by King Zoser during the Old Kingdom—the age of the pyramids.

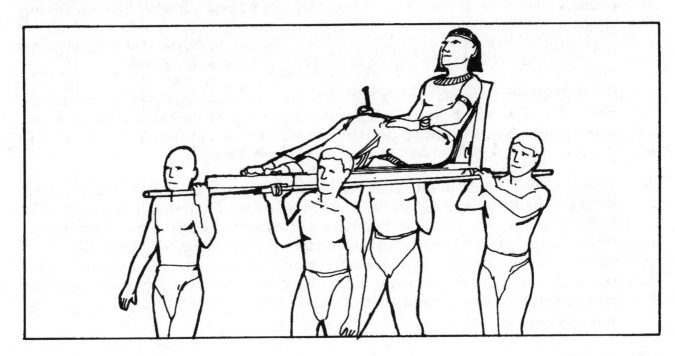

# Building the Pyramids *(cont.)*

**Zoser:** Welcome to my land! I am the pharaoh of all Egypt. Now that I have come to the throne, I have decided that I shall be buried in a grand tomb that will last forever. Previous tombs, like the mastaba for King Menes, were made of mud bricks that crumble over time. To keep my ba content, I will be preserved in stone in a new manner befitting my status. For this, I call on my vizier, Imhotep.

**Narrator 3:** Imhotep was a man of great intellect and courage. Besides being the king's chief architect, he also held the revered status of chief sculptor and chief carpenter. He was an astronomer, doctor, and advisor in the ways of the gods. Because of his great knowledge and talents, he had reached the second-highest office in the land—vizier to the pharaoh.

**Imhotep:** I hold my position of great power as an honor. Being the vizier is much like being a prime minister or president. I am a friend to the pharaoh and consult with him on matters of government, religion, and the people. I accepted the building of King Zoser's tomb as a privilege and will design the greatest tomb the world has ever seen.

One way to accomplish this feat is to build upwards. The base will remain a mastaba, a complex of temples and other rooms. However, for the remainder of the tomb I have something more ambitious in mind. I will build five more mastabas, one on top of the other, with each succeeding mastaba being slightly smaller than the one beneath it. The six steps will reach a height of nearly 2,000 feet. I call my new style of tomb a **step pyramid**.

**Narrator 4:** No one knows for certain if Imhotep planned his design in advance or thought of it as the work progressed. It is also uncertain why he chose this particular shape. Some experts believe that the shape of Imhotep's step pyramid created a stairway to heaven for the pharaoh's ba. Most agree it is a very stable and strong shape, therefore having a good chance of lasting a long time. It is also a sensible shape since the majority of the stone is in the bottom half. Hence, the higher you go, the fewer stones you have to move.

Later pyramids would continue with Imhotep's basic shape but with smooth sides. This was said to represent the rays of the sun shining down on the desert and creating a pathway to the sky. Other experts believe the shape to represent the ben-ben stone, or the first sacred mound of earth, which rose out of the waters and was used by the sun god to stand upon and create the universe.

**Imhotep:** The entire step pyramid complex will eventually include temples, chapels, other buildings, and courtyards. Like the other burial grounds, it will be on the west bank of the Nile, where the sun sets and leaves for other worlds. Each person's ba must make the same journey. To assist, we build all of our tombs as close as possible to the spot where the sun leaves the earth.

**Narrator 5:** The Step Pyramid of King Zoser still stands today in Saqqara near the ancient capital of Memphis in northern Egypt. Although the base mastaba has crumbled, it is still an impressive sight and a tribute to early architecture. King Zoser began an age of pyramid building that would last for over 600 years. Pyramid building reached its height during the Old Kingdom period. More than 80 pyramids still exist today, reminders of the ingenuity and perseverance of these ancient people. King Khufu also decided to build a pyramid that would be bigger, better, and more magnificent than anything built before. We join him now during the reign of the Fourth Dynasty, about 2573 B.C.

# Building the Pyramids *(cont.)*

**Khufu:** My father, King Sneferu, built the first pyramid with smooth sides. It is in the desert at Dahshur, a few miles south of Saqqara. I will build my tomb at **Giza**, a few miles north of Saqqara. My pyramid will be so grand as to be truly worthy of my greatness and power. The plans for my Great Pyramid show it will cover 13 acres. Thousands of laborers will be needed, along with skilled craftsmen, stonemasons, carpenters, surveyors, foremen, engineers, and overseers to make sure everything is done correctly and the results are magnificent beyond anything anyone has seen before.

**Cabal:** I am the chief surveyor for the king. My tasks require knowledge of geometry and astronomy. Our first step in building the Great Pyramid is to select a proper site on which to build. It must be on the west bank of the Nile and above flood level but close enough to the water so that the huge building stones can be transported by ship from the limestone quarries across the Nile and then moved by sleds to the building site.

To begin, we need a solid foundation. All of the sand, gravel, and loose rock must be removed until the solid rock floor of the desert lays bare. It is also very important that the four sides of the pyramid face exactly in the four directions—north, south, east, and west. To do this we build a circular wall on the rock base. At night, I mark the place on the wall where a star rises in the sky. After the star sets, I draw another line on the wall. I then draw a line from both of my marks to the center of the circle. By bisecting this angle, I will be able to find true north. The foundation must also be perfectly level. I call on Wasat for this bit of engineering.

**Wasat:** When any sort of container is filled with water, the surface of the water is level. We use this principle on a huge scale. Once the four sides of the base have been marked out, we dig a vast network of trenches that crisscross the marked area. The trenches are then filled with water, and the water naturally finds its own level. The water line is marked, the water is drained from the trenches, and the land is excavated to the waterlines. We end up with a perfectly level site. I am very proud of the work that we do, for this is by far the largest site ever to be leveled. Now we are ready to square and measure the sides.

**Narrator 6:** How accurate were the Ancient Egyptians at measuring and leveling? The base of King Khufu's Great Pyramid was off level by only five-eighths of an inch between the southeast and northwest corners.

**Cabal:** Once again I am needed to make sure the base is a perfect square. This is done using measuring cords made from flax fibers. We take a length of cord and divide it into 12 equal units. A knot is made at the third unit, the seventh unit, and at the end. The cord is then formed into a perfect right triangle and fitted into the corners. The length of each side can also be measured using these cords.

**Narrator 6:** The Egyptians' use of geometry was astounding. Although flax stretched when it was used, the difference between the longest and shortest sides of the Great Pyramid was only 7.9 inches. Considering each side is more than 750 feet long, the error is remarkably small. Many experts believe that such accuracy could only have been achieved by the use of astronomy as well.

# Building the Pyramids *(cont.)*

**Sadah:** While the site is being prepared and marked, I am hard at work at the limestone quarries, overseeing the cutting of the slabs. I am only one of hundreds of stonemasons working on the Great Pyramid. The only tools we use are metal chisels and saws and wooden mallets, hammers, and wedges.

My first task is to outline carefully on the slab where it will be cut. Then, using the mallet and chisel, I punch a number of cracks along the outline. Next, I drive wooden wedges into the cracks and soak them with water. The wedges absorb the water and expand, thus splitting the slab. We then lift the huge slabs with wooden levers, using a rock as a pivot, or fulcrum. With these simple tools and methods, we stonemasons will cut over 2,300,000 blocks of limestone, some weighing as much as 33,000 pounds!

**Factah:** As chief foreman, I have the responsibility of seeing that the slabs of limestone are placed exactly where the architects want them. The inside of the pyramid is made from limestone quarried in Giza, but the better-quality limestone for the outside comes from Tura, on the east bank. These blocks are put on logs and rolled to the edge of the Nile. There they are loaded onto barges and rowed down the river. This is done when the Nile is at its highest, during the inundation. During this time the Nile is only one quarter mile from the pyramid building site. Once at Giza, they are mounted on sleds and dragged into place along ramps, or inclined planes, that encircle the rising pyramid. Mud and mortar are used to help reduce the friction from the dragging sleds.

This is not an easy task. The laborers sometimes pull the slab over rollers to go up more difficult ramps. Although we try to be as careful as possible, there are still numerous accidents, and hardly a day goes by without some of the laborers being killed or injured. Eventually, one by one, the slabs are put into place.

46

# Building the Pyramids *(cont.)*

**Khufu:** Many people believe that my pyramids are built by slaves, but that is only partly true. In addition to these workers, peasant farmers help out for three or four months every year when the Nile floods their fields. They are paid for their services with food, oil, and cloth. The farmers hope that by helping with my preparation for death, they will please the gods and be rewarded in the next world.

**Factah:** I have the greatest admiration for the architects. Most of the blocks fit together so well that no mortar is needed to hold them in place. Some of the joints between the slabs are so tight you can't even slide the blade of a knife between them.

**Sadah:** The very last stone to be put into place is called the capstone. Its sides slope to end in a common point. The very top level of the pyramid has a hole. A plug is carved on the underside of the capstone. This plug fits into the hole and holds the capstone in place. When it is time for the capstone to be fitted, there is great rejoicing, for we know that the pyramid is almost finished. The sides of the Great Pyramid will be smoothed and polished. The stonemasons will work downwards from the top, removing the dirt ramps as they work toward the base. Finally, the work is complete. The pharaoh has his pathway to the gods, and we all believe that the fruits of our labor will last forever.

**Narrator 7: King Khufu's Great Pyramid of Giza** is one of the Seven Wonders of the Ancient World. It stands 481 feet high, about the height of a 40-story building. It is reported that over 10,000 laborers worked every day for over 20 years to complete it. If you view the pyramid from the outside, it appears to be solid stone. But inside are many tunnels and rooms used for the burial.

**Asashti:** I am the king's chief architect. I work out the details for the tunnels and **burial chambers**. The interior contains three burial chambers, each intended at one time to be the final resting place for the king. One chamber, mistakenly called the Queen's Chamber, was never intended for Khufu's wife, who was, in fact, buried outside the Great Pyramid. King Khufu's burial chamber, unlike many other kings' burial chambers, is inside the pyramid itself and not hidden underground.

Originally planned on a much smaller scale, Khufu's pyramid was enlarged as the king's reign was prolonged, until the final burial chamber was established in the midsection of the pyramid at the end of a steeply ascending Grand Gallery. It is here in the burial chamber that the **sarcophagus**, or stone coffin containing the king's body, will lie. The chamber walls are carved with descriptions of the changes that the king will go through until he becomes a god. It also contains false doors and openings to the outer world through which the king's ba can pass.

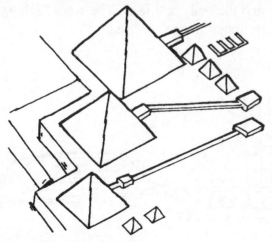
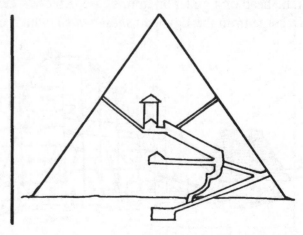

# Building the Pyramids *(cont.)*

**Narrator 8:** **The Grand Gallery** contains the most treasured possessions of the pharaoh for him to use in the afterlife. To prevent violation of the royal tomb, the passage leading to the Grand Gallery is sealed by plug stones. Workers slide the plug stones into place and make their way to the exit through an **escape shaft.** However, even the most secretive and complex plans can't deter thieves, and the Great Pyramid failed to give the pharaoh's mummy the protection intended. Many treasures and large quantities of gold were buried with each pharaoh. With so many people working on one phase of the pyramid or another, it was difficult to ensure security for such sought-after riches. In addition to stealing funeral items, robbers hacked away at the mummified body to steal the jewelry inside the wrappings. Sometimes they even set fire to gold coffins to melt off the metal.

**Khufu:** Still, the pyramid is only part of my entire funeral site. There is also a temple for the mummification rituals and a roofed causeway, carved with scenes from my life, that leads to the temple at the foot of the pyramid. This is where the priests will make offerings to feed my spirit. Also, near the base of the Great Pyramid, my "solar boats" are buried. My spirit will need these to move about the many lakes and rivers in the next world. Coming from a land so dependent upon the waters of the Nile, it is only logical that our heaven will also be filled with water.

**Narrator 9:** King Khufu is best known today by his Greek name, Cheops. Although King Khufu as the pharaoh was worshiped as a god-king, he was also a tyrant and oppressor who forced his people to build the Great Pyramid. He was disliked and even hated. When King Khufu died, his body was carried from his palace to Giza, the site of the Great Pyramid. It was prepared for burial, and his mummified body was placed on a funeral boat and pulled by workmen to the pyramid. Khufu's son, King Khafre, had his pyramid built next to that of his father's.

**Khafre:** I will follow tradition and build another pyramid. But I also want to leave a lasting memorial of myself in a way that no one else has. How do I create something different from anything seen before and protect my tomb at the same time? I know—I will have the likeness of my face carved in the form of a huge statue and place it before my tomb. This **Great Sphinx** will scare off thieves and protect my dead body.

**Narrator 10:** The Great Sphinx stands about 200 feet high. It was common for a deity to be represented by a huge statue or sculpture in Egypt. Usually the statue was of a human body with an animal head. The most popular animal was a lion, and there are statues with a lion's head guarding many temples and tombs. The Great Sphinx differs in that it is so immense and its form is reversed. It has the head of a god—or, in this case, Khafre's face—and the body of a lion. The word "sphinx" may have come from the Egyptian *shesep ankh*, which means "living image" or "statue."

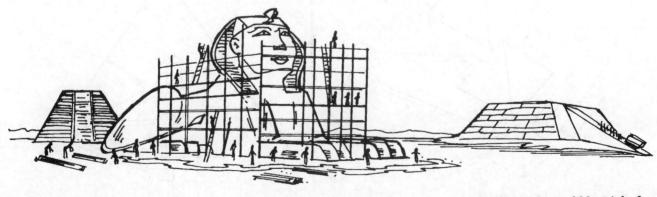

# Building the Pyramids *(cont.)*

**Narrator 11:**  Not all the kings who built the pyramids enslaved their people in the way Khufu did. The third pyramid at Giza was built by King Khafre's son-in-law, Menkaure. Here was an honest, just, and compassionate ruler greatly admired and loved by his people. Of course, not all pharaohs built pyramids for their tombs, either. Building such a large burial tomb required vast amounts of work by hundreds of workers over many years. Sometimes the pharaoh would die before his pyramid was completed, leaving the royal family in quite a predicament. They also realized that the enormous cost of building did not ensure them a sacred and untouched burial. Therefore, pharaohs ruling after the Old Kingdom began hiding their tombs in the desert cliffs near Thebes. This region eventually became known as the **Valley of the Kings**. King Tutankhamen was just one of the many pharaohs of the New Kingdom to be buried in these sacred cliffs.

**Tutankhamen:**  The tombs cut into the rock cliffs, with their underground tunnels and passageways, are more complex than the pyramids. A well, or shaft, is sunk in the main corridor of the tomb. In addition, a false wall is built on the other side of the shaft to make it look as if the tomb has come to an end. The tombs are also protected by strict laws. When thieves are caught, they are put on trial and forced to confess how they got into the tomb. The accused are then brutally executed by being thrust upon the points of sharp stakes stuck into the ground and left to die in agony.

**Narrator 12:**  But the tomb thieves of Ancient Egypt were not even discouraged by this cruel form of punishment. All the royal tombs have been robbed except those of Tutankhamen at Thebes and Psusennes at Tannis. The Ancient Egyptians left so much behind for us to admire. Wonderful buildings, artifacts, art, and written texts have survived over the centuries. The most famous of these, however, are the pyramids, which truly represent some of man's greatest technological achievements and which helped make Ancient Egypt one of the great civilizations.

# Building the Pyramids—Vocabulary and Comprehension

Write the following words on the chalkboard for students to copy on index cards for their picture dictionary. Remind them to research and write a complete definition, explanation, or example and draw a picture.

| | | |
|---|---|---|
| King Zoser, Imhotep, and the Step Pyramid | mastaba | burial chamber |
| King Khufu and the Great Pyramid at Giza | sarcophagus | escape shaft |
| King Khafre and the Great Sphinx | Grand Gallery | |
| Valley of the Kings | Pyramid | |

Use some or all of the following questions for whole-class discussion, small-group work, or individual written assessment. Allow students to refer to *Building the Pyramids* to answer them.

1. Name three different types of tombs used in Ancient Egypt. *(the mastaba, the pyramid, and a tomb in the Valley of the Kings)*

2. Describe the steps followed to build a pyramid. *(First select a site. Then clear the foundation of loose sand, gravel, or rock. Next, find true north to ensure that the sides face exactly north, south, east, and west. Dig channels and fill them with water to ensure that the foundation is level. Drain the water and level the foundation. Make sure the base is exactly square. In the meantime, have large limestone slabs measured, cut, and transported across the Nile to the building site. Load them onto sleds, drag them up dirt ramps to position, and place them. When each stone is properly placed, fit the capstone onto the very top. Then, working from the top down, smooth and polish the sides. Remove the dirt ramps.)*

3. Give at least two examples of geometry used by the pyramid builders. *(using a circle to find true north and forming right triangles to make sure the base was square)*

4. Give at least two examples of simple machines used by the pyramid builders. *(wedge to split limestone slabs, lever to lift the slabs, inclined plane used to move the slabs to the proper place on the pyramid)*

5. What people actually built the pyramids? Why? *(slaves and peasant farmers during the flooding of their fields when they could not work on their farms) they hoped that by helping the pharaoh the gods would look upon them favorably)*

6. What else is at Giza besides pyramids? *(the Great Sphinx)*

7. Why did pharaohs stop using pyramids for their burial tombs, and what did they do instead? *(Pyramids were easily robbed and took too much time, effort, and expense to build. Later pharaohs were buried in the Valley of the Kings in tombs carved into cliffs.)*

# Pyramid Building

Students love the challenge of building. In this lesson, students will experiment with designs for building the tallest and strongest pyramid.

## Preparing for the lesson:

1. Gather two identical sets of blocks—unifix cubes, base ten blocks, wooden or plastic blocks, or whatever you have available. The sets should have many blocks since it takes a large number to build a tall pyramid.

2. Provide a digital clock that students can watch to keep track of time and gather several large books for placing on top of the pyramids to test their strength.

3. Designate two safe work areas for building.

4. Reproduce "Design a Pyramid" (page 52) and "Pyramid Pattern" (page 53) for students to work on while they are not building and assemble the materials they will need. (See the materials list on page 52.)

## Teaching the lesson:

1. Tell students that they will be working in teams to see who can build the strongest and tallest pyramid. Tell them they will have 20 minutes to experiment and build. Then their pyramids will be measured to see how tall they are and tested to see how strong they are. The team that builds the tallest and strongest pyramid will be awarded the contract for building the pharaoh's pyramid.

2. Divide the class into six or eight teams. Assign them a number so you can chart their results on the chalkboard—team, height of pyramid, and strength of pyramid (how many books it holds before falling apart).

3. Distribute a "Design a Pyramid" and a "Pyramid Pattern" activity sheet to each student. Tell students they will work at their desks on this activity when their group is not building.

4. Assign two groups to the building areas. Remind them they have 20 minutes. Give a 10-minute warning to let groups know when their time is half over.

5. After 20 minutes, have the groups stop. Measure and chart the heights (measure in centimeters or count the number of layers) of their pyramids. Then test and chart strength by placing one book at a time on top of each pyramid to see how many it will hold.

6. Designate two new groups to build and have the previous building teams start on their activity sheets at their desks. Continue until all groups have had a chance to build.

7. When all groups have had a turn to build, use the results recorded on the chalkboard chart to determine the winner. If there is a tie for winner, hold 10-minute build-offs until the best team wins.

8. Discuss as a class the difficulties of and secrets to building a tall and strong pyramid.

# Design a Pyramid

Imagine that we still build pyramids today like the great pharaohs who ruled during the Old Kingdom. Design a pyramid for your own burial, complete with a model and cross-section, and describe the architecture and contents.

## Materials:

- pyramid pattern
- 12" x 18" (30 cm x 46 cm) light-colored construction paper
- scissors

- tape
- crayons or markers
- glue

## Directions:

1. Cut out the pyramid pattern and decorate the four sides. Remember, this is a modern pyramid, so it can be made from and look like anything you want.
2. Fold up and tape the sides of the pyramid. Glue it onto a corner of the construction paper.
3. Draw and clearly label a large cross-section of your pyramid. Show the burial chamber, Grand Gallery, air shafts, escape shafts, capstone, and any other passageway (real or false) you want.
4. Outline the cross-section in dark crayon or marker so that it can be clearly seen.
5. Color your drawing.
6. Describe the possessions you want buried with you and tell why you have chosen these particular items. Be detailed and specific.
7. Share your pyramid with the rest of the class or display it with others on a bulletin board.

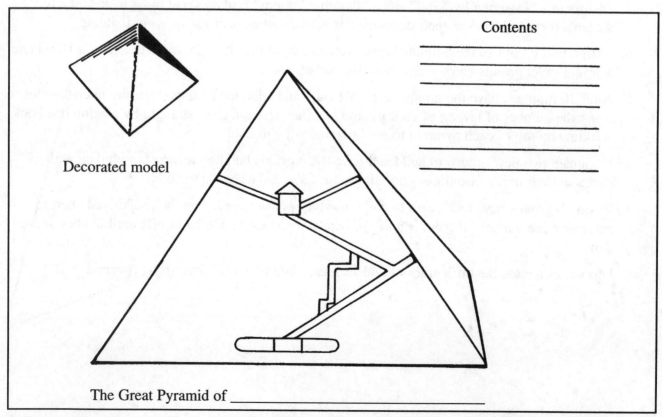

Decorated model

Contents
_____
_____
_____
_____
_____
_____

The Great Pyramid of _____

# Pyramid Pattern

Cut around the edges of the pattern. Decorate the four pointed sides. Fold along the dotted lines so that the decorations are outside. Tape the edges together to form a pyramid.

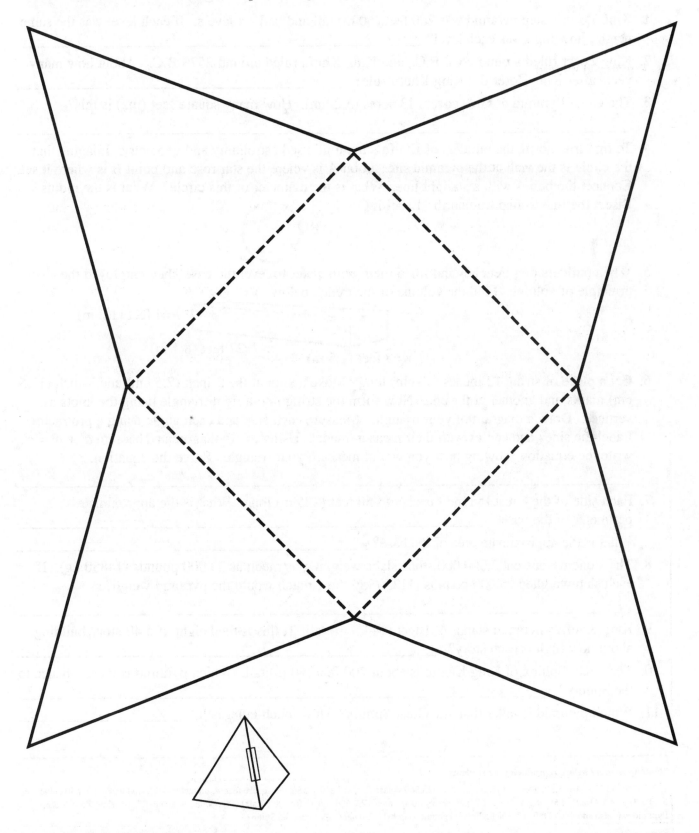

# Pyramid Math

Solve the following problems. You may refer to *Building the Pyramids*. Do your calculations on the back of this sheet. You will need to use a protractor or ruler and right angle.

1. King Zoser's step pyramid was 200 feet (60 m) tall and had six levels. If each level was the same height, how high was each level? _____

2. King Zoser ruled around 2650 B.C., and King Khufu ruled around 2573 B.C. About how many years after King Zoser did King Khufu rule? _____

3. The Great Pyramid of Giza covers 13 acres (5.2 hm). How many square feet (m2) is this?

   _____

4. To find true north, the builders of Khufu's pyramid used astronomy and geometry. Imagine that the circle is the wall at the pyramid site. Point A is where the star rose and point B is where it set. Connect the points with a straight line. What is the diameter of this circle? What is the radius? Bisect the line to find true north. Label it C.

   B ●      ● A

5. When builders dug trenches and filled them with water to level the base, they employed the principle of volume. Find the volume of the trench below. V=*l* x *w* x *h*

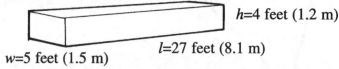

   h=4 feet (1.2 m)

   l=27 feet (8.1 m)

   w=5 feet (1.5 m)

6. Get a piece of string 12 inches (30 cm) long. Make a knot at the 3-inch (7.5 cm) and 7-inch (17.5 cm) marks and another at the end. Now form the string into a right triangle using the knots as vertices. Draw a diagram of your triangle. Measure each side and each angle using a protractor. Label the sides and angles with their measurements. Using the Pythagorean Theorem $a^2 + b^2 = c^2$, write the equation showing how you would measure your triangle. Solve the equation.

   _____

7. Each side of the Great Pyramid is about 750 feet (225 m) long. What is the approximate perimeter of the base? _____

   What is the approximate area of the base? _____

8. The stonemasons cut 2,300,000 stone slabs weighing as much as 33,000 pounds (14850 kg). If each slab weighed 25,000 pounds (11250 kg), how much would the pyramid weigh?

   _____

9. King Khufu's pyramid stands 481 feet (144.3 m) tall. If this is the height of a 40-story building, about how high is each story? _____

10. The Great Sphinx of King Khafre is about 200 feet (60 m) tall. Which pyramid is closer in size to the Sphinx? _____

11. Which pyramid is taller than the Great Sphinx? How much taller is it? _____

---

**\*Fold up answers before reproducing for students.**

1. 33' 4", or 33.333' (10 m); 2. about 77 years; 3. 1 acre=43,560 square feet, 13 acres=566,280 square feet; 4. diameter=1¼", radius=⅝"; 5. 540 cubic feet, 6. (3 x 3) + (4 x 4) = (5 x 5), or 9 + 16 = 25; 7. perimeter=3,000', area=562,500 square feet; 8. 57,500,000,000 lb.; 9. about 12'; 10. King Zoser's Step Pyramid was also about 200' tall; 11. King Khufu's Pyramid was 481', 281 feet taller than the Sphinx.

# Building the Pyramids Puzzle

The king's vizier planned to build a new pyramid. He was carrying the plan papers, written in step-by-step order when he tripped and dropped them. Help him put the steps back in order by placing a number on the proper line in the pyramid below.

A. Use geometry to make sure the leveled base is perfectly square.

B. Clear the foundation of loose sand, gravel, and rock.

C. Starting at the top, smooth and polish the sides, removing the dirt ramps as you work to the base.

D. Once at the building site, transport the limestone slabs on sleds and up ramps to their position on the pyramid.

E. Using astronomy and geometry, find true north to ensure that the four sides of the pyramid face north, south, east, and west.

F. Select the proper site to build the pyramid.

G. Measure, cut, and transport the limestone slabs onto boats, using logs as rollers.

H. Place the capstone atop the pyramid.

I. On boats, transport the limestone slabs across the Nile to the building site.

J. Make sure the site is level by digging channels and filling them with water. Mark the water level and clear excess dirt.

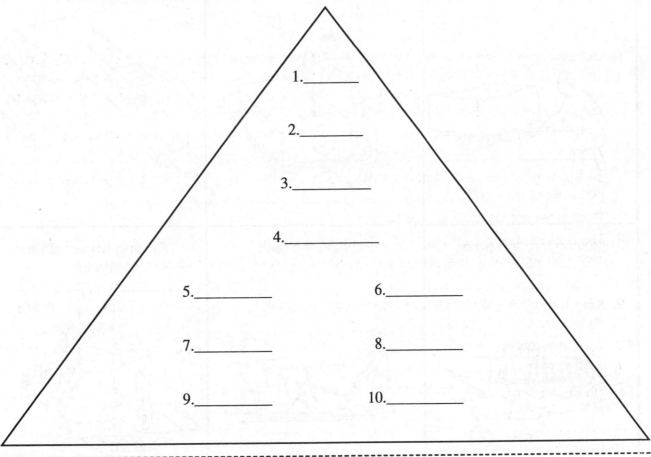

---

**\*Fold up answers before reproducing for students.**

1. F, 2. B, 3. E, 4. J, 5. A, 6. G, 7. I, 8. D, 9. H, 10. C

# Simple Machines

All machines, no matter how complex, are made of one or more simple machines. The six simple machines are the inclined plane, wedge, screw, lever, wheel and axle, and pulley. People use machines because they provide an advantage over doing work without a machine. When we work we use force (effort) to overcome a resistance (load). When we work, we use effort over a distance to move a load. When you lift a book from the floor to a table, you are working!

Lifting one book may not be very hard work, but what about lifting ten books? How could you lift something too heavy for you to pick up? You need something to give you more force. You need a simple machine. Simple machines can give you more force, give you more distance, or give you more speed. For example, you can walk to school, or you can use a machine—a bike. With a bike, you can use less effort over the same distance in less time. It's easier and it's faster.

The Ancient Egyptians understood these principles and used simple machines to do work such as irrigating, plowing, and building. Below are some pictures of Egyptians using simple machines in their daily lives. Three of them have been labeled to show the load and the direction of the effort applied. Look at the other pictures and identify the load and the direction of effort.

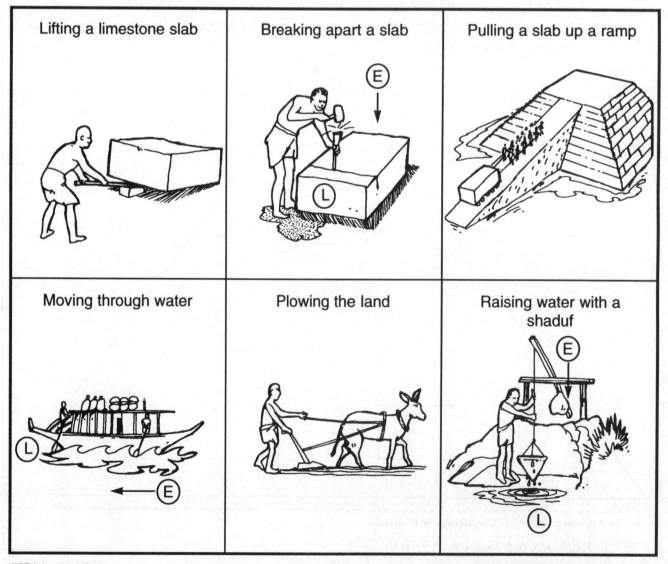

Lifting a limestone slab

Breaking apart a slab

Pulling a slab up a ramp

Moving through water

Plowing the land

Raising water with a shaduf

# Load and Effort

Look around your home to find examples of any form of the simple machines below. In each box, draw a picture of the machine. Tell how you would use it by labeling and describing the direction of the load (resistance to be overcome) and the direction of the effort (force) used to move the load. Share your findings and drawings with the class.

| Screw | Pulley | Wheel and Axle |
|---|---|---|
| | | |
| **Lever** | **Wedge** | **Inclined Plane** |
| | | |

# The Inclined Plane: An Experiment

One type of simple machine used by the Ancient Egyptians was the inclined plane, or ramp. Remember that they built dirt ramps around the pyramids to enable them to pull the heavy limestone slabs into place. An inclined plane is a sloped surface. A slanted board propped up for skateboarding and a path leading up a hill are types of inclined planes. Inclined planes are used in many ways to make work easier.

Some inclined planes are very steep; others are not. You know that it takes a great deal of effort to walk or ride a bike up a steep hill. That is why roads or paths going up steep mountains or hills wind back and forth. To go straight up, you must use more effort over a shorter distance. If you take a winding road, you use less effort, but you must travel a longer distance.

Just how does an inclined plane make work easier? Inclined planes don't move, but they can help you move or lift heavy things. Working cooperatively in a small group, perform the experiment below. Use the scientific method as shown to discover the advantage of using an inclined plane. Although force (effort) is really measured with a weight scale (showing grams, ounces, pounds, etc.), in this experiment you will measure *differences* in the amount of force you need, using a rubber band as a scale and the distance it stretches as the effort.

**Purpose:** (What are you trying to prove?) _____

**Hypothesis:** (What you think the experiment will show?) _____

_____

**Materials:**

- flat board
- 4 books approximately the same thickness
- large paper clip
- pair of round-point scissors
- metric ruler
- rubber band

**Procedure:**

1. Attach the rubber band to the scissors, as shown. The scissors are the load.

2. Attach the large paper clip to the other end of the rubber band.

3. Holding on to the paper clip, lift the scissors about 25 cm off the desk. Using the metric ruler, measure the rubber band from one end to the other. Record this number on your observation chart (page 59). This measurement represents the amount of effort (force) needed to overcome the load (scissors).

4. Make an inclined plane by placing one end of the board on the floor and the other on a book. Slowly pull the scissors up the ramp and measure the rubber band again from end to end. Record this measurement on your observation chart.

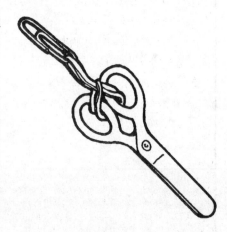

# The Inclined Plane: An Experiment *(cont.)*

5. Place another book on top of the first one to make the inclined plane steeper, and repeat the procedure. Record your observations on the chart.

6. Continue the experiment with three and four books. Record your results.

**Observation Chart:**

| **Effort** (length of rubber band, in centimeters) | **No book** | **1 book** | **2 books** | **3 books** | **4 books** |
|---|---|---|---|---|---|
| **Distance** (height of inclined plane, in books) | | | | | |

**Graph Your Results**

*Effort in books* (y-axis 0 to 4)
*Distance in cm* (x-axis 1 to 20)

## Conclusions (write your answers on the back of this page):

1. Was your hypothesis correct? Why or why not?

2. When was the most effort needed to move the load?

3. When was the least effort needed to move the load?

4. How does the steepness (slope) of an inclined plane affect effort?

5. If the inclined plane were twice as long, would it take more or less effort to lift the load four books high? Why?

6. The Ancient Egyptians used inclined planes to move heavy limestone slabs into place on the pyramids. Do you think the ramps were very steep? Why or why not?

7. You want to lift a certain load to a certain height. Describe the tradeoff between effort and distance that you get using an inclined plane.

- - - - - - - - - - - - - - - - - - - - - - - - - - - - - - - - - - - - - - - - - - - - - - - - - - - - - - - - -

**\* Fold up before reproducing for students.**

1. Accept reasonable answers. 2. The most effort is required when there is no inclined plane and/or when the scissors are lifted the highest distance. 3. The least effort is required when the scissors are lifted the shortest distance. 4. The steeper the inclined plane, the more effort is required. 5. If the inclined plane were longer, it would require less effort because it would not be as steep. (But it would require effort [moving the load] over a farther distance.), 6. No, the ramps were probably not very steep, because the slabs were extremely heavy and it would be easier to move them a longer distance than to move them a shorter distance but up a steeper incline; 7. The trade off is the amount of effort applied for the amount of distance over which the effort is applied. If you want to use less effort to move the load, you must apply the effort over a farther distance (longer incline). If you want to move the load a shorter distance (steeper incline), you must use more effort.

# The Screw: An Experiment

A screw is another type of simple machine—it is an inclined plane wrapped around a center post, or cylinder. A screw can be used to hold things together or to lift things. Screws are used in building, and some jar lids screw on. Some car jacks are screws that enable a single person to lift a car, and some screws bring liquids up from a lower source, such as drilling for water. Do the following experiment and answer the questions. (*Note to Teacher*: Reproduce enough copies of page 61 for half the class; cut the pages in half and give a set of two patterns to each student.)

**Materials:**

- 2 pencils   • crayon   • scissors   • 2 inclined plane patterns

A

B

**Procedure:**

1. Cut out triangles A and B. The sloped sides are like inclined planes. Which would require less effort to walk up? Why? _____
   _____

2. Which inclined plane would be shorter to walk up? Why? _____
   _____

3. Color a strip along the sloped side of each triangle. Beginning with the fat end of the triangles, wrap each around the end of a pencil, as shown.

4. What does each pencil now resemble? _____

5. Which screw would require less effort to insert into wood? Why? _____
   _____

6. Which screw would take less time to insert into wood? Why? _____
   _____

7. Carefully remove the pencils from the papers. Stand the papers on end. What do they remind you of? _____

8. List five ways the screw is commonly used. _____
   _____
   _____

- - - - - - - - - - - - - - - - - - - - - - - - - - - - - - - - - - - - - - - - - - - - - - - - - - - - - - - - - - - - - -

**\*Fold up before reproducing for students.**

1. B, because it is not as steep. 2. A, because it is a shorter distance. 4. It looks like a screw. 5. B would require less effort because the inclined plane is not as steep. 6. A would take less time because the inclined plane is shorter. 7. Accept reasonable answers, such as a spiral staircase or a seashell. 8. Accept reasonable answers.

# Inclined Plane Patterns

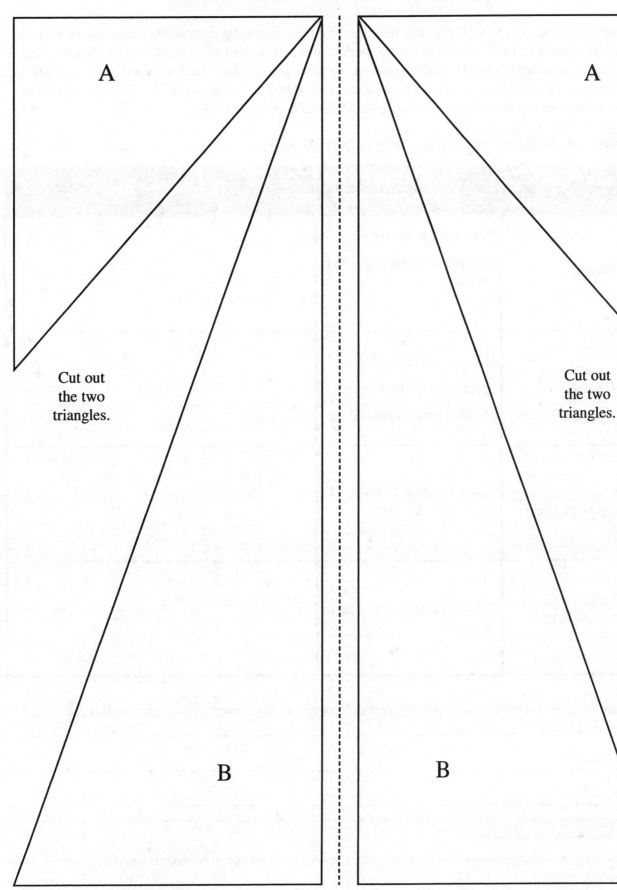

A

A

Cut out
the two
triangles.

Cut out
the two
triangles.

B

B

*Science and Achievements*

# The Wedge

The wedge is another type of simple machine used by the Ancient Egyptians. A wedge is two inclined planes placed back to back. A wedge makes work easier and is most often used to push things apart. For example, a wedge is used for splitting or cutting through resistance such as wood, rock, or cloth. Forming part of a solid body, such as a boat or car, into a wedge "streamlines" it. Then the solid body can move more easily through the resistance—a fluid such as water or air.

**Complete the chart and then answer the question below.**

|  | The Wedge in Ancient Egypt | The Wedge Today |
|---|---|---|
| **At Work** | Plow used to till the soil<br><br>Digging tools used to plant seeds | |
| **At Home** | Knives used to cut food<br><br>Axes used to chop wood<br><br>Needles used to sew fabric | |
| **For Transportation** | Boats designed to glide easily through water | |
| **For Building** | Pounded into rock to break off slabs | |

What are some of the similarities and differences between wedges used by the Ancient Egyptians and wedges used today? _____

_____

_____

- - - - - - - - - - - - - - - - - - - - - - - - - - - - - - - - - - - - - - - - - - - - - - - - - - - - - - - - - - - - - - - -

**\*Fold up before reproducing for students.**

Similarities/Differences—Accept reasonable answers. We still use many of them in the same way today; technology has expanded the ways we use wedges today.

# The Lever

A lever is a simple machine consisting of a beam (lever arm) that is free to rotate around or pivot on a fixed point (fulcrum). The lever arm moves, but the fulcrum doesn't. The lever makes work easier by using force and distance to move a load. The pictures below show some common uses of levers in Ancient Egypt and today. Some of the pictures have been labeled to show the fulcrum (F), load (L), and effort (E). Study them carefully. Then label the fulcrum, load, and effort on the other pictures.

**shaduf**

**teeter-totter**

**fishing pole**

**lever to lift limestone slabs**

**wheelbarrow**

**bottle opener**

On the back of this paper draw and label as many different levers as you can. Think of examples in the kitchen, in your garage, at school, and at play. How many different levers were you able to describe? Share your answers with the class.

# The Lever Advantage

Archimedes, a Greek mathematician who lived from 287 B.C. to 212 B.C., said about the lever, "Give me a place to stand, and I will move the earth." What do you think he meant? When you finish studying levers, you will know the answer.

The Ancient Egyptians discovered the advantages of the lever and used it in many ways. The shaduf was probably the first water-lifting machine invented. It was made of a beam balanced on a pillar as the fulcrum. A bucket hung from one end of the beam and a heavy weight hung from the other end. The person getting water would apply force to pull and lower the bucket into the water. As the bucket lowered, the weight would rise. When the person quit applying force, the weight would lower, and the bucket would rise, full of water. This simple machine is still used in Egypt today.

Another type of lever used by the Egyptians was a form of crowbar. Workers split apart slabs of limestone, using wooden wedges soaked in water. To move the slabs, they used a lever. They would stick a long wooden plank under a corner of a slab. Then, using a rock as a fulcrum, they would lift the slab by applying force to the other end of the plank.

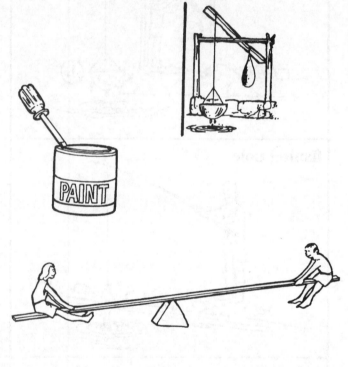

In many types of levers, the fulcrum is between the load and the effort. When you use a hammer to pull a nail out of a board, the nail is the load, the head of the hammer is the fulcrum, and effort you use is on the handle. The handle (effort) must move farther than the nail (load), but it is easier to pull the nail out. When you pry the lid off a can of paint with a screwdriver, the lid is the load, the place where the screwdriver blade rests on the can is the fulcrum, and the effort you use is on the handle. The handle moves farther than the lid, but the lid is easier to lift off.

A teeter-totter is also a lever with the fulcrum between the load and effort. It might be too much work for you to lift your sister by yourself. But with a lever—the teeter-totter—you can. If your sister sits in the middle of her end and you push in the middle of your end, you still may not be able to move her. But if you move to the far end of your side, you can lift her. By using the advantage of a lever arm, a lighter person can lift a heavier one. You move farther than your sister, but she is easier to lift.

In all of these examples, you trade distance for effort. In other words, the effort moves farther than the load, but less effort is required to move the load than not using a lever at all. This lesson will help you better understand the advantages that using a lever to do work can provide.

64

# The Lever Advantage: An Experiment

Provide students the opportunity to experience and understand the relationship between load, effort, and the fulcrum.

## Preparing for the lesson:

1. Gather the following materials for each group: a meterstick, masking tape, permanent marker, long pencil and removable eraser, binder clip, two medium rubber bands, metric ruler, load—object that can be attached to and supported by a rubber band (two or three pairs of student scissors taped together will work).

2. Reproduce pages 67–70 for each student, and make overhead transparencies of the graphs (pages 69 and 70) to use as a model for students.

3. Set up a lever system as a model. Make sure the rubber bands can handle the load you choose.

## Teaching the lesson:

1. Divide the class into groups of four or five students.

2. Show students the model lever and tell them they will be making a similar one with which to experiment with load and effort.

3. Distribute pages 67–70 to students. Tell them they will use the scientific method to experiment with levers and record their results. Allow students time to discuss and write their hypotheses.

4. Distribute materials to each group. Have each group check to make sure they have all the materials they need as listed on page 67.

5. Direct groups to cover the bottom half of their meterstick with masking tape. Have each group mark with 0 the center of the meterstick on the masking taped edge. Show how to mark intervals of 10 cm in both directions from the center point (0) along the taped edge.

6. Prepare the loads. If you are using student scissors, have students tape them together with masking tape. Then have them loop one of the rubber bands through the finger holes. Remind them to make sure the load is not so heavy that it breaks the rubber band. (You may wish to have students cover the tips of the scissors with tape to reduce the possibility of injury.)

| 0 | 10 | 20 | 30 | 40 | 50 | 60 | 70 | 80 | 90 | 100 |
|---|----|----|----|----|----|----|----|----|----|-----|
| 50 | 40 | 30 | 20 | 10 | 0 | 10 | 20 | 30 | 40 | 50 |

# The Lever Advantage: An Experiment *(cont.)*

7. Model how to set up the lever by following these steps:

   • Tape one end of the pencil to a desk top so the other end extends beyond the surface. (You may need a volunteer to also hold the pencil down on the desk.)

   • Attach the binder clip at 0 on the meterstick, and slide it over the end of the pencil extending from the surface. Elicit from students the response that this represents the fulcrum.

   • Place the removable eraser on that end of the pencil to prevent the clip and meterstick from sliding off.

   • Check to make sure that the lever is balanced evenly.

8. Have students review the Procedure section on page 67 and have someone assigned to each job.

9. Ask another volunteer to help you model the experiment by stabilizing the meter stick as you add the load by looping the rubber band attached to the scissors over one end of the meterstick. Then add to the effort by looping the other rubber band over the other end.

10. Model the experiment:

    • Place the load at the 40-cm mark on one side of the fulcrum and the effort at the 10-cm mark on the other side of the fulcrum.

    • Have the volunteer who is stabilizing the meterstick hold onto the end of the rubber band (effort) and let go of the meterstick. (The meterstick will move as the load weighs down on its end.)

    • Ask the volunteer applying the effort to pull down on the rubber band until the meter-stick is level.

    • Measure the effort again and record it on the chart transparency.

11. Instruct groups to continue following the procedures on page 67. Allow groups time to experiment and record their results.

12. When everyone is finished, discuss the groups' findings as a class.

13. As an extension to this lesson, have students build a model of a shaduf for the classroom, label its parts, and describe the advantages to the Egyptians when using this machine.

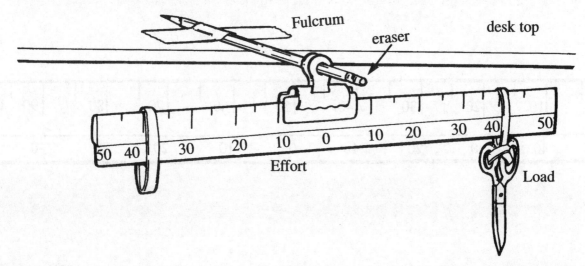

# The Lever Advantage: Experiments

**Purpose:** To discover how to lift the load in the easiest way possible using the given lever system

**Hypothesis:** (What do you think will be the easiest way? Why?) _____

_____

_____

**Materials:** meterstick, long pencil and removable eraser, binder clip, two medium rubber bands, metric ruler, load (scissors), masking tape, permanent marker

**Procedure:**

1. Assign these jobs to people in the group:

   • Prepare the lever arm, following your teacher's instructions.

   • Prepare the load.

   • Make sure the lever is balanced and secure on the desk.

   • Make sure the effort (rubber band) is in the proper place and pull down on it.

   • Measure the effort (stretch of the rubber band).

   • Make sure the load is in the proper place and to record the results on a chart

2. Place the load 40 cm from the fulcrum. Place the effort 10 cm from the fulcrum on the other side. Pull on the effort until the lever arm is balanced (level). Measure the length of the effort from the top of the rubber band all the way to the bottom. Record your findings on the chart on page 69.

3. Keep the load at 40 cm but move the effort to 20 cm. When the lever is balanced, measure and chart the effort. Did it require more or less effort this time?_____

4. Continue the procedure with the load at 40 cm and the effort at 30, 40, and 50 cm. Record your results. Could you predict what was going to happen? Why or why not? _____

   _____

5. Use the information from your chart, graph the results, and complete the Conclusions part of the experiment (page 68).

6. Try Experiment #2 with your group. Record your findings on page 70.

7. Try Experiment #3 with your group. Answer the questions.

# The Lever Advantage: Experiments *(cont.)*

## Conclusions:

1. Was your hypothesis correct? Why or why not? _____

   _____

2. What were the four main parts of your lever system? _____

   _____

3. In what ways can a lever provide an advantage? _____

   _____

4. How do load and effort differ? Which remains constant and which changes? _____

   _____

5. What could this kind of lever be used for? _____

   _____

6. What did you learn about the relationship between load and effort on this type of lever system? What is the easiest way to lift the load? _____

   _____

**Experiment #2:** Keep the effort in a constant position 40 cm from the fulcrum and move the load. Record your results (page 70).

1. What happened as you moved the load farther from the fulcrum?_____

   _____

2. What does this tell you about the relationship between load and effort on this type of lever system?_____

   _____

**Experiment #3:** Move the load, effort, and fulcrum to a variety of positions but always keeping the fulcrum between the load and the effort. Answer these questions:

1. What would be the best positioning of the load, effort, and fulcrum if I wanted to use the least amount of effort possible? _____

   _____

2. What would be the best positioning of the load, effort, and fulcrum if I wanted to lift a load really high?_____

   _____

3. How do these two situations differ? _____

   _____

# The Lever Advantage: Results of Experiments

## Observations—Experiment #1
(Load always 40 cm from fulcrum at 0)

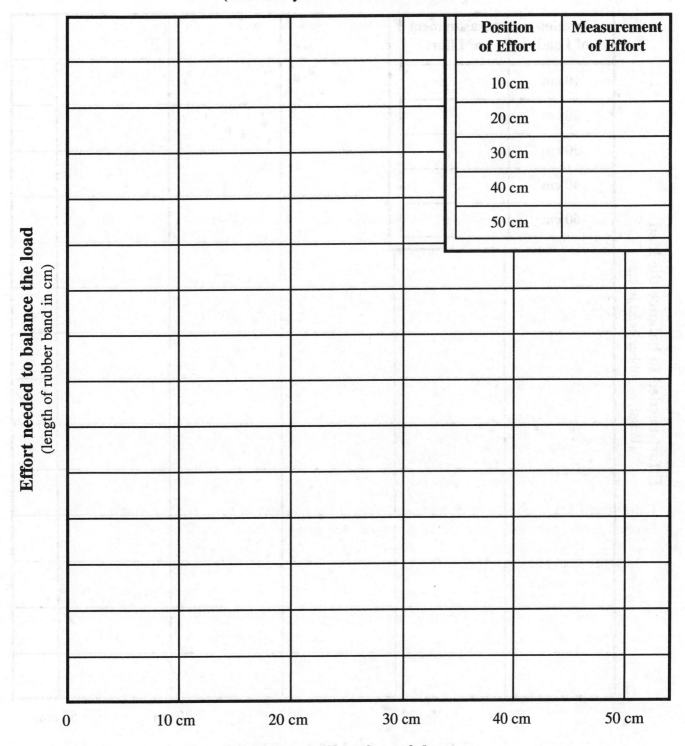

| Position of Effort | Measurement of Effort |
| --- | --- |
| 10 cm | |
| 20 cm | |
| 30 cm | |
| 40 cm | |
| 50 cm | |

*Effort needed to balance the load*
(length of rubber band in cm)

0          10 cm          20 cm          30 cm          40 cm          50 cm

**Distance of effort from fulcrum**

# The Lever Advantage: Results of Experiments *(cont.)*

## Observations—Experiment #2
(Effort always 40 cm from fulcrum at 0)

| Position of Load | Measurement of Effort |
|---|---|
| 10 cm | |
| 20 cm | |
| 30 cm | |
| 40 cm | |
| 50 cm | |

**Effort needed to balance the load** (length of rubber band in cm)

| 0 | 10 cm | 20 cm | 30 cm | 40 cm | 50 cm |
|---|---|---|---|---|---|

**Distance of load from fulcrum**

# Answer Key

## The Lever (page 63)

Teeter-totter— E F L—load=one person, effort=other person, fulcrum=triangle in middle

Fishing pole—E F L—load=fish, effort=hands on handle, fulcrum=elbow

Bottle opener—E F L—load=bottle cap, effort=hand lifting handle, fulcrum=end of opener over the cap

## The Lever Advantage—Experiment #1 (page 67)

**Hypothesis**—Accept reasonable answers.

**Procedure:**

3. Less effort

4. Yes; it seemed to require less effort to move the load as the effort moved farther from the fulcrum.

## Conclusions: (page 68)

1. Accept reasonable answers

2. Lever arm, load, effort, and fulcrum

3. It can make lifting an object easier than trying to lift it without a simple machine.

4. Weight refers to the load and it never changes. Effort refers to how much energy is needed to move the object. The effort changes depending on where it is applied along the lever arm.

5. Accept reasonable answers.

6. On this type of lever, the farther you moved the effort away from the load and fulcrum, the easier it was to lift.

## Experiment #2 (page 68)

1. Required more effort

2. The farther the load is from the fulcrum, the more effort required to lift the load.

## Experiment #3 (page 68)

1. Put the load and fulcrum at one end and the effort at the other.

2. Put the load at one end and the fulcrum and the effort at the other.

3. One uses little effort but doesn't move the load very far (height). The other moves the load more distance (farther/higher) but requires much more effort.

# Exploring Types of Levers

Have students explore and experiment with other types of lever systems by rearranging the load, effort, and fulcrum. Have students discover the advantages of different levers and record their findings.

## Preparing for the lesson:

1. Gather materials (same as on page 65).

2. Reproduce page 73 for each student.

## Teaching the lesson:

1. Divide the class into groups of 4 or 5 students and tell them they will be experimenting with different types of levers, using the same materials as they did in "The Lever Advantage" experiments. Elicit from students that in their lever systems, the fulcrum is the binder clip and pencil, the load is the scissors, and the effort is the rubber band.

2. Distribute page 73. On the chalkboard, draw and label the lever diagram as shown below— fulcrum (F), load (L), and effort (E). **Do not draw the direction arrows at this time.**

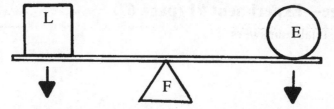

3. Have students tell the direction of the load and the direction the effort must be applied to move the load. **Add arrows showing these directions.** Then ask students to name some examples of this type of lever system (teeter-totter, crowbar, shaduf).

4. Ask students to describe other ways to arrange the load, effort, and fulcrum along a lever arm. On the chalkboard, draw and label these diagrams, as shown below (**leave off the direction arrows**). Make sure one shows the load in the middle and one shows the effort in the middle.

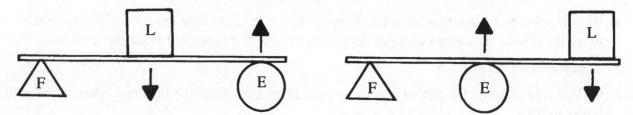

5. Have students tell the direction of the load and the direction the effort must be applied to move the load in these diagrams. **Add arrows showing these directions.**

6. Elicit from students the response that in both these lever systems, the fulcrum remains at one end of the lever arm. Tell students that they will be working in groups to explore using the three types of lever systems. They will need to move the load and effort around to find the best ways to lift the load the easiest and to lift the load the highest.

7. Distribute the materials. Allow groups time to experiment with both systems and record their findings. Circulate around the room to help as needed.

8. Discuss the findings as a class. Have volunteers draw on the chalkboard the lever systems that meet the requirements shown on page 73.

# Exploring Types of Levers *(cont.)*

| | Requires least effort | Lifts load the highest |
|---|---|---|
| **Fulcrum in middle** <br><br> F | | |
| **Load in middle** <br><br> L | | |
| **Effort in middle** <br><br> E | | |

What did you learn about the relationship between fulcrum, load, and effort in the three types of lever systems?

# Real-World Levers

This lesson will allow students to transfer their knowledge of levers to those used in the real world.

## Preparing for the lesson:

1. Reproduce pages 75–77 for students. Make an overhead transparency of page 77 to model how to draw and label diagrams.

2. Gather materials for bulletin board display: three large pieces of poster board or butcher paper in three different colors, construction paper, markers, crayons, scissors, and glue.

3. (Optional) Gather samples of machines that incorporate lever systems: boat oar/paddle, paper cutter, broom, rake, wheelbarrow, golf club, garlic press, baseball bat, crowbar, can opener, stapler, staple remover, scissors, bottle opener, tennis racket, fishing pole, hammer, mallet, fly swatter, nutcracker, tweezers, pliers, hole puncher.

## Teaching the lesson:

1. On the chalkboard, draw diagrams of the three classes of lever systems, as shown on pages 75 and 76. Label the fulcrum (F), the load (L), and the effort (E) in each.

2. Distribute pages 75–77 to students and read them aloud together. Then have students identify the diagrams on the board by class. Label them. To help students remember the classes, give them the mnemonic device FLE (A). Tell students that the letters stand for the component that is in the middle of the lever system: **F** (fulcrum)=Class 1, **L** (load)=Class 2, **E** (effort)=Class 3. (Tell them the **A** is their grade for remembering the mnemonic!)

3. Have students look at page 77. Do the first three examples together as a class. Use your transparency to model how to draw and label the diagram.

4. Allow students time to work alone or in small groups to complete page 77.

5. If you desire, have students create a bulletin board display entitled "Real-World Levers," showing the three types of lever systems. Divide the class into three groups and assign each a class of lever. Give each group a sheet of poster board or butcher paper and instruct students to make a clearly labeled diagram of their levers. Have them make and glue on several different examples of their class of levers. Encourage students to think of levers from the past such as those used by the Egyptians, and levers used in the present. (If you brought in the optional samples of levers, display them for the groups to examine and use when drawing their diagrams.)

74

# Real-World Levers *(cont.)*

**Class 1 Lever Systems:** When you first think of a lever, you may conjure up images of teeter-totters and crowbars—or even the shaduf. In these lever systems, the fulcrum is in the middle, between the load and the effort. This type of lever is known as a Class 1 lever system. You have learned that one advantage of using a Class 1 lever system is that you can move a heavy load with little effort. You know that the closer the load is to the fulcrum and the farther the effort is from the fulcrum, the easier it is to move the load. You use effort over a greater distance than the load moves, but it is easier to move it. A Class 1 lever gives you more force.

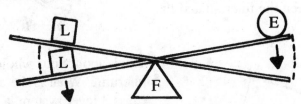

Another advantage of a Class 1 lever is its ability to lift objects a greater distance. The closer the effort is to the fulcrum and the farther the load is from the fulcrum, the higher the load will move. But again there is a tradeoff between effort and distance. To move the load higher, you must use more effort.

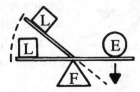

**Class 2 Lever Systems:** In this type of lever system, the load is in the middle, between the fulcrum and the effort. The wheelbarrow, dolly, and bottle opener are all examples of Class 2 lever systems. On a wheelbarrow, the wheel is the fulcrum, the load is in the middle, and the effort is applied at the handles.

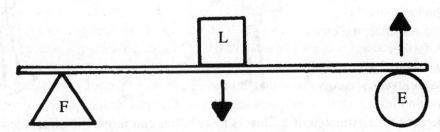

As with a Class 1 lever, you can increase the advantage of a Class 2 lever by moving the load closer to the fulcrum and applying the effort farther from the fulcrum. It is easier to lift a load with a long-handled wheelbarrow than a short-handled one. It is easier to open a bottle with a long-handled opener. It is easier to move a dolly if you put the heaviest objects nearest the fulcrum. A Class 2 lever gives you more force.

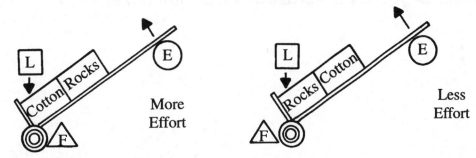

More Effort

Less Effort

# Real-World Levers *(cont.)*

**Class 3 Lever Systems:** In the third type of lever system, the effort is in the middle, between the fulcrum and the load. Examples of Class 3 levers are a fishing pole, a hoe, and your arm itself. With a hoe, the fulcrum is your elbow, and the load is the ground. The effort is the weight of the hoe itself and the amount of pressure applied by the other hand—the one between the fulcrum and the load.

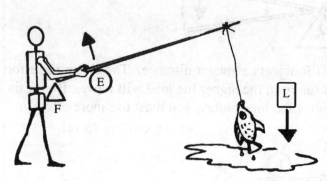

Think about your whole arm as a lever. What is the fulcrum? What is the effort? What is the load? In a Class 3 lever system, a great deal of effort is needed to move the load. How can this be an advantage? As with the other levers, you trade force for distance. Though you must use more force to move the load, you can move the load farther. You may be able to lift a heavy fish with your hand, but you can lift it farther with a fishing pole. A Class 3 lever can give you more distance.

Another advantage of a Class 3 lever is you can use it to move a load faster. If you swing a baseball bat, your shoulder is the fulcrum and your arms/hands are the effort. The weight of the bat is the load. To cover the same distance, the end of the bat moves farther—and faster—than your arm. A Class 3 lever can also give you more speed.

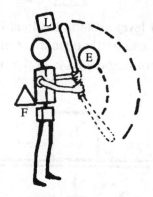

How can you increase the advantage of a Class 3 lever? You can move the effort closer to the load. It is easier to swing a heavy baseball bat if you "choke up" on the handle, or move your arms/hands (effort) closer to the load (end of the bat). Of course, you trade effort for distance and speed. The bat will not travel as far nor as fast, but it is easier to swing.

Remember that Archimedes said, "Give me a place to stand and I will move the earth." What do you think he meant? Do you think he was correct? Explain your answer.

76

# Identifying Real-World Levers

Study the following real-world levers. Label the fulcrum, effort, and load of each. Indicate the class of lever each represents. Then draw a diagram of the lever system below each picture. The first one has been done for you.

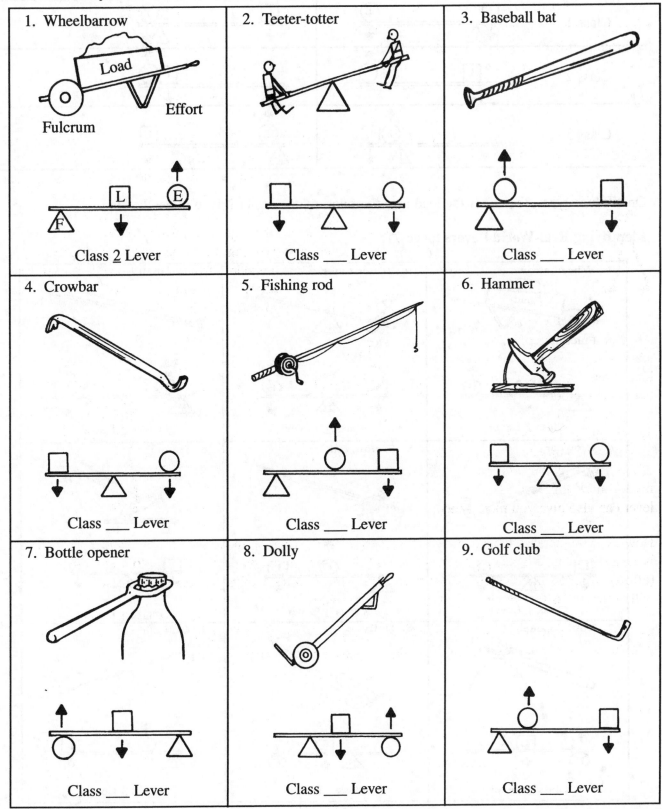

# Answer Key

## Exploring Types of Levers (page 73)

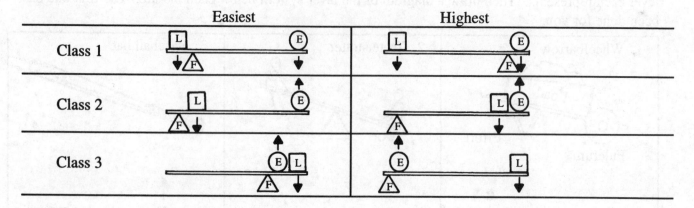

|  | Easiest | Highest |
|---|---|---|
| Class 1 | | |
| Class 2 | | |
| Class 3 | | |

On all three types, the closer the load is to the fulcrum, the easier it is to move the load.

## Identifying Real-World Levers (page 77)

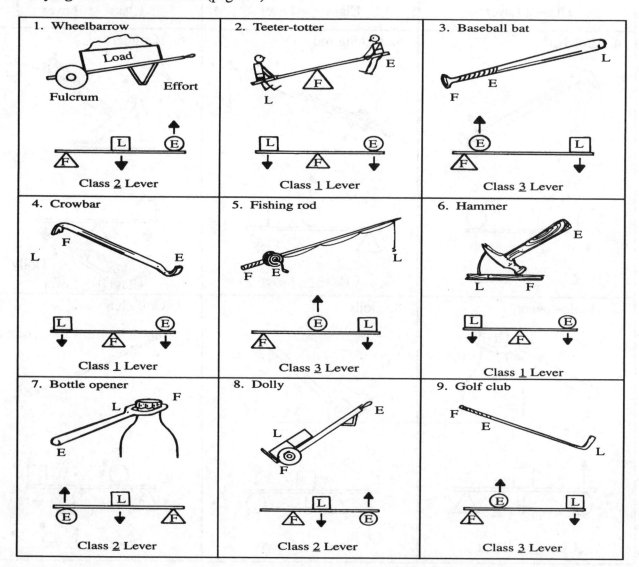

1. Wheelbarrow — Class 2 Lever
2. Teeter-totter — Class 1 Lever
3. Baseball bat — Class 3 Lever
4. Crowbar — Class 1 Lever
5. Fishing rod — Class 3 Lever
6. Hammer — Class 1 Lever
7. Bottle opener — Class 2 Lever
8. Dolly — Class 2 Lever
9. Golf club — Class 3 Lever

# Simple Machines: Assessment

1. Label the load and effort in these three pictures.

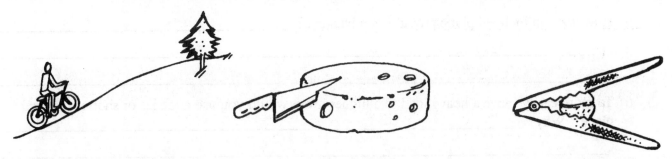

2. In each set of pictures, circle the picture of the item that requires the least amount of effort to move the load.

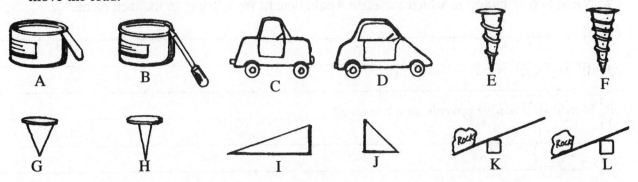

3. Identify the following levers as Class 1, Class 2, or Class 3.

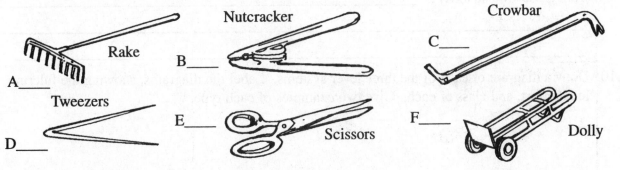

4. Draw a diagram of each class of lever, showing the placement of the load, effort, and fulcrum that would require the least amount of effort to move the load.

Class 1                    Class 2                    Class 3

# Simple Machines: Assessment *(cont.)*

**Answer the following questions.  Be as specific and thorough as possible.  Use complete sentences.**

5.  How does an inclined plane provide an advantage? _____

   _____

   _____

6.  To more easily move a heavy load to a higher lever, would you use a longer or shorter inclined plane?  Why? _____

   _____

   _____

7.  Name two situations in which someone would benefit from using an inclined plane.

   _____

   _____

   _____

8.  How does a wedge provide an advantage? _____

   _____

   _____

9.  Give three examples of wedges used by the Egyptians.  How are they the same as or different from those we use today? _____

   _____

   _____

10.  Draw a diagram of each of the three lever systems.  Label the diagrams, showing the fulcrum, load, effort, and class of each.  Give two examples of each type.

11.  How do levers provide an advantage? _____

   _____

   _____

12.  Do you think Archimedes was correct?  Why or why not? _____

   _____

   _____

# Simple Machines: Assessment *(cont.)*

## Vocabulary

Read the clues to fill in the blanks. Then use the words formed by the letters in the boxes to answer the question.

1. ☐ __ __ __ __
2. __ __ __ ☐ __ __ __ __ __
3. __ __ __ __ __ __ ☐
4. __ __ __ __ ☐
5. ☐ __ __ __
6. __ ☐ __ __ __
7. __ __ __ __ __ __ ☐ __ __ __ __
8. __ __ __ __ __ ☐ __ __
9. __ __ ☐ __ __ __ __ __ __ __ __ __ __
10. __ ☐ __ __ __ __
11. __ ☐ __ __ __ __ __
12. __ __ __ __ ☐ __ __ __ __
13. ☐ __ __ __ __ __

1. An inclined plane wrapped around a center post

2. Load refers to weight or _____.

3. The pivot point on a lever system

4. If you are an Egyptian pulling a stone slab up an inclined plane, you will not want the inclined plane to be this.

5. On a shaduf, it is the bucket of water.

6. Two inclined planes back-to-back

7. This helps a boat slice through water or a plane to move through the air more quickly.

8. What the load and the effort sit upon in a Class 1 lever system

9. Scientific name for a ramp

10. An Ancient Egyptian Class 1 lever system used to lift buckets of water

11. The _____ of the load from the fulcrum affects the effort required to move the load.

12. Levers provide this to their users.

13. Another word for "work"

14. To what do all the vocabulary words relate?

# Simple Machines Assessment: Answer Key

(pages 79–81)

1. L=weight of person; E=pedals

L=cheese; E=push on handle

L=nut; E=push on handles

2. Students should circle these items: **B D F H I K**

3. A. Class 3

   B. Class 2

   C. Class 1

   D. Class 3

   E. Class 1

   F. Class 2

4. Class 1

   Class 2

   Class 3

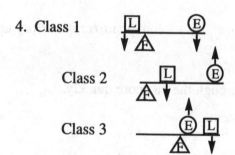

5. It makes it easier to move a heavy object up to a higher level rather than picking it up and lifting it.

6. A longer inclined plane requires less effort since it is not as steep.

7. Accept reasonable answers.

8. It makes it easier to pierce, cut, or slide through resistance.

9. Answers might include plow, hoe, knife, wedge, or boat.

# Simple Machines Assessment:
# Answer Key *(cont.)*

10. Class 1—L F E

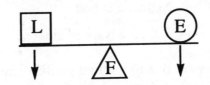

   Teeter totter

   Hammer pulling nail

   Crowbar

   Shaduf

   Paint lid prier (screwdriver)

   Scissor

   Class 2—F L E

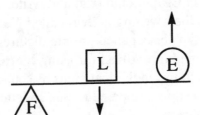

   Wheelbarrow

   Garlic press

   Waffle iron

   Bottle opener

   Dolly

   Class 3—F E L

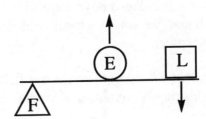

   Fly swatter

   Fishing rod

   Golf club

   Rake

   Tweezers

11. Levers allow you to lift heavy objects you could not lift alone.  They allow you to crush or pry apart objects that you could not crush or pry alone.

12. Accept reasonable answers.

**Vocabulary**

| | | | |
|---|---|---|---|
| 1. | screw | 8. | lever arm |
| 2. | resistance | 9. | inclined plane |
| 3. | fulcrum | 10. | shaduf |
| 4. | steep | 11. | distance |
| 5. | load | 12. | advantage |
| 6. | wedge | 13. | effort |
| 7. | streamlining | 14. | simple machines |

# Shunat the Scribe Student

**Narrators 1–10**

**Shunat,** the student      **Tarine,** his sister

**Akhmed,** his brother      **Nekht,** a friend      **Renof,** a tutor

**Thorin,** a friend      **Jaf,** an advanced student      **Rashid,** the scribe master

**Narrator 1:** The Egyptians were one of the first civilizations to use written language, and their earliest writing dates back to 3100 B.C. They recorded information on temple walls, tombs, and papyrus scrolls. Thousands of complete and fragmented ancient papyrus scrolls exist today, preserved by the dry climate in Egypt. Because of this, historians are able to learn many interesting facts about life in Ancient Egypt.

**Narrator 2:** Not everyone in Egypt could read and write. Special training was required to learn the complex signs that made up their writing system called hieroglyphics—a Greek term meaning "sacred carved inscription." Hieroglyphics began as simple picture-writing with a picture or sign representing a particular object. Slowly a method evolved for using **hieroglyphs** to represent ideas and actions. Eventually, it was expanded to use individual signs as sounds, much like our alphabet today. However, hieroglyphics comprises 750 signs compared to our 26 letters. Most of the hieroglyphs are pictures of people, animals, plants, or objects.

**Narrator 1:** Learning all of these different signs required ten years of laborious education in the temple schools, and only a few privileged boys were fortunate enough to attend. Join us for a journey into a day at school with Shunat, the son of a local nobleman. It is sunrise, and he eats his breakfast with his sister and younger brother.

**Shunat:** We must hurry so that we are not late for our first lesson. You know how angry Rashid, the scribe master, gets if all of his pupils are not in place and ready to receive the morning's dictation.

**Akhmed:** Yes, and today I will be working with Old Renof, the tutor. He is more patient than Rashid, but he can still swing a mean cane.

**Tarine:** I don't know how you can waste your time so. Every day you go off to the temple school. You work from sunrise to sundown, learning the different hieroglyphic signs and memorizing the exercises. I consider myself lucky to be a girl. I stay at home and work each day with Mother, learning to run our household. I help the servants with the cooking and sewing chores. I learn how to be a good wife and hostess so that I might marry a wealthy nobleman and entertain his friends properly. Today Mother is going to teach me a new song, and we will practice some of the special dance steps for the Festival of the Nile. You see, it is not necessary for me to bother myself with such nonsense as learning to read and write. I will be a wealthy noblewoman someday, and my husband will hire a scribe to do it for me.

# Shunat the Scribe Student *(cont.)*

**Narrator 3:** According to historical records, girls did not attend temple schools. They stayed at home, learned household skills, and got some training in the arts. Girls from wealthy families also learned how to deal with the servants and run a larger household. However, some girls did learn to read and write. In the tomb of Kenamun there is a painting of a woman with a scribe's palette beneath her chair, and letters written by women have also been discovered.

**Shunat:** Dream on, little sister, and hope that your wealthy husband has also "wasted" his time at the temple school. Do you not understand the advantages of learning to read and becoming a **scribe**? A scribe is everybody's boss. He sits in the shade and writes while others do the backbreaking labor. A scribe does not have to work on the building sites or irrigation canals. Instead he records the materials used and names of workers. Wealth and success are the future for any good student!

**Akhmed:** How true. Only those who learn to read and write can ever hope to achieve a high status such as a scribe, state official, priest, or one who works in medicine. Scribes collect taxes for the pharaoh and wealthy landowners. They can leave school and work at the temples or on a nobleman's estate. If they prove to be good record keepers, they can even be promoted to a position overseeing the accountants or possibly a position in the royal household, writing official letters and drawing up legal documents.

**Shunat:** The ultimate position for a scribe is to become the vizier to the pharaoh. But look how you have wasted our time. We will be late now for sure. Come, Akhmed, we must hurry.

**Narrator 4:** As the boys dash down the street to the temple school, known as the **House of Life**, they encounter their friend Thorin, who is also late. Unlike the brothers, Thorin is not a son of a wealthy nobleman or official. Although school is expensive, his fees are being paid by a local landowner who felt he showed some promise of becoming a good student. Possibly later Thorin will return the favor by working for him as his scribe.

**Thorin:** I see you also run to attend the morning's lesson. Rashid will be angry, and I cannot disappoint the landowner who has been kind enough to pay my way. Very few boys like me are privileged enough to enter the House of Life. If it weren't for him I would be home learning to be a mason like my father. It is a respectable profession, to be sure, but I dream of someday becoming a scribe responsible for many important tasks.

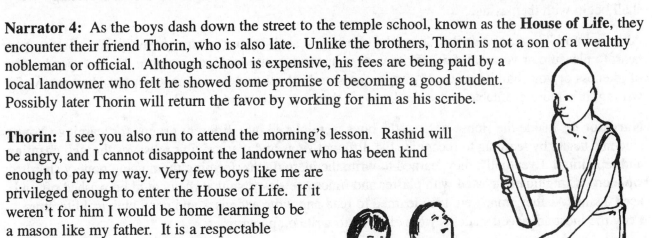

# Shunat the Scribe Student *(cont.)*

**Akhmed:** We sometimes forget how lucky we are. Most boys must learn the craft of their father or pay to be an **apprentice** at a shop and learn its trade. Some boys do not have a school nearby and are sent away from their families for many years. Others are so wealthy and privileged that they are allowed to attend school at the palace along with the royal children.

**Shunat:** We will not be so fortunate if Rashid catches us sneaking in late. Be quiet and find your place on the floor with Renof. I must gather my writing tools.

**Narrator 5:** The House of Life contained no desks, chairs, or blackboards. The students all sat cross-legged on the floor and stretched their linen *shenti*, or kilt, across their knees to make a firm writing surface. They wrote with a reed brush and a palette of red and black ink. The black ink was used for standard information and made from soot and water. The red ink was made from desert ocher and used for special headings and more important items.

**Renof:** I see Thorin and Akhmed have decided to join us this morning. You are lucky that we have not yet begun our early recitation. It is also most fortunate that Rashid, the master, is busy preparing for the advanced students and did not notice these two snakes who are so knowledgeable they do not need a full day of learning come slithering in. Perhaps the two of you could enlighten the class by reviewing all of the symbols we learned yesterday and the passage you memorized in class regarding advice to youthful scribes.

**Thorin:** Thank you, kind tutor, for not alerting the master and allowing us to escape a beating. We shall begin with the passage.

**Akhmed and Thorin:** O scribe, do not be idle or you shall be cursed straight away. Do not give your heart to pleasure or you shall fail. Write with your hand; recite with your mouth. Do not spend a day of idleness or you shall be beaten. A boy's ear is on his back and he listens when he is beaten. As for writing, it is more profitable to he who knows it than any other trade.

**Narrator 6:** Inside the House of Life, the boys were placed into different groups for learning. Young students began by learning to recognize the different signs and memorizing passages through chanting and repetition. Eventually, they learned to write the hieroglyphs, forming them using pottery shards or wooden writing boards coated with plaster and limestone flakes so that they could be washed off and used again. As they improved, they learned to read and write exercises and copy classical literature. Only the most advanced students were allowed to write on papyrus.

**Narrator 7:** Since all learning was by rote practice and repetition, it was very long and boring work. Sometimes young minds strayed, and the boys received harsh punishment from their teachers, such as beatings, reciting, or being made to write long proverbs. Students who ran away were caught and had wooden blocks tied to their ankles to keep them from doing it again.

86

# Shunat the Scribe Student *(cont.)*

**Renof:** Very good, young students. I hope this reminds you about the great importance of your schooling and the consequences for idle workers. When you feel jealous of your friends out playing in the fields, remember that they can never aspire to advance their status. It is only those chosen to read and write that will acquire the positions of wealth and power. Let us now review the different hieroglyphic signs, and then we shall move on to the morning lesson.

**Narrator 7:** While the young boys read the different signs put before them by their tutor, Shunat tries to appear inconspicuous and join his group of advanced students. Luckily, Rashid has his back to the students as he gathers the scrolls of text to be copied for the day. Shunat is able to slide in between his friends Jaf and Nekht.

**Jaf:** "That was cutting it close," said the wheat to the plow. Do you not remember what special day it is? This is the day we advance to writing on papyrus. I could hardly sleep all night, dreaming of the beautiful marks my reed will make on this sacred paper.

**Nekht:** Yes, he was waiting at the door even before the teachers had lit the entry lamps. I have never seen a boy so anxious to write. I think he plans to replace the king's vizier. Do you think we should warn the vizier that his job is at stake?

**Jaf:** You joke now, but it is I who will be doing the laughing in the future. I take my years of education seriously, and it shows in my work. The Master himself said he has never seen finer strokes. Your work looks more like scratches from a goose. What position do you ever hope to attain—recorder for the pharaoh's layer of eggs?

**Shunat:** Quiet, both of you, or we will all be in for a beating. Master Rashid is approaching with the daily scrolls to be copied. I hope mine will be something more interesting than yesterday. I spent seven tedious hours copying calculations for a landowner's expenses. Perhaps today I will be more fortunate and be handed the tale of *A Thousand and One Nights*.

**Narrator 8:** The different scrolls that have been found show that the Egyptians recorded a variety of information. Since educated people read for pleasure, some scribes copied stories, proverbs, and love poems. Other writings were referred to as "wisdom literature," which usually consisted of instructions and advice from older and wiser scribes. Scientific papyrus scrolls detailing instructions and information about math, medicine, surgery, and astronomy have also been found.

**Rashid:** Good morning. As you know, today is the day we begin on papyrus. You must work diligently and not waste your ink. Take special care to pull your shenti tight since writing on paper is far less stable than your wooden writing boards. Before we begin I would like our star pupil to review the different types of hieroglyphic signs. I noticed that several of you were still making careless mistakes when I reviewed yesterday's dictation. Jaf, please bring your writing board to the front of the group and show the three different meanings for "ro," or "mouth."

**Jaf:** When I draw a picture of a mouth it can mean mouth, the object. This is using the hieroglyph to represent an idea, and we call it a sense-sign. But this same hieroglyph can also mean the word "toward," since it has the same sound—"ro." In this way it is used as a word-sign. And this same hieroglyph can also be used to form a sound-sign for the "r" sound. So you see, it is quite simple.

# Shunat the Scribe Student *(cont.)*

**Narrator 9:** Obviously, it is not very simple at all, and that is why deciphering these complex hieroglyphics eluded scholars for hundreds of years. After Alexander the Great's conquest of Egypt, its rulers were all Greek. Therefore, the royal language was also Greek. Some inscriptions during this period were recorded in both Egyptian and Greek. Gradually, fewer and fewer people knew how to write Egyptian hieroglyphics. Eventually, the Romans conquered Egypt and spread Christianity throughout the land. By then all knowledge of the old ways of writing had vanished.

**Narrator 10:** Luckily, in 1799 French soldiers were digging near the Nile delta and made a marvelous discovery. They found a stone tablet with inscriptions that had been written by priests back in 196 B.C. The tablet, called the **Rosetta Stone**, contained a royal decree written in Greek, hieroglyphics, and a later form of Egyptian writing. Champollion, a brilliant young French scholar of ancient languages, used the other two languages to decode the hieroglyphic signs and symbols. By 1822 the world knew of his magnificent discovery. Although there was still a great deal of work to be done, this ancient language could be read once more.

**Rashid:** I hope you each take Jaf's example and study hard to learn the many intricacies of our hieroglyphic signs. Today is a special day, and I have chosen a special text. We will write on fresh papyrus the first chapter of the Arabian story, *A Thousand and One Nights*. Please prepare your palettes and writing surfaces.

**Shunat:** Ah, Lord Re has heard my words and smiles upon us today.

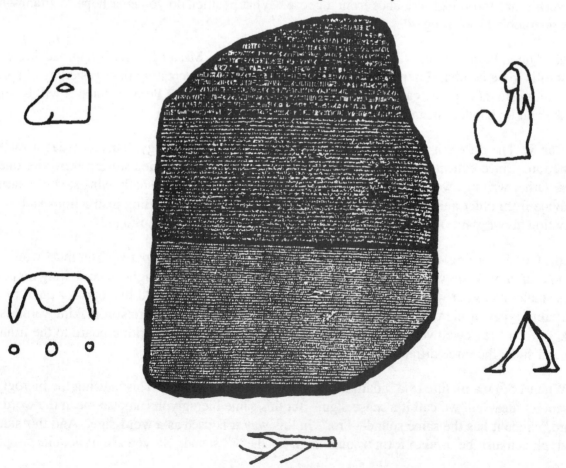

# Shunat the Scribe Student—
# Vocabulary and Comprehension

Write the following words on the chalkboard for students to copy on index cards for their picture dictionary. Remind them to research and write a complete definition, explanation, or example and draw a picture.

**scribe**      **Rosetta Stone**      **hieroglyphics**      **House of Life**      **apprentice**

Use some or all of the following questions for whole-class discussion, small-group work, or individual written assessment. Allow students to refer to *Shunat the Scribe Student* to answer them.

1. Describe the education of an Ancient Egyptian girl. *(She did not go to school. She stayed at home and learned from her mother how to run a household. She learned to cook, sew, and tend to the daily chores. If she was from a wealthy family, she was also taught how to manage the servants and entertain for her husband's guests. Girls were taught how to sing, play music, and dance. Some girls learned to read and write using hieroglyphics.)*

2. Name the three different ways a boy might be educated or learn a trade. *(A boy might be sent to school at the House of Life or the royal palace, he might learn a trade from his father, or he might pay to be an apprentice at a shop and learn a different trade or craft than his father.)*

3. What were some of the advantages of becoming a scribe? *(It was the only profession that allowed a person to better himself socially. A scribe had many opportunities to become wealthy and powerful since all landowners, temples, and wealthy merchants needed someone who could read and write to keep their records. A scribe did not have to do hard labor in the fields or on the building projects.)*

4. What did scribe students write with, and what did they write on? *(Scribes wrote with black and red ink, using a reed pen or stylus. Depending on their level, they wrote on pottery shards, a wooden writing board covered in plaster, or papyrus. They did not have desks, so they stretched their shenti, or kilt, across their knees to make a solid writing surface.)*

5. How was scribe school different from school today? How was it the same? *(Accept reasonable answers.)*

6. Why were hieroglyphics more difficult to learn than our alphabet? *(The signs were more complex than our letters, and there were over 750 signs to memorize. Hieroglyphics were also difficult to master since they could be used in a variety of ways. They could be sound-signs, word-signs, or sense-signs.)*

7. Why was the Rosetta Stone such an important discovery? *(It allowed scholars to decode the hieroglyphic text and read many documents that could not be deciphered earlier.)*

8. Why do you think the instructors used such strict discipline methods? *(Accept reasonable answers.)*

# School Days Then and Now

A day at school for Shunat and his Ancient Egyptian friends was similar and yet different from school today. Have students write a comparison about what school is like now and what scribe school was like back in Ancient Egypt.

## Preparing for the lesson:

1. Reproduce a Compare and Contrast Chart (page 92), an Illustration Page (page 95), and an Editing Checklist (page 25) for each student.

2. Make overhead transparencies of The Writing Process (page 24) and the Compare and Contrast Chart.

3. On the chalkboard, write the Compare and Contrast Words from page 91.

## Teaching the lesson:

1. Use the overhead transparency of The Writing Process to review the steps with students.

2. Distribute a Compare and Contrast Chart to each student. Tell them that they will use this chart for the prewriting stage of their composition comparing school today and school in Ancient Egypt.

3. Display the overhead transparency Compare and Contrast Chart. Write "Scribe School" for Subject #1 and "School Today" for Subject #2.

4. Brainstorm with the class a list of categories to compare the subjects. Possible categories include: time and years spent in class, subjects taught, seating students, materials used, rules in the classroom, consequences, availability to rich or poor, boys and girls, etc. Write several of these categories in the middle column of the transparency.

5. Divide the class into small groups. Allow students to use information from *Shunat the Scribe Student* to find and write supporting details about scribe school. Have them use their personal experiences to write supporting details about school today. Allow time for them to complete the chart.

6. Have groups share their information with the class. Encourage them to add information to their charts as facts are shared.

7. Distribute the Editing Checklist. Review how to use the checklist to improve writing.

8. Review with students the information on Write a Compare and Contrast Composition, page 91. Use the same transparencies you made for this part of the lesson.

# Write a Compare and Contrast Composition

Discuss with the class the following points to help students learn how to use their Compare and Contrast charts to write a composition that compares and contrasts scribe school to school today.

1. Display the transparency of the "Compare and Contrast Chart" (page 92). Point out that the introduction should provide interesting background information that will make the reader want to read the rest of the composition. It should also let the reader know the two subjects (scribe school and school today) that are going to be compared and contrasted in the composition.

2. Tell students to begin a new paragraph by writing a sentence that describes the first category on their charts.

3. Show students how to provide specific supporting details in each category and for each subject. Review the compare and contrast words you have written on the chalkboard (taken from the bottom of this page).

4. Then tell students that they should begin new paragraphs for two to three more categories. Be sure students understand that they should provide specific supporting details for each subject. Students may have categories written on their charts that they don't choose to use in their compositions. Encourage students to use the categories for which they have the most information. This will make the composition much easier to write.

5. Call attention to the conclusion section at the bottom of the "Compare and Contrast Chart." Explain that a conclusion should restate the subject, give a short summary of points covered in the composition, and provide any closing remarks.

6. Display the transparency of "The Writing Process" as students write.

7. Allow ample time for students to use their "Editing Checklist" to improve their rough drafts before making their final drafts.

8. Distribute the "School Days Now and Then Illustration Page" (page 95). You may wish to have students create composition booklets by stapling their final drafts on the right sides of pieces of construction paper, stapling their illustration pages on the left side, folding the in half, and adding titles and their names to the covers.

9. Allow time for students to share their compositions with the class. Then display the compositions in the classroom or in the library for other classes to enjoy.

## Words for Comparing

| | | | |
|---|---|---|---|
| same | similar | also | alike |
| in common | much like | as well as | similarly |
| likewise | too | each | both |

## Words for Contrasting

| | | | | |
|---|---|---|---|---|
| different | however | on the other hand | although | but |
| differently | unlike | differ | differences | yet |

# Compare and Contrast Chart

| Introduction: | | |
|---|---|---|
| **Subject #1:** | | **Subject #2:** |
| **Supporting Details** | **Categories** | **Supporting Details** |
| | | |
| | | |
| | | |
| | | |
| | | |
| Conclusion: | | |

# Hieroglyphics Code

Not all hieroglyphic signs translate into our English alphabet, but this code is a close representation for hieroglyphic sound-signs.

A vulture

B foot

C (use "S" or "K" depending on the sound)

D hand

E 2 reed leaves

F viper

G pot stand

H rope

I reed leaf

J cobra

K basket

L lion

M owl

N water

O wheat

P stool

Q hillside

R open mouth

S folded cloth

T bread loaf

U reed leaf + quail chick

V viper

W quail chick

X basket + folded cloth

Y 2 reed leaves

Z door bolt

SH lake

TH cow belly

CH hobble rope

# Scribe School Sentences

Use the hieroglyphic code to decipher these sentences from the Book of the Dead.

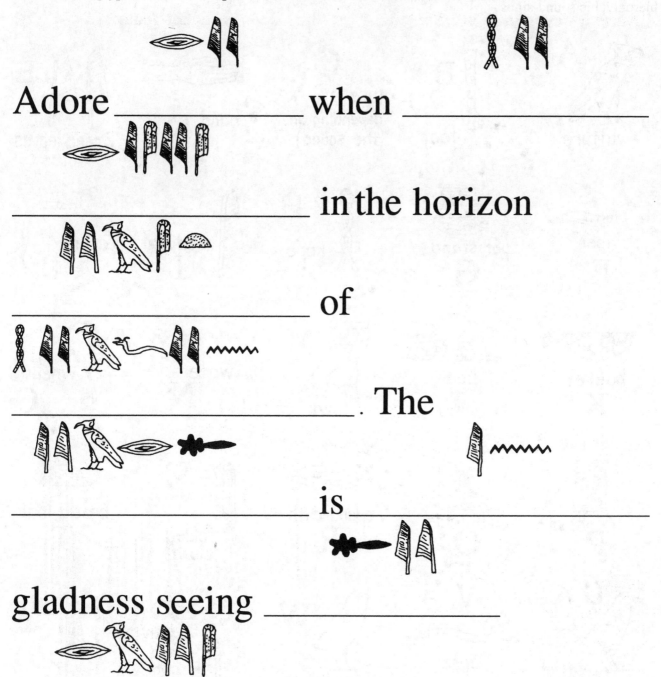

Adore _____ when _____

_____ in the horizon

_____ of

_____ . The

_____ is _____

gladness seeing _____

_____ .

--------------------------------------------------------------------------------

Fold over before reproducing. Adore Re when he rises in the horizon east of heaven. The earth is in gladness seeing thy rays.

# School Days Then and Now Illustration Page

Complete and color each student. Label clothing and school supplies.

**Ancient Egyptian Scribe Student**          **Student Today**

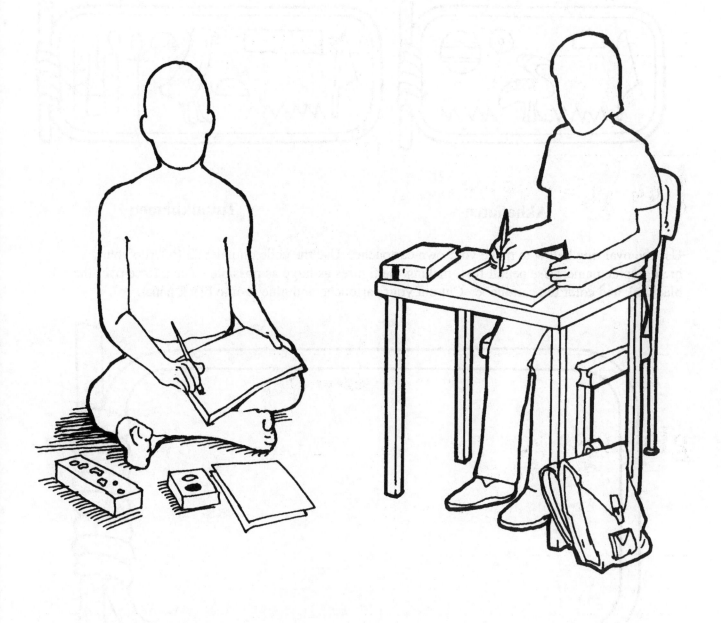

# Make a Personal Cartouche

The individual rulers of Ancient Egypt each had their own personal signatures in the form of cartouches. A royal cartouche consisted of the name of the ruler written in hieroglyphics enclosed in an oval ring. The different royal cartouches were invaluable to early scholars attempting to translate the various hieroglyphic texts. By comparing these early cartouches, Champollion was able to crack the code on the Rosetta Stone, making a momentous breakthrough for further understanding of this ancient written language. Below are two examples of royal cartouches. Words were written right to left, left to right, or top to bottom, and the characters always faced the beginning of the word.

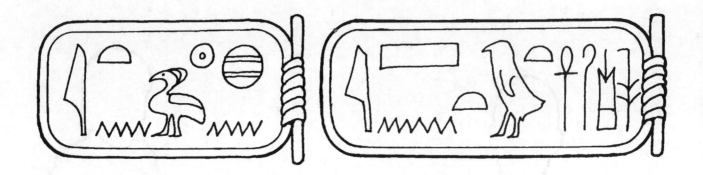

**Akhenaten**                    **Tutankhamen**

Use the oval ring below to make your own cartouche. Use the code on page 93 to write your hieroglyphic name. Use pencil first, making the figures as large as possible. Then, trace over them in black ink and color the cartouche. Cut out your cartouche and glue it onto black paper.

# Make a Scarab Seal Stamp

The Egyptians sometimes used seals to stamp information onto a papyrus scroll or clay tablet. The seal allowed them to quickly write the information needed over and over again without having to handwrite each hieroglyphic sign. The seals were decorated with sacred symbols such as the cat, hippo, or scarab beetle. The scarab was used extensively by Egyptians in their art and for decorating everyday items because the scarab represented the sun god Amon-Re and everlasting life. Like Amon-Re, who carried his daily ball of fire across the sky, the scarab beetle diligently rolled his ball of dung across the desert. Have students create a seal to sign their documents.

## Preparing for the lesson:

1. Bring a portable oven and cookie sheets to class, if possible. (You may wish to just bring the cookie sheets and aluminum foil to hold the stamps on the sheets and then take the stamps home with you to bake.)
2. Gather ink pads and paper for printing with the seals.
3. Gather materials for each student: modeling clay, thin plastic knife, pencil or ballpoint pen, and paper to cover the work area.
4. Gather pictures of scarabs used in Egyptian art to show students as examples.
5. Use some of the modeling clay to make an example of the stamp for yourself.

## Teaching the lesson:

1. Tell students they will be making personal scarab seal stamps, and distribute the materials.
2. Have students use half of their modeling clay to form a scarab beetle. Remind them to press all of the joints together well so the stamp doesn't fall apart while baking. Make sure they press the bottoms onto their work surfaces so that they are flat.

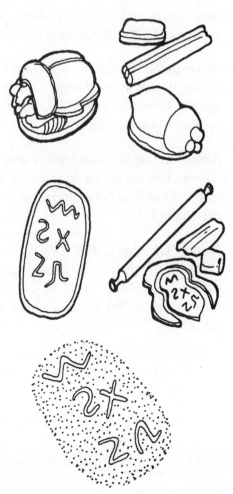

3. Have students press the rest of their clay into bases that are flat on both sides and big enough to attach their scarab models to. Tell them to place their scarabs on top of the flattened clay bases and cut around the scarabs, either in the shape of the scarab outlines or as ovals.
4. Have students lift their scarabs off the bases. Have them use pens or pencils to carve picture hieroglyphics and their initials onto the base. (Remind students that they must carve backwards for the seal to be correct after printing!)
5. When they finish carving, have them carefully lift the bases and attach their scarab beetles to the flat, uncarved side of the bases. The beetle will serve as a handle for the stamp.
6. Place the finished seals on cookie sheets and bake them at 300° F/150° C for ten minutes.
7. When the seals have cooled, have students use them to stamp sign a writing project or piece of art. Let them experiment with different colors of ink and paper. Gold, red, turquoise, royal blue, and black look especially Egyptian.

# Anen the Artist

**Narrators 1–10**    **Hapu,** a stonemason    **Smenkh,** a carpenter    **Ramose,** a potter

**Anen,** an artist    **Tuyu,** a stone crafter    **Penthu,** a goldsmith    **Maya,** a weaver

**Harem,** a friend    **Merit,** a metal worker    **Ay,** a leather worker    **Huy,** a painter

**Narrator 1:** Painters, metal workers, sculptors, and carpenters were all types of craftsmen in Ancient Egypt. Although each was a highly skilled artist, each was trained as a specialist in his field. Therefore, it took several specialists to create any one piece of art. For example, to build a statue for a temple, a stonemason was needed to cut the right-sized block. Then a trained stone crafter would carve the statue, and an inscriber would add hieroglyphics. Perhaps gold or precious gems would be added, requiring the skills of a goldsmith or stone crafter. Finally, since all statues were painted, a skilled painter would add the finishing touches. Join us on a journey through the intricate web of the temple workshops where skilled craftsmen labor to create works of art for the temple, tombs, and royal family.

**Anen:** Greetings, and welcome to the temple workshops! There is much work and commotion among the many artists here, and each craftsman has earned the special privilege of being part of these shops. Only the best artists and craftsmen work on tombs, in the great temple workshops, or on the royal palace.

**Harem:** We were lucky to be considered two of the painters fit for such labor. Many other artists are very capable and work for wealthy noblemen on their vast estates. Some lesser-trained artists work in small towns and villages, making objects to sell locally in the market. Even the common man needs statues and amulets for daily worship.

**Narrator 2:** Egyptians were highly religious and superstitious. All of them kept statues of the different gods in their homes and wore **amulets** around their necks or wrists to protect them from evil spirits. Often the amulet was in the shape of an **ankh,** or a cross with a loop at the top. This was a symbol of everlasting life.

**Anen:** Let us take our friends around to see the various crafts we produce. As everyone knows, Egypt is quite famous for its magnificent artwork. Our first stop will be at the stonemason shop where a new shipment of limestone has just been delivered for carving statues. Ah, I see Hapu is seated at his carving bench.

**Hapu:** Greetings. Today we are carving limestone statues for the royal tomb. Limestone is easier to carve than is the granite from Aswan that was used to build the great **obelisks.** Some of those granite towers stand almost 100 feet (30 m) tall with their pyramid tops covered in precious metals to reflect the sun's rays. We also work with sandstone to build temples, but it doesn't hold up well for smaller statues.

# Anen the Artist *(cont.)*

**Harem:** I am always amazed at the skill of the stone carvers. Some shape enormous blocks of stone standing hundreds of feet high, while others hollow out delicate vases and jars used for cosmetics.

**Hapu:** From the earliest of times, stonemasons have used the simplest of tools to craft fine art pieces from the beautiful minerals found in the Egyptian hills and desert. Saws are used to cut enormous blocks down to the right size, and chisels and drills are used to shape the piece. On this statue, you can see the markings in red ocher that guide my chisel. A stone sculptor must have much patience and a steady hand to keep his carving true and his hands safe from injury. Take a look at Tuyu's beads before you go. They are truly stunning!

**Anen:** Tuyu, Hapu has been bragging about your fine beadwork. We Egyptians love jewelry and wear as much as we can afford. You must be kept especially busy working for the wife of the pharaoh.

**Tuyu:** How true, Anen. The most popular stones from the desert mines are blue-green turquoise, red and orange carnelian, green feldspar or malachite, mauve amethyst, and the most highly prized deep-blue lapis lazuli, imported from as far east as Afghanistan. A cheap substitute for the lapis lazuli can be made by firing copper ore and silica together to make a rough glass. Then we grind it into a powder, sprinkle it into settings, and melt it to make shiny inlays of blue glass. The queen gets nothing but the real thing, of course.

**Harem:** Of course. I see you are working with some lapis beads now. How do you get them so round and shiny?

**Tuyu:** The stones are broken down and roughly shaped by rolling. Then, they are smoothed by rubbing them together. We make a hole using a bow drill. This is a bow that is pulled back and forth rapidly, spinning a stick with a piece of sharp metal on the end. Once the holes are made, we polish the stones and string them together.

**Anen:** I see. And are these blue amulets, plates, and beads also made of lapis lazuli?

**Tuyu:** No, those all are made from **faience**, a glazed ceramic material. If we take the glass powder and mix it further with narton, or sodium carbonate, we can paint it on clay items such as beads, drinking vessels, mummy plaques, and plates. Once it is fired, it gives off the rich, shiny blue color you see.

# Anen the Artist *(cont.)*

**Narrator 3:** Today, faience can be found in the form of Egyptian paste, a claylike substance that forms crystals when it dries. Once fired, the crystals create the blue glaze of the faience. Stonemasons also worked on more delicate projects, such as vases, jars, cosmetic holders, and the canopic jars with sculpted animal-face lids that hold the internal organs of the deceased.

**Anen:** Thank you for the lesson. We must be on our way to the metalwork shops. Come, Harem, let us find our friend Merit. Perhaps he is working on a fine copper or bronze sculpture today.

**Merit:** Good day, friends. I have saved the unveiling of my latest work for your arrival. Earlier this month I formed a model out of beeswax. Then I carefully covered the model with clay, leaving a small hole in the base. Once the clay was completely dry, it was ready for bronze smelted in a bellow-powered furnace. I poured the molten bronze through a funnel into the clay mold. You can see the wax around the bottom that drained out the hole in the base. Today it is cool enough to break off the mold. Stand back while I carefully crack the clay with my hammer.

**Harem:** What a stunning likeness of Osiris! You have used such detail and precision that it must be for the pharaoh's tomb. Is that the way all metal objects are made?

**Merit:** Some tools, decorative tomb items, and statuettes require molds. For example, an ax is cast in a mold and then sharpened to produce the sharp cutting blade. It is then lashed with leather thongs to a wooden handle. Other metal items, such as farming tools, weapons, cooking utensils, and jars, are made by hammering the metal to the desired thickness and shape.

**Harem:** I see your supervisor over by the scales. Has there been a shortage of metal?

**Merit:** No, but weighing the metals is always a serious business and carried out only in the presence of the overseer. In Egypt, all metals are precious because they are rare and difficult to mine. Each morning we are given a precise amount of metal that is carefully weighed and recorded. It is even more strict in the goldsmith shops.

**Penthu:** Gold is the most precious of all the metals. Gold objects are made in a variety of ways. Over by the furnace you can see a worker melting ingots to pour into a cast, or mold. This method is used for smaller objects, such as jewelry, small statues, or amulets. Even the smallest shavings of gold are swept from the ground, cleaned, heated, and repoured to make fresh ingots. Some ingots are made into gold wire. The workers heat the ingot so that it is flexible. Then, using tongs, they pull it through a hole on an annealing board. Each time, they draw it through a smaller and smaller hole, stretching out the gold into a thin, long wire. Different thicknesses of wire are then used to make chains and add decorations to objects.

**Harem:** How do you make a larger item such as a mummy mask, bowl, or goblet?

**Penthu:** For larger items the ingots are beaten into thin sheets and then formed to their desired shape. Here, take a look at these goblets for the temple. It takes much skill to form the vessel without marring the surface with the hammer. Ah, here comes the head priest now to check the goblets. I must say farewell.

# Anen the Artist *(cont.)*

**Narrator 4:** When you study artwork from famous excavations such as King Tut's tomb, it may appear that gold was plentiful in Egypt. In reality, all metal was rare and difficult to acquire. Gold was mined in Nubia and the eastern desert. The conditions of the mines were so outrageous that criminals sent there to labor for their crimes rarely returned. All of the gold was sent only to the temple or pharaoh's workshops, since it belonged to the god-king, and he could choose what and how items would be made.

**Anen:** We must go on and stop by the carpenters' benches. I understand they have been building some furniture for the temple, and it is of the latest design.

**Harem:** One artist cannot help but admire the work of another. I am anxious to see this furniture. I understand it is made completely from imported cedar from Lebanon! Then let's go visit the craft quarter where everyday objects such as cloth, pots, and leather rope are made. The noise in these workshops is giving me a headache. I can't wait to get back to the quiet of the temple where we can paint in peace.

**Narrator 5:** There are many paintings depicting the highly organized workshops of the temple and palace. The pictures show many different craftsmen working under the care of supervisors who inspect the finished art and goods. Although these paintings show the workshops to be clean and orderly, most likely they were hot, noisy, smelly, and crowded with smoldering metals, smoking pots of fatty glue, dust from grinding-stone drills and wooden projects, as well as the bustling of workers passing off pieces to be finished by other specialists.

**Narrator 6:** High-quality imported wood was very expensive. Therefore, imported wood was usually mixed with locally grown wood to build most items. Then it was painted or inlaid with ebony or ivory to mask the different wood grains. The poor-quality local wood was also carved into statues that had to be covered with gesso, a mixture of chalk and glue, to make the surface smooth for painting.

**Smenkh:** Be careful as you walk. A carpenter uses many sharp blades in his craft, and the many planks of wood are easy to stumble upon. We produce a wide variety of projects in our shop. The carpenters build boats, furniture, funeral statues, coffins, and even the grand doors for the palace and temples. We rely on many tools for carving, cutting, and splitting. The group of men over there is preparing planks for a boat. One uses an adze and mallet, one uses a bow drill, and another uses a saw. We also use a variety of chisels, axes, and hammers.

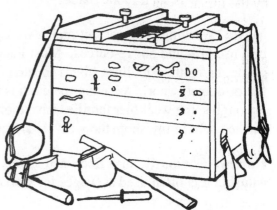

**Anen:** We have come to see the new temple furniture.

**Smenkh:** Unfortunately, the last piece was finished today and delivered to the temple. The pieces were truly works of art. I was not allowed to work on them myself since I am only an **apprentice**, but someday I hope to make the coffin for the pharaoh himself.

# Anen the Artist *(cont.)*

**Narrator 7:** Sons of craftsmen always followed their fathers' trades and were trained from a very early age. But one could also pay to become an apprentice or student at a particular workshop. If a boy could not afford the apprentice fee, he might be sponsored by a wealthy landowner or nobleman. Of course, only those showing the most promise were allowed to apprentice at the temple workshops or those for the royal palace.

**Anen:** Here we are at the tannery. I see Ay is preparing a skin to make rope. Greetings, Ay. How goes the leather work today?

**Ay:** Fine. Lord Re shines brightly upon our animal skins. I am cutting leather strips, while other workers stretch and weave the strips into a sturdy rope to be used by farmers and builders. People tend to take my work for granted, but leather is used for many tasks and on many tools. Blades are attached to handles with leather, shields and armor are crafted from thick leather hides, and the sandals made for the wealthy are also cut from leather. It seems my work is never done.

**Harem:** Well, we shall leave you to your work then, friend, and visit the weavers and potters. My wife's friend Maya said we should stop in today on our tour. I hope she is on the loom and can show us how to weave the linen Egypt is so famous for.

**Anen:** We are in luck, for there is Maya now. Look at the beautiful cloth she is carrying. It must be linen for the royal family; see how it shimmers with gold.

**Maya:** Hello, Harem. How is your dear wife? I have been expecting you.

**Harem:** My wife is well and would be most envious of the fine cloth you carry. We assume it is destined for the royal tailors.

**Maya:** Yes, it was woven just today. Here in the temple workshop we make plain cloth for daily use and also the fine linens used for royal garments and ceremonies. This cloth has fine golden threads woven through it.

**Anen:** How is such fabric made?

**Maya:** Weaving is an ancient craft. We Egyptians did not invent the loom, but I believe we make the best use of it and our resources. Most linen cloth is made from flax, and many people are needed to create the cloth. The linen fiber is beaten from the flax plant and then spun on a stick weighted with a flat or domed whorl. Weaving the cloth is more professional work. Looms take up much space, although some wealthier families have looms in their courtyards and employ full-time weavers. As you can see here in my shop, the weavers are generally women, which is unusual for craft shops.

**Harem:** Obviously, such fine linen as this requires finishing by a special craftsperson. Linen is so valuable it is often used as wages for workers.

**Maya:** This is true. And we weave not only cloth from flax but also rope, mats, baskets, and sandals. Palm fiber and grasses are also used. Baskets are needed by all for storage in the home. We make baskets of various shapes and sizes, many with lids. We have even made small tables, using woven reeds.

# Anen the Artist *(cont.)*

**Anen:** You are right, Maya. Egyptians do use their resources well. Now we must move on. We have time only for a quick stop at the potter's stall and perhaps a bite to eat.

**Ramose:** I heard you were touring about. Let me show you my shop. Here you can see some smaller pots being made with coils of clay. Once the coils are wound about, they are carefully joined and sealed. We create a wide variety of vessels. Some are buff colored with red designs painted in ocher. Others are formed from red clay and then placed upside down over the fire's smoldering ashes to create black insides and rims. Over here is one of our latest inventions. It is a circular platform that can be spun around with your hand or foot. This is very helpful when making the large pots needed for storing water and grains. You can see one of the potters flattening and smoothing the sides, using a large wooden paddle.

**Anen:** Your pots are some of the finest in Egypt. You have many beautiful funerary vessels fit for a pharaoh's tomb. Thank you for showing us your work.

**Narrator 8:** The two men went back to the temple where they sat in the shade and ate their meager lunches brought from home. After drinking some water, they went into the temple and gathered their paints and reed brushes.

**Narrator 9:** Paints were made from egg yolk or gummy glue mixed with color from powdered minerals and water. Artists followed strict rules of color and form. Black, made from soot, represented life in the afterworld. Statues of dead people were often painted black before being placed in a tomb. Green was made from malachite, or copper ore, and represented resurrection. Red, made from iron ore and ocher, meant evil. White represented hope and was made from chalk, gypsum, or limestone. Statues of the gods were painted with yellow ocher to represent their golden skin. Shades of brown were made from various soils, while blue was created using azurite.

**Narrator 8:** The Egyptians also melted beeswax and spread it over their paintings. They then fused it into a smooth surface by holding it over the embers of a charcoal fire. These ancient artists believed this method allowed their work to last forever. And some paintings have lasted more than 5,000 years.

# Anen the Artist *(cont.)*

**Anen:** The temple wall has been prepared and marked for our grid painting. First the wall is smoothed and covered with gesso. Then a special grid of lines is drawn horizontally and vertically using twine soaked in paint. The twine is held taut against the wall and plucked, leaving a straight line. The individual squares determine the form of the painting—one square represents the size of a fist of the painted figure.

**Harem:** Today we will sketch the different figures in the painting. Each part of the body fits a certain number of squares. Each figure, from the hairline to the base of the foot, equals 18 squares. The figures must be painted in profile, with two very important exceptions—the shoulders and eye always face forward so they are visible. For other items there are other rules. Objects from nature are painted in profile. Garden pools or the Nile are painted from above. Baskets and tables are shown from the side with food and items piled up sideways into the air.

**Narrator 10:** You may wonder why all figures in Egyptian art were drawn this way. It is not because the artists were unskilled. Art was a means of religious expression rather than a purely artistic one. To the Egyptians, paintings were not symbolic but magical. Tomb paintings were believed to become real in the afterlife, so they had to be depicted as clearly as possible and show all important features at the same time. Therefore, artists were not free to paint what they saw; they had to follow strict rules. It wasn't until the reign of Akhenaten in the New Kingdom that artists were encouraged to paint and sculpt using perspective.

**Anen:** We sometimes carve the walls deep in the recesses of a tomb. We use the artificial light of a bronze reflector or oil lamp. These paintings are called reliefs since they are carved as well as painted. Usually reliefs depict scenes of daily life and objects the deceased might need in the afterlife.

**Harem:** On a relief the grid is also formed to guide the drawing. Then, the background is carved away so that the figure stands out from the wall. Next, the carving is also painted. On outside walls we carve an outline deep into the stone so that the sun can make strong shadows. Sometimes the figure itself is carved away so that the background stands out.

**Anen:** Harem and I must get back to work. We hope that our brief visit helps you appreciate and want to learn more about our splendid artwork and crafts.

# Anen the Artist—Vocabulary and Comprehension

Write the following words on the chalkboard for students to copy on index cards for their picture dictionary. Remind them to research and write a complete definition, explanation, or example and draw a picture.

| | | |
|---|---|---|
| **amulet** | **ankh** | **obelisk** |
| **faience** | **apprentice** | **grid painting and reliefs** |

Use some or all of the following questions for whole-class discussion, small-group work, or individual written assessment. Allow students to refer to *Anen the Artist* to answer them.

1. Name five different types of arts or crafts in Ancient Egypt. *(any five—items made from carved stone, rocks, or minerals; items crafted from metals, wood, gold, leather, pottery or clay, weaving, and painting)*

2. Why do you think the Egyptians carved their statues, buildings, and objects such as bowls and vases out of stone rather than wood? *(They did not have a ready wood supply, but they did have an ample supply of different stones from the vast desert.)*

3. Describe the steps for making a bronze, copper, or gold object using a mold. *(First, a model is carved out of beeswax. Then it is covered with clay, leaving a hole in the bottom for drainage. Once the clay hardens, the melted metal is poured into the clay mold. The wax melts and runs out of the bottom. Once the metal is completely cooled, the clay mold is broken off to reveal the metal object.)*

4. Name at least three items built by carpenters. *(any three—boats, coffins, statues, doors, furniture, and other decorative items)*

5. How could a boy become an artist or craftsman in Ancient Egypt? *(He could be trained by his father. A boy could also pay to be an apprentice in a particular craft shop or be sponsored to become an apprentice.)*

6. How did a boy get to work in the temple or palace workshops? *(He had to develop a high level of skill, as only the most highly skilled artists were chosen to work in the temple or palace workshops.)*

7. Describe the steps Ancient Egyptians used to make a gold chain. *(A gold ingot is heated and then pulled through a series of holes on an annealing board. This stretches the gold into wire. The wire is pulled through smaller and smaller holes until it is the desired thickness. Then, it is cut and shaped to form a chain.)*

8. Which trade was typically run by women? *(weaving)*

9. Why do you think most Egyptian cloth was woven from flax rather than cotton or wool? *(Flax grew in abundance in Egypt and could be used in a wide variety of ways. It was also a cooler cloth.)*

10. Why did the Egyptians follow a strict mathematical code for pictures? *(Art was considered magical and religious rather than a form of artistic expression. It was important to show many features of the person or objects all at once, so all artists were trained in and used the same techniques.)*

# Build Temple Workshops

Many Egyptian paintings depict the intricate workings of the temple and palace arts and crafts workshops. Have your students design a bulletin board showing the different skills and objects made by the Ancient Egyptians.

## Preparing for the lesson:

1. Divide the class into nine groups and provide a work space for each. Choose a vertical or horizontal bulletin-board display format so students know which direction their papers should be placed for drawing.

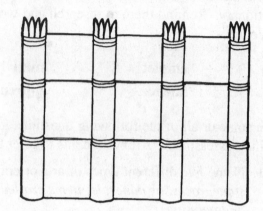

2. Gather white poster board or large sheets of white drawing paper, pencils, erasers, crayons, thin black markers, and colored markers for each group.

3. Assemble pictures from books showing artists and craftsmen at work. Students can also use the pictures from *Anen the Artist* as a reference guide.

## Teaching the lesson:

1. Assign each group a craft shop:

   - stonemason shop—carve large statues, large building blocks, obelisks, etc.
   - stone worker shop—make stone jewelry, vases, bowls, plates, canopic jars, faience, etc.
   - metal worker shop—make copper and bronze items such as weapons, statues, pans, etc.
   - carpenter shop—carve boats, furniture, statues, doors, etc.
   - goldsmith shop—make jewelry, goblets, bowls, collars, mummy masks, etc.
   - tannery shop—make leather items such as rope, sandals, armor, etc.
   - pottery shop—make pots, jars, bowls, plates, statues, faience, etc.
   - weaving shop—show a loom and weaving of different types of cloth
   - painters shop—tomb paintings, reliefs, painted statues, etc.

2. Distribute the materials. Remind students to draw vertically or horizontally on their paper or poster board, whichever you have determined will be the format of your bulletin board. Have students label their craft shop and fill the entire sheet of paper with pictures showing the methods for making the craft and the different types of objects that are made there. Tell students to outline their drawings in black marker and use bold colors so that they can be seen from a distance. Have them sign their posters on the front.

3. Review rules for group work and circulate around the room, helping as needed.

4. Arrange completed posters in a grid on the bulletin board. Have the first four groups finished make four large, colorful Egyptian columns out of butcher paper to place between the workshops.

5. Title the bulletin board "Egyptian Arts and Crafts—The Temple Workshops." Add artwork to the bulletin board as you complete different projects.

106

# Mathematical Grid Egyptian Portraits

The painters of the famous temples and tombs in Egypt followed a strict set of rules to create their works of art. Have your students create colorful Egyptian portraits following these same guidelines.

## Preparing for the lesson:

1. Gather for each student a sheet of graph paper with half-inch (1 cm) grids, a fine-point black marker, colored markers (including flesh colors), and gold and silver fine-point paint pens, available at art or office supply stores. You may wish to ask students to provide their own.

2. Make an overhead transparency of the seated and standing portrait example (page 108), showing the dimensions.

3. Gather other examples of portraits.

## Teaching the lesson:

1. Tell students that they will be creating an Egyptian portrait, using the same methods and guidelines as the Ancient Egyptians.

2. Display portrait examples with dimensions. Point out the specific dimensions and copy the chart below onto the chalkboard for reference.

3. Have students review many different samples to get ideas for their portraits.

4. Distribute the graph paper. Have students decide to each make a seated or standing figure. (The standing figure is easiest!) Have students mark and label their graph papers with the proper dimensions as shown on the overhead transparency.

5. Check to make sure students' graph paper is properly labeled and then have students sketch their figures in pencil. Circulate around the room and offer help as needed.

6. When students have completed their sketches, check them. If they are okay, have them outline the sketches in permanent black marker. Have students trace their outlines onto white copy paper before coloring.

7. Have students add details, an Egyptian-design border, and color their drawings. Have students choose color schemes that use no more than five colors on their entire portraits. The background color will need to be a contrasting color not used on the figure.

8. Display portraits on a bulletin board or have students use them as a cover for a writing piece.

### Egyptian Portrait Grid Chart

1 square = the width of the fist of the figure

18 squares = wig line/forehead to the soles of the feet

3 squares = sole of the foot to the middle of the calf

3 squares = middle of the calf to just above the knee

3 squares = just above the knee to the wrist

3 squares = wrist or mid-figure to the elbow

3 squares = elbow to the shoulders

3 squares = shoulders to the wig line/forehead

2 squares = the face

3 squares = length of the foot

5 squares = shoulders to approximately the waistline

# Mathematical Grid Egyptian Portraits *(cont.)*

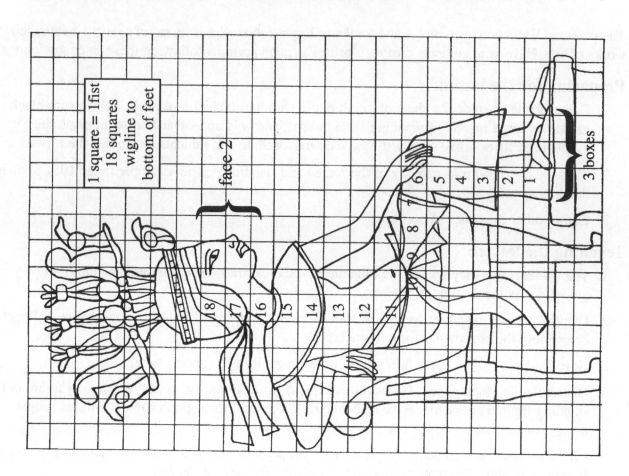

1 square = 1fist
18 squares
wigline to
bottom of feet

face 2

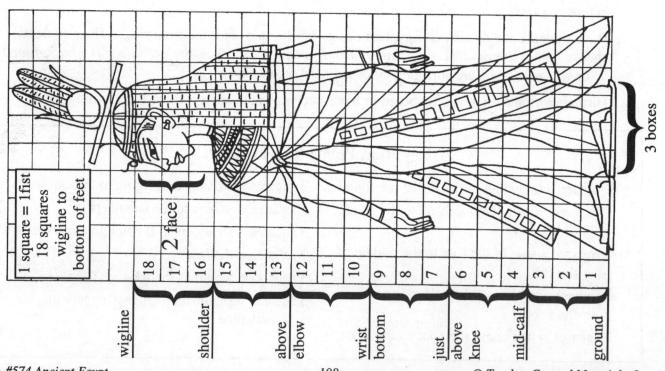

1 square = 1fist
18 squares
wigline to
bottom of feet

2 face

3 boxes

| | |
|---|---|
| 18 | wigline |
| 17 | |
| 16 | shoulder |
| 15 | |
| 14 | |
| 13 | above |
| 12 | elbow |
| 11 | |
| 10 | |
| 9 | wrist |
| 8 | bottom |
| 7 | |
| 6 | just above |
| 5 | knee |
| 4 | |
| 3 | mid-calf |
| 2 | |
| 1 | ground |

108

# Make a Relief Carving

Another popular form of art was carving the walls inside the tombs or temples before painting them. Have students create their own relief carvings.

## Preparing for the lesson:

1. Prepare the tile grout at least one day ahead of time. Gather a plastic tub, sturdy spoon, and a medium-sized bag of white tile grout. Mix the tile grout, following the directions on the bag. Pour the prepared grout mix into Styrofoam meat trays (one for each student; one for your sample) to about a half-inch (1.25 cm) thick. Let the grout set overnight.

2. Make a sample. Gather samples of Egyptian art to use as other samples.

3. Gather scratch paper and a carving tool for each student (thick paper clips work well).

4. Assemble water color paints, cans of water, and brushes.

5. Cover work areas with paper or plastic to catch tile grout dust as students carve.

## Teaching the lesson:

1. Tell students that they each will be making an Egyptian relief painting by carving and painting a plasterlike surface. Display the samples.

2. Distribute scratch paper and have students draw the images they want to carve onto the tile grout. Remind them to keep it simple—a face, animal, Egyptian symbol, or part of a picture that is like a broken fragment from a tomb wall.

3. Distribute a slab of dried tile grout to each student. Have students keep the tile grout in the tray until the project is completed.

4. Have students lightly pencil-sketch their drawings onto the tile grout.

5. Distribute paper clips. Have students carve out the outlines of their pictures or carve away the backgrounds, leaving their pictures standing out in relief.

6. Once the carvings are complete, invite students to paint their carvings, using very little water, since the colors will bleed. Have students practice on the backs of their carvings before painting the fronts. Have them carve their initials on the backs, too.

7. Display the painted reliefs on a counter by removing them from the trays and placing them on a small sheet of colored construction paper. Have students write their names and titles on the construction paper. Some students may choose to carefully break away the edges to give a rough, authentic look to their relief.

8. Option: use light-brown tile grout and have the students make an unpainted carving.

# Make Clay Coil Pottery

Early Egyptian pottery was made by winding coils of clay on top of each other to form a shape. Have students create small Egyptian pottery, using the coil method.

## Preparing for the lesson:

1. Gather white or red clay, string, round-tipped plastic knives, paints, and paintbrushes.

2. Assemble pictures of Egyptian pottery. Make a transparency of page 111.

3. With water, thin the paint so that it is thinner than tempera but not as watery as a wash. If you are using white clay, mix a little red and brown paint together. If you are using red clay, thin down black paint.

4. Make a sample pot.

5. Cover the work areas with plastic or paper and place a small container of water at each work area to keep the clay moist.

## Teaching the lesson:

1. Tell students that they will be creating a small pot using the coil method. Display the transparency, your sample pot, and other examples of Egyptian pottery. Have students note the shape and designs found on Egyptian pottery.

2. Using a piece of string, cut each student a slab of clay.

3. Have students roll the clay into long "snakes" about as thick as a finger.

4. Have students wind the clay around to form a closed, coiled circle to form the base. Have them coil more clay snakes around the perimeter of the base. Remind students to keep the clay moist (but not wet) while working. Have students pinch the coils together as they stack them.

5. When the desired shape has been achieved, have students use the plastic knives to smooth out the coils on the outside. Then, have them add handles or other features.

6. Allow the pottery to dry completely before baking it in a kiln. Drying time depends on the weather and thickness of the clay. (Clay that has been fired in a kiln is much more durable and less likely to break. However, air-dried clay objects can be painted.)

7. Have students paint designs onto their pots. Use red/brown paint on white clay or black paint on red clay.

8. Display the pottery on a counter or shelves.

# Clay Coil Pottery Examples

# Egyptian Paste (Faience) Amulets or Shabti Sculptures

Faience, or Egyptian paste, was used by the craftsmen in Ancient Egypt as a cheaper alternative to lapis-lazuli. Provide students the opportunity to experiment with this claylike substance to create amulets or shabti figures like those in the Egyptian tombs. (Note: You must order the Egyptian paste at least two weeks prior to the lesson. You must also have access to a kiln to bake the objects for this lesson.)

## Preparing for the lesson:

1. Order five pounds (2 to 3 kg) of powdered Copper Blue Egyptian by calling **Laguna Clay Company, Ceramic Research and Supplies, 14400 Lomitas Avenue, City of Industry, CA 91746, 1-800-338-8846.** Make sure you ask the current price, cost for shipping, and if they can include any special instructions for mixing with water or for firing in a kiln.

2. Gather pictures of shabti figures, scarab beetles, ankhs, or any other simple Egyptian figure to use as examples for the students.

3. In a large plastic tub, mix the powder with water to the consistency of clay. If there is too much water, the objects will not hold their shapes. Use your hands to thoroughly combine the powder and water.

4. Cover student work areas with plastic or paper.

## Teaching the lesson:

1. Review with students what Egyptian paste, or faience, is. Describe the different types of items made from this material. Display the sample pictures. Tell students that every year people were required to help with the farming. However, wealthy Egyptians could pay someone to do their work for them. When the deceased arrived in heaven, they, too, were required to help with the farming. Therefore, wealthy people were buried with shabti sculptures to do their work after death. The quality and quantity of shabtis in a tomb gave clues to archaeologists as to the social status of the deceased. By 1000 B.C., rich Egyptians were being buried with 401 shabtis to ensure a fresh worker for each day of the calendar year and bosses to oversee the workers as they toiled in the afterworld. Historians have found stories that claim the dead person would chant, "O Ushabti. If I am called upon to pull weeds or water the river banks or plow the fields, you will say, 'Here I am.'"

2. Distribute to each student a ball of paste the size of an oversized golf ball. Have students form their object, making sure all pieces are connected securely. Tell students to construct Shabtis lying down rather than standing.

3. Allow the objects to dry for about a week. Small crystals will form on the surfaces as the paste dries. These crystals become the glaze when the objects are fired, so handle the dried paste carefully.

4. Follow the instructions from the Laguna Clay Company for firing in the kiln.

5. The objects will emerge from the kiln a bright, shiny blue. Display them on bright red construction paper with the students' names and titles of their sculptures.

# Pentah the Priest

| | | | |
|---|---|---|---|
| **Narrators 1–7** | **Satu,** a man | **Trindad,** his wife | **Banthur,** his son |
| **Sinkha,** his daughter | **Hapshet,** a scribe | **Pentah,** a priest | **Darzun,** the vizier |
| **Semat,** a priest | **Iphoter,** the architect | **Reshep,** a reader priest | |

**Narrator 1:** Religion played a very important role in the daily lives of Ancient Egyptians. They believed that by worshiping their gods in special ways they could protect themselves from their enemies, sickness, evil spirits, and the forces of nature.

**Pentah:** We will start our tour today in the family home of Satu. Ordinary people do not normally visit the temples of the great gods.

**Satu:** We believe that these great gods are too remote to be concerned with the everyday troubles of ordinary people. Only the pharaoh and the rich and powerful priests are allowed to take part in the secret and intricate ceremonies inside the grand temple walls. But every family worships daily within its household and community.

**Trindad:** Come see the statues that honor our gods. Although our gods do not have temples, we offer them prayers and gifts within our homes and at small local **shrines**. There are a number of gods that watch over the family and protect us from wrongdoing. We worship these gods to help us with common problems at home and at work. One of the most popular gods is Bes.

**Sinkha:** Bes is a joyful family god associated with feasting, dancing, and music. He looks like a plump little dwarf with the mane, ears, and tail of a lion. We paint his image inside our homes and wear amulets of his likeness to ward off evil.

**Banthur:** We Egyptians are very superstitious people. We wear jewelry and amulets for protection. Workmen in the desert pray to the cobra goddess, Meretseger, and carry magical batons shaped like boomerangs to draw a circle around their sleeping areas to ward off snakes or scorpions with their spell.

**Sinkha:** Other statues and objects within our homes are carved with pictures and spells to protect our families.

**Satu:** Of course, all Egyptians like to enjoy themselves with singing, dancing, eating, and drinking. That is why we especially enjoy the holidays when we have a **festival** to the gods. It is only on these festival days that we might catch a glimpse of the shrine containing a divine statue of one of the great gods as it is carried from one temple to another. The statue is encased within a shrine because the image is too sacred for ordinary people to see.

**Trindad:** During the festival, the statue or shrine is paraded through the streets on a boat called a *bark*. People can ask advice of the god, and they look for a response in the form of a dip or movement in the boat. The pharaoh, priests, and noblemen accompany the procession. Sometimes the procession is followed by a reenactment of a story or **myth** important to our religion. Most celebrations coincide with important events during the year, such as the flooding of the Nile or harvesting of crops. We also arrange festivals for when one god visits another in a nearby neighboring temple.

# Pentah the Priest *(cont.)*

**Narrator 2:** The Egyptians worshiped many gods—a practice known as **polytheism**. Some lists found have named more than 80 gods. Before Egypt became a unified region, each small band of people living along the Nile worshiped an animal as their protective emblem, or totem. They also had their own hero that performed good deeds. They built temples where they believed these heroes had been buried. Eventually, the animals and the hero became one. They now had gods with powerful abilities, and they depicted them accordingly so that they could be identified.

**Narrator 3:** Certain gods were identified as the patrons of specific arts and occupations. Other gods were assigned to perform specific duties for humans. In time, stories about the different gods were shared, and different beliefs became intermixed. Therefore, certain gods and goddesses became confused with others and took on properties and attributes that were not theirs in the beginning.

**Narrator 4:** During the New Kingdom, the pharaoh Akhenaten made his people worship only one god—the sun disc, Aten. But once Akhenaten died, the people destroyed most of the temples and returned to polytheism. Egyptian religion evolved for over 3,000 years. This makes understanding the different gods and their duties very confusing!

**Banthur:** Of course, household gods such as Bes do not have great festivals organized by the priests. Instead, we honor them in unofficial ways with parades in our local community. On these days, people wear masks and dance, shake tambourines, and beat ivory clappers. The community sings and follows the dancers. Then, there is usually a great feast. Everyone is involved in some manner.

**Pentah:** Thank you for sharing with us. We must go meet with the pharaoh's vizier and temple architect.

**Darzun:** Hello. Are you ready to tour the temple grounds? The pharaoh is the gods' son on earth, so he is owed much respect and honor. It is his duty to feed and protect the gods, as well as keep everything in proper order for them. By doing this, the pharaoh can preserve the harmony of the world so that the gods might look favorably upon Egypt and its people. Without this balance, there would be disorder and chaos for all.

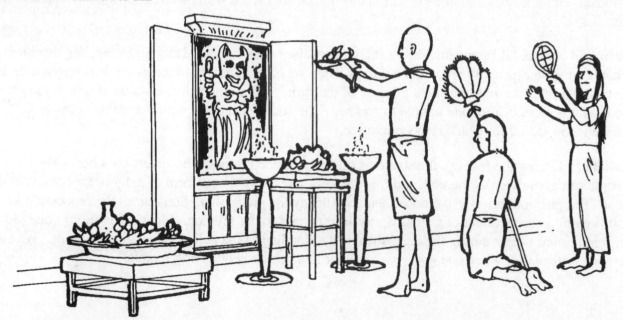

# Pentah the Priest *(cont.)*

**Pentah:** The pharaoh is the real high priest of each god. In every temple is a picture of the pharaoh making his daily offerings. But with so many other functions to perform, his daily religious duties are often carried out by priests acting in his behalf.

**Iphoter:** Every town in Egypt has a temple dedicated to its local god or family of gods. Large or small, temples have a similar design based on the first temples ever built—believed to have been built by the gods themselves. Temples symbolize the world. The lower portion represents the earth. From it extend tall columns with tops shaped like lotus blossoms, papyrus, and palms. The columns stretch to the ceiling, which symbolizes heaven and is painted with birds and stars.

**Darzun:** Each temple is built on the spot where the god is believed to dwell. According to legend, the gods once roamed the earth but are now in the land of the dead. Therefore, the temple represents the home of their spirit, or ka. The daily rituals are designed to awaken the god's ka so that its power can help Egypt.

**Iphoter:** The inside of the temple contains a series of courtyards and halls with many columns. The innermost sanctuary containing the god's statue is small and dark. Priests enter the sanctuary with torches to light their way and perform the daily rituals.

**Semat:** Come, Pentah, we will let your friends get a usually forbidden look at the inner workings of the temple. Each day begins the same, and there are many grades of priests under the high priest, with many separate duties. Before Re appears over the horizon, the temple kitchens are abuzz with the commotion of preparing the meat and bread for the god's meals. At dawn, a choir of priests and priestesses awake the god's ka with song as they proceed toward the inner sanctuary containing the golden statue. The priestesses also play ritual music on their sacred rattles or necklaces adorned with beads.

**Pentah:** Only priests who have purified themselves are allowed into the inner room. Purification is achieved by bathing twice a day and twice each night in the sacred lake.

**Narrator 5:** Washing was only one part of the purification process. Each priest was also required to shave his body and head every three days to free himself from possible infestations of lice. This was also why they dressed only in white linen; animal skin clothing was forbidden. However, there was one type of priest who was allowed to wear a panther skin over his linen robes.

**Semat:** Once inside the torchlit sanctuary, we break the clay seals to the shrine and reveal the statue. Then we remove the statue and take off the clothing and makeup from the previous day. The statue is then washed and anointed with sweet-smelling oils. Incense is burned to purify the room.

**Pentah:** Next, we dress the statue in fresh linens, makeup, and jewelry before presenting it with the morning meal.

**Narrator 6:** Naturally, the statue of the god didn't really eat and drink. It was believed that the ka ate the "spirit" of the food, and, therefore, it was later removed and eaten by the priests as a form of payment. This ritual of meals occurred again at midday and in the evening.

# Pentah the Priest *(cont.)*

**Semat:** At the end of the day, the god's statue is put to rest back in the shrine and sealed. The room is then purified with incense, and all footprints are carefully swept away. Throughout all of these ceremonies we chant while a reader priest recites from a sacred scroll. Reshep is one of the reader priests.

**Reshep:** Most priests spend about three months of the year working in the temple. The rest of the year we live at home with our families, where we work as scribes, lawyers, and doctors. Although we are to live a simple life, we are well paid, well educated, and highly respected by the public and pharaoh. Priests in Egypt have become a very powerful group. Priests are not the only people working at the temple, however. We also employ scribes, librarians, doctors, teachers, cooks, and craftspeople of all kinds. Hapshet is one of our temple scribes.

**Hapshet:** Our temple stands inside a walled enclosure surrounded by a large estate of many buildings and farms requiring many types of laborers. Much of this land was left to the temple through the wills of ordinary people wishing to gain favor in their afterlife. Because they donated land, priests will make regular offerings at their tombs. Sometimes a statue of the deceased is allowed to stand within the temple walls and share the god's food a few days out of the year.

**Reshep:** Our farm provides the food needed for the god and other temple workers. Workshops help to provide all of the necessary items for daily living, ritual, and decoration of the temple. The estate is very much like a small town in that we are able to provide for all of our own needs.

**Narrator 7:** As you can see, the lives of the priests and workings of the temples were highly organized and sophisticated. Ordinary Egyptian citizens carried on with their own household rituals, unaware of the workings behind these sacred walls. The belief system within Egypt evolved and changed over thousands of years, disappearing completely by the time the Greeks and Romans ruled the land. Fortunately, the Egyptians left many papyrus documents and colorfully painted reminders that help unlock the mysteries of their ancient religious ways.

116

# Pentah the Priest—Vocabulary and Comprehension

Write the following words on the chalkboard for students to copy on index cards for their picture dictionary. Tell students to write each word on a card. Remind them to research and write a complete definition, explanation, or example and draw a picture.

shrine        religious festivals        myth        polytheism

Use some or all of the following questions for whole-class discussion, small-group work, or individual written assessment. Allow students to refer to *Pentah the Priest* to answer them.

1. Who were the only people allowed inside the temple? Why? *(the temple priests, because they purified themselves through cleansing rituals)*

2. How did ordinary people practice their religion? *(They did not visit temples. They worshiped at local shrines and at shrines at their homes. They had statues and amulets to protect them. They usually worshiped gods that protected the family and helped them with common household and work-related problems.)*

3. What happened during a religious festival? *(During a festival the statue of a temple god was placed in a shrine and paraded through the street. There was much singing and dancing as the shrine and priests moved through the village. Usually there was also a feast and, sometimes, some reenacting of famous myths.)*

4. What was unusual about the religious beliefs of Akhenaten compared to previous pharaohs? *(He believed there was only one real god, Aten. The other pharaohs worshipped many gods, a practice known as polytheism.)*

5. Why is it difficult to remember the different gods in the ancient Egyptian religion? *(There were so many of them; they changed over time, taking on different characteristics; and they used a variety of names.)*

6. Describe a typical Egyptian temple. *(The temple represents the world. The floors and lower portion represent the earth. Tall columns support the ceiling and are designed like large lotus blossoms, papyrus, and palms. The ceiling is painted like heaven with stars and birds. Inside is a series of courtyards and halls. The innermost sanctuary where the god's statue is housed is very small and dark.)*

7. Describe the steps of the daily rituals to awaken the god's ka at the temple. *(Food is prepared for an offering. Then the god's ka is awakened by singing and music as the priests make their way to the inner sanctuary. The statue is then removed from the shrine, cleaned with sweet oils, and redressed. The statue is then presented the meal as an offering.)*

8. What happens to the food given to the statue during the ceremony? *(The food is eaten later by the priests as their payment for working in the temple.)*

9. Why must the priests shave their heads and bodies? *(to be pure and to eliminate any possibility of carrying lice into the temple)*

10. Name at least three types of workers on the temple grounds. *(any three—scribes, librarians, doctors, teachers, cooks, and craftspeople)*

# The Many Egyptian Gods

**Horus**—son of Isis and Osiris. In mythology, he avenged the death of his father by killing Seth. During the battle he lost an eye, which was renewed by Isis. You see the Eye of Horus in paintings, amulets, and jewelry, representing renewal and protection. When people die, he leads them into the Underworld to be judged by weighing their hearts. He is sometimes depicted as the head of a falcon or as an entire falcon wearing a crown.

**Osiris**—one of the chief gods representing immortality. He presides over the Underworld, where he is the judge of the dead. A son of Nut and Geb, he married his sister, Isis, with whom he had a son, Horus. He is represented as a mummy in a royal crown, holding the crook and flail, the signs of sovereignty and power. Sometimes he is white (mummy wrappings), sometimes he is black (the Underworld), and sometimes he is green (spring and resurrection).

**Anubis**—messenger to Osiris and guard of the scales during the weighing of the heart ceremony. He is the god of embalming and presides over the mummification process. Priests wear his jackal head during rituals performed when working on a mummy.

**Isis**—sister and wife to Osiris, the goddess of magic and healing. She wears a headdress shaped like a seat. Some believe it is her tears for her dead husband that flood the Nile each year.

**Thoth** (Troth)—the god of wisdom and science. He is the scribe of the god world, recording all writing, counting, and measurement. Since he records time, he is also the god of the moon. He is husband to Ma'at and represented by the head of an ibis. Many times he is holding tools for writing or measuring.

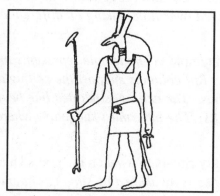

**Seth** (Set)—evil brother of Osiris and therefore another son of Nut and Geb. Seth represents the lord of the desert and the god of storms, violence, and disorder. His battle with Horus illustrates the battle of night with day and the conquest of good over evil. He is represented with the head of an unidentified animal.

**Ammit**—not a god per se but a little monster who devours the souls of anyone judged impure or evil. He is part crocodile, part hippopotamus, and part lion.

# The Many Egyptian Gods *(cont.)*

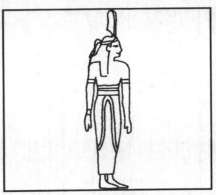

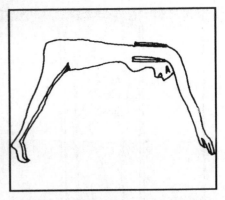

**Re/Amon/Amon-Re** (Ra, pronounced ray)—the original god of the sun. He sails his boat across the sky between heaven and earth. Amon is the chief god in Thebes, the capital of Egypt during the New Kingdom. Eventually Re and Amon merged together to make Amon-Re, the supreme state god of Egypt. He is usually depicted with a large crown. Sometimes the crown also has the sun disc. Many pharaohs during the New Kingdom are also shown wearing this crown, representing their devotion to Amon-Re.

**Ma'at**—goddess of law and order and truth and balance. The Egyptians required precise order in their daily lives; they believed that without this balance and harmony, the world would be filled with destruction and chaos. Ma'at is the daughter of Re and wife of Thoth. The ostrich feather she wears on her head is put on the scales during the judgment ceremony. Sometimes Ma'at is shown sitting on the tip of the scales, and sometimes her entire body is being weighed on the scales itself.

**Nut**—represents the heavens as the sky goddess. She is sister and wife to Geb and mother of Osiris and Seth. Nut is believed to be one of the first gods. Usually she is represented as a lady arching over the earth god, Geb. Sometimes she is seen as a large cow, and sometimes she is depicted with stars, representing the night sky.

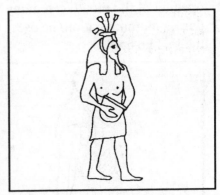

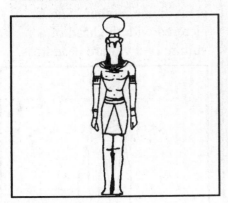

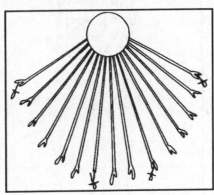

**Re-Harakhti**—merging of Horus and Re. Just as Amon-Re became the supreme state god, Re-Harakhti became seen as one of the sun gods. The falcon had the sun disc on his head, showing that he flies across the sky, carrying the sun.

**Aten**—another form of the sun god, this god is unlike any of the others—neither human nor animal. This sun disc with outstretched arms holds an ankh, representing everlasting life. He is the one and only god worshiped during the reign of King Akhenaten.

**H'apy** (Hapi)—god of the Nile and responsible for the proper workings of this precious river. He is usually shown as a long-haired man with papyrus and lotus flowers growing from the top of his head. He also has the chest of a woman, depicting fertility. He lives in a cave at the head of the Nile.

# The Many Egyptian Gods *(cont.)*

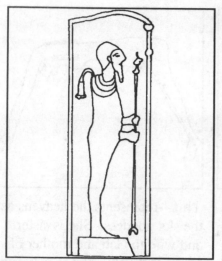

**Ptah**—local god of Memphis, one of the ancient capitals of Egypt, and husband to Sekhmet. He is the parson of craftsmen, since it is believed that he invented the arts. He is shown as a hairless mummylike figure holding a large tool, and at the opening of the mouth ceremony during mummification, he uses the tool he holds.

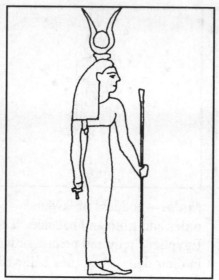

**Hathor**—goddess of love, beauty, dancing, and music and protector of children and birth. She is often shown as a beautiful woman with the sun disc and horns of a cow. Sometimes she is depicted as a cow with the sun disc between her horns.

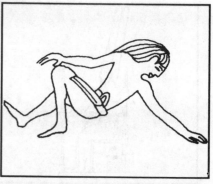

**Geb** (Seb)—the god of the earth. He usually poses below his sister/wife, Nut. Sometimes he is shown with a goose on his head, representing one of the many creation myths in which he laid the egg from which the world sprang.

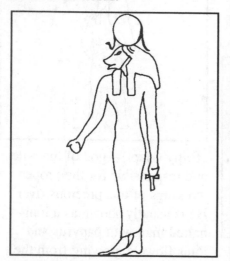

**Sakhnet**—brings destruction to all enemies of Re. She is the goddess of war and consulted by pharaohs. It was believed that her fiery breath was the hot winds of the Egyptian desert. She is wife to Ptah and has the head of a lion.

**Nepthys**—the nature goddess who represents the day, both before sunrise and after sunset. She is daughter of Nut and Geb, sister to Isis, wife to Seth, and mother of Anubis by Osiris. She wears on her head hieroglyphics that mean "lady of the house."

**Mut**—goddess of Thebes and a great divine mother. She is pictured with the head of a vulture or a vulture headdress.

**Bastet** (Bast)—household goddess representing joy and music. She is depicted as a cat—a prized animal in Ancient Egypt because rodents infested the granaries.

# Identify Egyptian Gods

The Ancient Egyptians practiced polytheism, or the worship of many gods. Their first gods represented the natural elements that affected their daily lives, such as the sun, storms, river, and death. Each had to be encouraged and thanked in order for the people to prosper. Animals, both fierce and helpful, were also worshiped to help protect the people.

Over time, the Egyptians began to think of the gods as having human qualities, and, therefore, they were depicted with human shapes. But some of the gods retained the head of an animal. Each region in Egypt had its own special god, although gradually a few of these became worshiped throughout the land as universal gods.

As the many stories and myths were told about the gods and how they came into being, they became mixed together and changed. Therefore, many of the gods' names, duties, and characteristics can vary from place to place, making the study of ancient religion very complex.

Use pages 118–120 to identify the figures in the Egyptian art below.

# The Puzzling Egyptian Gods

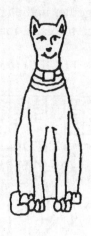

(See page 140 for answers.)

## Across

1. I am the sky goddess and gave birth to Osiris.
3. I am the god of death and the Underworld.
7. I am the god who presides over the mummification process.
8. I am the goddess of love and beauty.
9. I am the sun god who wears a tall crown.
11. I killed my brother Osiris and represent evil.
13. I am the creator of the arts.
15. I am the goddess with the face of a cat.

## Down

2. I am responsible for the record keeping of time and measurement.
4. I am the goddess of war with the face of a lion.
5. I am wife to Osiris and goddess of magic.
6. I am the god of the earth and brother to Nut.
8. I am the guide to the Underworld and son of Isis.
10. I wear the feather of truth on my head.
12. I am the bringer of the Nile waters each year.
14. I am the one and only god of King Akhenaten.
16. I devour evil souls who do not pass the weighing of the heart ceremony.

# Write Poems About the Gods

Historians have found many scrolls of Egyptian poems. These ancient people used a variety of poetic forms to express their feelings about loved ones, gods, and nature. Use the examples below to have students write poems about the Ancient Egyptian gods. Have the class choose as many different gods as possible and have them illustrate their poems with drawings of the gods they write about. Allow time for students to share their poems and drawings.

## Title Poem

Use each letter of the god's name to begin a sentence or phrase describing the attributes, duties, or life of that god.

**O**siris, god of death and resurrection,
**S**entenced to abide in the dark Underworld
**I**nside your chamber with crook and flail
**R**uling and judging the dead
**I**sis, your wife, healed with magic the doom
**S**eth contrived.

## Diamonte

This type of poem has two subjects. The poem leads from one subject to the other and forms a diamond shape.

| | |
|---|---|
| **Osiris** | (subject # 1) |
| green, dead | (2 adjectives describing subject #1) |
| ruling, judging, waiting | (3 -*ing* words for subject #1) |
| powerful, husband, gentle, wife | (2 adjectives for subject #1 and 2 for subject #2) |
| healing, flying, caring | (3 -*ing* words for subject #2) |
| beautiful, magical | (2 adjectives describing subject #2) |
| Isis | (subject #2) |

## Couplet

A couplet is two lines that rhyme. Challenge students to write at least two couplets about their subjects.

Osiris, god of resurrection and death,
Tricked and killed by brother Seth.

Brought back to life to rule the dead,
By Isis, his sister, whom he wed.

# Write an Egyptian Story or Myth

The Ancient Egyptians were polytheistic and fascinated by magic and mysticism. Many myths and stories were told to explain creation and existence. Read to your students some Egyptian myths and stories. After discussion, have students create myths of their own.

## Preparing for the lesson:

1. Gather samples of Egyptian stories or myths. The story of how Osiris was murdered by his brother Seth is probably the most well known and easy to find. You can find different versions in the following sources: *The Egyptian Book of the Dead* by E. A. Wallis Budge; *The Ancient World*, a Scholastic World History Program; *Ancient Egypt* by George Hart; and *A Message of Ancient Days,* a Houghton Mifflin social studies textbook. Two other recommended sources for stories include *The Egyptian Cinderella* by Shirley Climo and *The Winged Cat* by Deborah Nourse. These stories are not myths but use elements such as magic and refer to the different gods.

2. Make an overhead transparency of the "Story Plot Outline" (page 125) and "The Writing Process" (page 24).

3. Reproduce a "Story Plot Outline" and "Editing Checklist" (page 25) for each student.

4. Gather writing and illustrating materials. Decide how you plan to bind and display the stories.

## Teaching the lesson:

1. Read some myths or stories from Ancient Egypt. Discuss the common elements found in these myths and stories, such as reference to the many different gods, the use of magic, good overcoming evil, and the explanation of natural phenomena. Note also the character and setting descriptions that let the reader know the story takes place in Ancient Egypt.

2. Display the transparency of the "Story Plot Outline." Discuss the sections of the outline. Ask students to use one of the myths to provide examples of the types of information that should go into each part of the outline.

3. Tell students that they will be writing their own myths or stories that take place in Ancient Egypt. They should take special care to include the elements that you discussed as a class.

4. Distribute a "Story Plot Outline" to each student and have them use this format to prewrite their stories. Discuss together possible problems for a story or different natural phenomena that their myths might explain.

5. Review "The Writing Process" and allow students time to write their drafts.

6. Distribute an "Editing Checklist" to each student. Have students follow these steps to complete their compositions.

7. Have students illustrate and bind their stories to share with classmates or other classes.

# Story Plot Outline

I. Introduction

   A. Character Description _____

         _____

         _____

   B. Setting Description _____

         _____

         _____

   C. Problem _____

         _____

         _____

II. Plot—sequence of events

   A. Obstacles/conflicts—scenes leading to the climax

      1. _____

         _____

      2. _____

         _____

      3. _____

         _____

   B. Climax—the exciting scene where the problem is solved _____

         _____

         _____

         _____

         _____

         _____

III. Conclusion

         _____

         _____

         _____

         _____

         _____

# Beshet the Burial Priest

**Narrators 1–5**

**Hapun, Haret, Naturik,**

**Mintah,** the priests

**Beshet, Alexus, Knunum,** the embalmer

**Imset,** Knunum's helpers

**Damutef, Atif**

**Narrator 1:** Many people believe the Ancient Egyptians were preoccupied with death. However, it was their love of life that dictated the extreme care given to those who died. The practice of mummification was a symbol of the Ancient Egyptians' desire to continue living in the next world as lavishly as they lived in this one. Beshet, one of the priests overseeing burial processes, will guide us as we learn about the many steps of the burial rites in Ancient Egypt.

**Beshet:** I am a priest, but rather than serve a god in a temple, I am responsible for supervising the many stages of burial. It is my job to make sure that the deceased is fully equipped to make the journey into the afterlife by observing the proper customs, rituals, and **mummification** steps. The entire process is quite complex.

**Mintah:** We believe that when a person dies, various spirits are released from the body. The **ka** is the person's spiritual double, or shadow. The ka is formed at birth and has an independent existence. It can move freely from place to place and enjoy life with the gods in heaven. The ka needs nourishment, so we bring offerings of food and drink to the tomb for its sustenance.

**Beshet:** The **ba** is like the soul and symbolizes the living personality. The ba has the body of a bird, because it flies out of the tomb during the day to visit its relatives and loved ones. The ba returns at night to its tomb.

**Mintah:** There is also the **akh**, or the supernatural power of the deceased. It is the akh that makes the perilous journey to the Underworld to be judged for the afterlife. With all of these spirits it is important that the body of the deceased be preserved so that its spirits can recognize it and return safely to it. Without its spirits, the deceased cannot exist in the afterlife. Here comes Alexus. He is a very old priest who remembers how things were done in the beginning.

**Alexus:** In the earliest days, a body was "put to rest" in the sleeping position with the elbows and knees drawn together. The body was placed in a pit dug into the hot sands. Items such as jars of food or tools were also placed in the pit for use in the afterlife. Sand was pushed over the body, allowing it to dry quickly and wither but not decay. However, these graves were subject to raids by hyenas and jackals, which dug up the bodies and chewed them to pieces. This would not do if the spirits were going to recognize the bodies and return. Therefore, we began protecting bodies in coffins made from reeds and wooden planks and sealed in tombs. Still, the coffins did not protect bodies from decay, and once again the spirits were left with no home.

126

# Beshet the Burial Priest *(cont.)*

**Mintah:** Through these many years, the technique of mummification has been perfected, allowing us to preserve the body and still bury it within a coffin and tomb for added protection. Now the spirits can enjoy a peaceful afterlife forever!

**Narrator 2:** Although the mummification process preserved the body, no means were ever developed to completely lay the body safely to rest. Tombs were robbed and pillaged for their riches. Even the mummies were robbed and destroyed. The word "mummy" comes from the Arabic word *mummiya,* which means "bitumen" or "resin." Medieval doctors believed the resin covering the mummies could cure illness. For this reason, mummies were scavenged and sent to Europe, where they were ground up and swallowed as medicine.

**Beshet:** Originally only the wealthy and noble received such elaborate mummification. Eventually all bodies were preserved in some manner. The complexity and care taken during the mummification process indicates a person's status. Let us head over to the west bank of the Nile to the **embalming pavilion**, or funerary workshop. Here Knunum and his helpers can explain the steps of the mummification process, which takes about 60–70 days.

**Knunum:** Once a body comes to our tent, we remove the clothing and lay it on a long, narrow, wooden board or table. Here you see Atif insert an instrument up through the nostrils to remove the brain.

**Atif:** The heart is the only organ that is saved and preserved inside the body cavity. We believe the heart is the center of all intelligence and emotions. The brain, however, is useless, and, therefore, it is removed in bits and discarded. Now I will clean the mouth and fill it with sweet-smelling oiled linens.

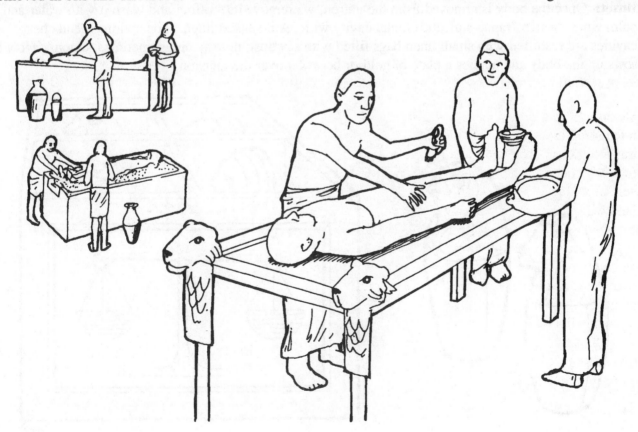

# Beshet the Burial Priest *(cont.)*

**Knunum:** Before an incision can be made in the body, a priest wearing the mask of Anubis, the god of embalming, draws a line down the body. Another will approach, make the incision, and then be chased from the area with curses. This ritual is performed to calm the spirits, since it is forbidden to injure another Egyptian. Haret and Naturik are working on another body that has already been opened.

**Haret:** This morning we made the incision into the abdomen and removed the contents. The intestines were put into a jar and presented with a prayer to the sun. The diaphragm was then cut, and we removed the contents of the chest cavity, except for the heart.

**Naturik:** Now we will wash the inside of the body with palm wine and spices. This works as a disinfectant, flushing away all materials that might cause decay. The internal organs are then sprinkled with perfume, treated with hot resin, packaged, and placed into four separate **canopic jars** representing the four sons of Horus.

**Haret:** The lids of these jars have the heads of the gods to protect the organs. The liver is placed in a human-headed jar and the lungs in an ape-headed jar. The stomach is sealed in a jar with the head of a jackal, and a hawk-headed jar hold the intestines. Then we pack the chest and abdomen cavities with straw, sand, and rags so that it will keep its shape as it dries with the **natron**, or salt. We then pack the canopic jars into a large trunk or chest.

**Naturik:** This body is on a sloping board so that any fluids can drip away without causing a puddle inside the body. The body will stay packed in heaps of natron for about 40 days. Then it will be dried and ready for further embalming. Imset and Hapun will describe the final embalming steps.

**Imset:** Once the body is removed from the natron, we remove its stuffing and wash it with water and palm wine. Watch Hapun stuff the cranial cavity with resin-soaked linen. The abdomen and chest cavities are restuffed with small linen bags filled with sawdust, myrrh, and, sometimes, onions. Now he sews up the body and applies a plate of gold or beeswax over the incision.

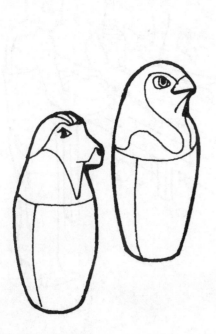

# Beshet the Burial Priest *(cont.)*

**Hapun:** Imset will now rub the body with cedar oil, cumin, wax, natron, gum, wine, and milk. He then dusts the body with crushed spices, such as myrrh and cassia. In order for the spirits to recognize the body, we make it look lifelike by padding the cheeks and eye sockets with linen. Finally, it is time to plug the nose and close the eyelids. We then cover the body with molten resin from local trees, which turns very black as it dries and hardens.

**Imset:** The last stage is to paint on eyebrows and wrap the body in linen. Damutef is our expert in this final ritual.

**Damutef:** Wrapping the body usually requires about 150 yards of linen. The attention to details while wrapping depends on the social class of the individual. Someone from a higher class will have each finger, toe, and limb individually wrapped before wrapping the body as a whole. About 100 protective amulets or pieces of jewelry are placed inside the bandages to strengthen the parts of the body.

The heart scarab represents rebirth, the pillar represents strength, and the Eye of Horus restores health. We also include fragrant herbs such as sprigs of rosemary and flower bulbs. The wrapped mummy is then brushed again with resin, and the mummy mask depicting the individual is placed over the face. The entire mummy is then placed into a coffin painted with the person's portrait so that the spirits will know where to return. During all of these steps, prayers are chanted to ensure proper preservation.

**Beshet:** On the day of the burial, friends and relatives come to the embalming pavilion. The corpse is carried across the Nile on a barge to the cemetery in the western desert. The funeral procession consists of priests, relatives, and professional mourners who are paid to wail and tear at their garments and hair. These actions show grief for the departed and also help ward evil away from the coffin.

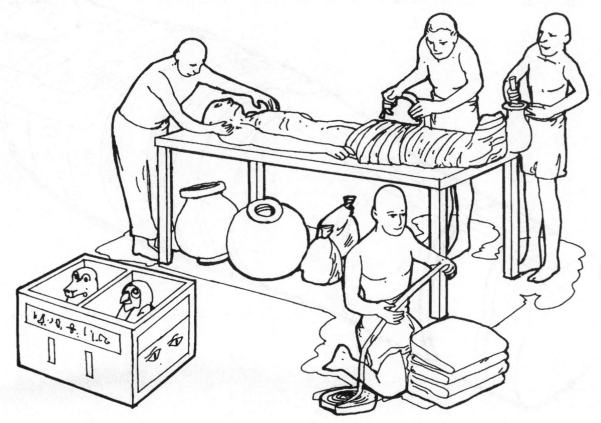

# Beshet the Burial Priest *(cont.)*

**Mintah:** The coffin is then placed in a boat-shaped sled and drawn by oxen to the tomb. It is attended by two women mourners who represent the goddesses Isis and Nephthys. A priest waving a censer and sprinkling milk heads the procession. Behind the coffin comes the chest containing the canopic jars, followed by the person's belongings that are to be buried with the body and used in the afterlife.

**Narrator 3:** The Egyptians believed that in their afterlife was a paradise known as the **Field of Reeds**. In this version of heaven the grain grew tall and the fruit was plentiful. The dead were required to plow and tend to these fields to keep everything in order. Therefore, small statues called shabtis, or "little servants," were also buried in order to work for the deceased in the afterlife.

**Alexus:** A number of spells and incantations are said during the procession, many of them chosen by the person before death. These are taken from the ***Book of the Dead***. This book contains over 200 verses, hymns, prayers, and magic spells to help the deceased make the trip to the Underworld, pass through to the Field of Reeds, and ensure a happy afterlife. Verses from the *Book of the Dead* are also painted on the coffin, tomb walls, and papyrus scrolls.

**Knunum:** Once we reach the tomb, we conduct the ceremony of the **Opening of the Mouth**. We stand the coffin upright, and it is supported by a priest wearing the mask of Anubis. Priests and the eldest son of the deceased then scatter water over the coffin, burn incense, and touch the mouth of the mummy case with special magical implements. Spells are recited in which the god Ptah gives the dead person the ability to eat, speak, and move as if still alive. Offerings are made. Then the afterlife can be enjoyed, because the spirits that left the corpse during mummification can now know where to return.

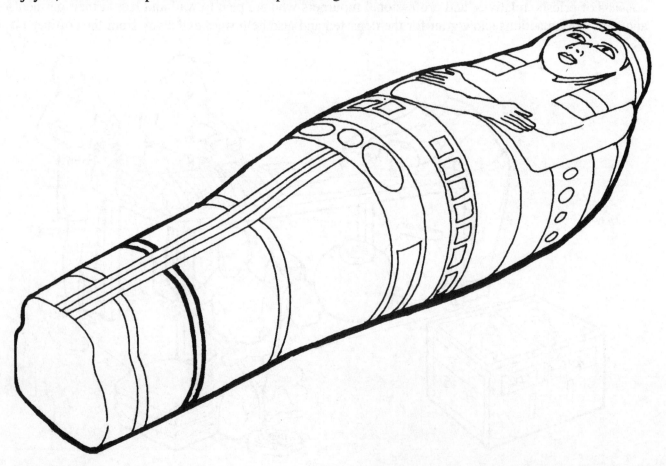

# Beshet the Burial Priest *(cont.)*

**Atif:** The coffin is then placed in an outer coffin, which is a series of two or three other coffins painted with magical texts and illustrations to help the deceased in the Underworld. This added protection varies, depending on the person's social class. Finally, the painted coffins are placed into a large stone **sarcophagus**, and the deceased's belongings are arranged around the tomb.

**Narrator 4:** The upper part of the tomb consisted of a chapel where the statues and paintings were situated. Here priests and relatives could visit on anniversaries and festival days. The burial site itself was located at the bottom of a deep shaft to discourage grave robbers.

**Naturik:** Once the mummy and its belongings are in place, we sweep the burial chamber to remove all traces of human life and to keep it free from evil. Then we carefully seal the tomb forever. We break weapons to keep harm away from the dead. Relatives enjoy a funerary feast outside the tomb as the akh travels through the floor of the burial chamber into the Underworld and the Hall of Judgment.

**Haret:** Using the verses from the *Book of the Dead,* the akh moves through gateways guarded by terrifying gods such as serpents, vultures, and hippopotamuses. They stop any unworthy akh. The worthy akh reaches the Hall of Judgment, or Two Truths. Here it is judged to see if it is fit to live forever in the kingdom of Osiris and enjoy paradise in the Field of Reeds. At the **judgment scene** are Anubis, the god of mummification, who presides over the judgment; Thoth, the god of wisdom, who records the events; and a set of scales. The heart of the deceased is put on one side of the scale, where it is weighed against Ma'at or her feather of truth.

**Imset:** Forty-two gods then question the heart, accusing its owner of unthinkable crimes. The heart denies all charges, but only the goddess of truth, Ma'at, can determine whether or not it is lying.

**Narrator 5:** Naturally, all Egyptians hope to pass this test. They always showed hearts balanced with Ma'at's truth and not weighed down with evil. This may have been a source of such phrases as having a "heavy heart" when we are troubled or feeling "light hearted" when we are happy. The Egyptians also gave us the heart as a symbol of emotion. Imagine what Valentine's Day would be like if they had known the brain was actually our center of emotion and intelligence!

**Imset:** If the heart does not pass the test, it is tossed to Ammit, the Devourer of the Dead, who sits beside the scales. She gobbles it up and brings complete destruction on all parts of the soul and prevents it from going on to an afterlife. If the heart is innocent, the akh passes into the throne room of Osiris. Once blessed by Osiris, the deceased can then proceed to paradise in the Field of Reeds.

**Beshet:** This is a celebration of the life that will continue eternally in a perfect world, free from hardships. Death is only the gateway into this world, and by providing the dead with all of these things, we ensure that life's pleasures will continue forever.

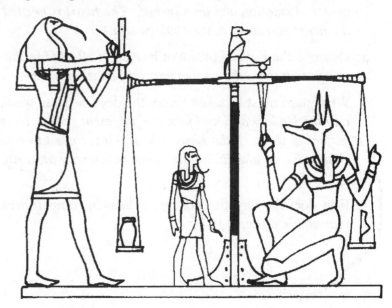

# Beshet the Burial Priest—Vocabulary and Comprehension

Write the following words on the chalkboard for students to copy on index cards for their picture dictionary. Tell students to write each word on a card. Remind them to research and write a complete definition, explanation, or example on and draw a picture.

| | | |
|---|---|---|
| **ba, ka, akh** | **mummification, natron** | **canopic jars** |
| *Book of the Dead* | **Opening of the Mouth ceremony** | **sarcophagus** |
| **judgment scene** | **Field of Reeds** | **embalming pavilion** |

Use some or all of the following questions for whole-class discussion, small-group work, or individual written assessment. Allow students to refer to *Beshet the Burial Priest* to answer them.

1. Why did the ancient Egyptians take such special care to preserve the body of the dead? *(They believed that spirits left the body at death. For the spirits to return to the correct body, it had to be well preserved so that the spirits could identify it. Without a preserved body, the spirits had no home, and the deceased would have no afterlife.)*

2. How did the earliest Egyptians preserve the bodies without mummifying them? *(Bodies were preserved by burying them in the hot desert sands to dry.)*

3. Briefly describe the steps for mummifying a body. *(The body is taken to the embalmer's pavilion. The brain is removed through the nostrils. The mouth is cleaned and stuffed with oiled linens. An incision is made in the torso, and all the internal organs except the heart are removed. Some are placed in special canopic jars to be buried with the deceased. The inside of the body is washed and stuffed to keep its shape. The entire body is covered in natron for 40 days and put on a slanting board to drain. The natron is removed, the body is cleaned again and restuffed with linen and herbs. The body is sewn up and covered with oils and spices. Finally, it is covered with resin and wrapped with yards of linen.)*

4. Why was the heart left in the body of the mummy? *(The ancient Egyptians believed it was the center of emotion and intelligence. The heart is needed by the deceased to pass the weighing of the heart ceremony in the Underworld.)*

5. Describe the Egyptian form of heaven. *(Afterlife in the Field of Reeds is just like life in Egypt except that there are no worries, problems, or sickness.)*

6. What steps must be taken before the deceased can reach heaven? *(The deceased's akh must pass into the Underworld and face the judgment scene. Here the heart is weighed against Ma'at's feather of truth. If the heart is heavy, it is tossed to Ammit, who gobbles it up and destroys a chance for an afterlife. If the heart balances with truth, the akh proceeds to Osiris and the Field of Reeds.)*

7. How does the Egyptian concept of heaven compare with that of some modern religions? *(Accept reasonable answers.)*

# Investigate Mummy-X

Mummies are extremely intriguing to students. Have your students work as teams of scientists to unlock the mysteries of a real 3,000-year-old mummy.

## Preparing for the lesson:

1. Reproduce the specialists's report (pages 135–138) so that there is one type of report for each group.

2. Reproduce an "Inquiry Page" (page 134) for each student. This can be used for individual assessment or class discussion.

3. Make an overhead transparency of the "Conclusions Chart" (page 139).

## Teaching the lesson:

1. Tell students they will be grouped into research teams to analyze information and put all of the clues together to learn about a real mummy. Read aloud the following newspaper article.

### News Flash! Mysterious Mummy Leaves Egypt
### for Scientific Testing in the United States

*Cairo*—The mysterious mummy of a person dead for over 3,000 years leaves today on an unexpected journey to the United States. Scientists and historians hope to discover more about the person who lived and learn the techniques Ancient Egyptians used for body preservation. Mummy-X, swathed in ancient linens, was shipped in a plain wooden box. It left the museum in a police van escorted by a heavily armed squad of police cars. Sirens wailed as the entourage made its way through the congested streets of Cairo to the airport. The entire world eagerly awaits the results of this unique opportunity to perform an autopsy on a person who lived so many centuries ago.

2. Distribute the "Inquiry Pages." Allow time for students to answer questions 1–4. Divide the class into four scientific research teams. Have each group choose a head scientist to lead the discussion of their information and a secretary to record their responses on their specialists' report. Distribute a "Specialists' Report" to each group. Allow the groups about 30 minutes to read the information, discuss, and respond.

3. Once all groups are finished, allow each to share its findings. Write the information on the "Conclusions Chart" transparency on the overhead.

4. Then have students answer questions 5–10 on their "Inquiry Page." Collect them or discuss them in class.

5. Read aloud this Postscript to the class.

## Postscript

Mummy-X is a real mummy. Based on hieroglyphics from her tomb, historians believe her name was Makare. Evidently she was a priestess of the god Amon-Re around the eleventh century B.C. Somehow she was able to elevate her status and work in the temple, which explains her diet and the elaborate burial process reserved for those of a higher class. Scientists speculate that Makare died in childbirth and that the baboon was buried with her to symbolize her baby, who probably lived. The information from the autopsy reports accurately reflect the life and death of a high-class person in Ancient Egypt. The evidence helped establish the person's age, sex, diet, and social status, as well as some common health hazards and diseases that existed for all Ancient Egyptians.

# Investigate Mummy-X *(cont.)*

## Inquiry Page

### Answer questions 1–4 before you begin your investigation.

1. You are a scientific specialist who will help analyze the body of an ancient, mummified person. How does this make you feel?_____

   _____

2. If Mummy-X were to come to life, how do you think it would feel about being taken from Egypt, its home?  Why? _____

   _____

3. Why do you think there was such a heavy police escort for the mummy?

   _____

   _____

4. As a scientist, what things would you look for to give you clues about the mummy's identity, lifestyle, and cause of death?_____

   _____

### Answer questions 5–10 after you complete your investigation.

5. What did the mummy reveal about daily living and hazards in Ancient Egypt?

   _____

   _____

6. What were some diseases common in Ancient Egypt?_____

   _____

7. What gender was this person?  How do you know? _____

   _____

   _____

8. How old was this person at death?  How do you know?

   _____

   _____

9. What was the social status of this person?  How do you know?

   _____

10. What is the most likely cause of death?  Why do you think this?

    _____

    _____

# Investigate Mummy-X *(cont.)*

## Chemical/Embalming and X-Ray Specialists' Report

1. Chemical analysis shows that the bones of Mummy-X contain a very low percentage of lead. It appears that the content is roughly one-tenth what is normal in a modern human.

2. The body was preserved by a prolonged soaking over a period of months in a solution of juniper resin, camphor oil, and myrrh.

3. The body was carefully wrapped and mummified. Fingers were individually wrapped. The brain had also been carefully and completely removed. You observe that the resin did not dry too quickly and crack the skin.

4. X-rays show the pelvic region is greatly enlarged, indicating a recent birth. A smaller mummy is attached to the body.

5. A fracture line shows that the person broke a leg at one time. It appears that the leg was properly set by a trained physician, since it seems to have healed and grown correctly.

6. The skeleton indicates the person was about 35–40 years old at the time of death.

7. After x-raying the smaller mummy, you find that it is the remains of a baboon, not a baby.

## Discuss the following questions and record your responses on the lines provided:

1. Lead is a deadly poison that seems to enter the body of all humans. How much lead was found in Mummy-X compared to humans today? _____

_____

2. Was it was safer to live in Ancient Egypt than today? Why or why not?

_____

_____

3. What were the age and the sex of the person who is Mummy-X? How do you know?

_____

_____

4. What do the x-rays tell us about doctors in Ancient Egypt? _____

_____

5. What might be a likely explanation for the attached baboon mummy?

_____

_____

6. What was the social class of this person? How do you know?

_____

_____

7. Did you find a possible cause of death? If so, what? _____

_____

Religion

# Investigate Mummy-X *(cont.)*

## Dental and Skull Specialists' Report

1. While examining the jaw region, you find the teeth very straight, with no apparent overlapping or overcrowding.

2. The teeth show no signs of cavities, but they are badly worn down. There is microscopic evidence of sand and grit embedded in the teeth.

3. The upper and lower jaws of this mummy are larger than those of modern Egyptians.

4. The mummy also appears to have more protruding cheekbones and larger eye sockets than those of modern Egyptians.

5. Based on the size of the skull, you conclude that this is an adult approximately 30–40 years old.

## Discuss the following questions and record your responses on the lines provided:

1. If this mummy were alive today, would a dentist be impressed by its dental records? Why or why not?

2. What might be your explanation as to why this mummy did not have any cavities? What does this tell you about our diet compared to food eaten in Ancient Egypt?

3. What do the teeth tell you about the geography and climate in Ancient Egypt?

4. What do the teeth tell you about how food was prepared? (Think about how bread was made.)

5. Based on the skull report, how did this person differ from humans today?

6. From your information, can you tell the age and sex of the mummy? Why or why not?

7. Did you find a possible cause of death? If so, what?

# Investigate Mummy-X *(cont.)*

### Lung and Parasite Specialists' Report

1. After viewing the lungs under a microscope, you find that the person had suffered a minor case of tuberculosis sometime during their life.

2. The inside of the lungs are coated with carbon, an element in smoke.

3. You also note a high concentration of very fine silicone particles, most likely sand.

4. Inside the intestines are the mummified remains of worm eggs most commonly found in pork.

5. You also find schistosomiasis (schisto) eggs in the blood vessels of the mummy. These eggs are from very small snails that live in the Nile River and can cause disease.

## Discuss the following questions and record your responses on the lines provided:

1. The signs from what disease was found in the mummy's lungs?

2. What do the lungs tell you about breathing hazards in Ancient Egypt?

3. Considering the pollution in the air we breathe today, how much different was the air of Ancient Egypt?

4 What did this person eat? What parasites were found because of this?

5. Why was this diet unusual? What does this tell you about the social status of this individual?

6. What other parasites were found? How do you think they got there?

7. Did you find a possible cause of death? If so, what?

# Investigate Mummy-X *(cont.)*

### Bone and Heart Specialists' Report

1. The skeleton measures between five feet two inches (155 cm) and five feet three inches (157.5 cm), a height more common for females.

2. The bones show traces of Harris lines around the major leg and arm bones. This indicates that the bones stopped growing for several months during early development. This usually happens due to starvation.

3. The bones show early signs of arthritis, which normally occur between the ages of 35 and 40.

4. An examination of the pelvis confirms that the mummy is female.

5. The heart also shows signs of middle age. The main arteries leading into the heart indicate the beginnings of hardening as a result of the buildup of cholesterol. This usually occurs in a diet heavy in meat.

## Discuss the following questions and record your responses on the lines provided:

1. What were the age and sex of the person at death? How do you know?

_____

_____

2. Is the mummy taller or shorter than the average person today? Why do you think this is the case?

_____

_____

3. Based on the bone reports, what can you say about the childhood of this individual?

_____

_____

4. Knowing that only the upper classes ate a lot of meat, how did this person's lifestyle change from childhood to adulthood? How do you know?_____

_____

5. How did diet affect this person? Do you think it benefited the upper classes to have more meat than other people? Why or why not? _____

_____

6. What diseases or ailments did this person suffer?

_____

_____

7. Did you find a possible cause of death? If so, what?

_____

_____

# Mummy-X Conclusions Chart

| |
|---|
| **Chemical/Embalming Report** |
| **X-Ray Report** |
| **Bone Report** |
| **Heart Report** |
| **Lung Report** |
| **Parasite Report** |
| **Dental Report** |
| **Skull Report** |

# Answer Key

## The Puzzling Egyptian Gods (page 122)

**Down:** 2. Thoth  4. Sakhnet  5. Isis  6. Geb  8. Horus  10. Maat  12. H'apy  14. Aten  16. Ammit

**Across:** 1. Nut  3. Osiris  7. Anubis  8. Hathor  9. Amon Re  11. Seth  13. Ptah  15. Bastet

## Investigate Mummy-X Inquiry Page (page 134)

1.–2. Accept reasonable answers.

3. Heavy security is needed because mummies are priceless and there may be people wishing to steal and sell one illegally.

4. Accept reasonable answers.

5. Daily living was difficult. There was not always enough food, and Egyptians seemed to eat an unbalanced diet. It was windy and dirty so the food was filled with sand. Parasites lived in the food because they did not have food preservation methods. Taking a bath in the Nile or drinking the water also gave you parasites. The air was smoky from oil lamps, filling lungs with debris. It was common to break a bone or catch other diseases. Although they had good medical treatments, they still did not live long lives. Childbirth was dangerous.

6. Tuberculosis, high cholesterol, schisto, food poisoning, and arthritis were common.

7. The person was a female. Evidence for this included its short height, its expanded pelvic area, and the small mummy attached to it.

8. The person was around 35–40 years old. Evidence for this included the size of the bones and the beginnings of arthritis, the size of the skull, and the onset of hardening of the arteries.

9. The person appears to have been a member of the upper class at death because she had such a thorough burial and mummification process. She also was eating a diet of pork, an upper-class food. However, at one time she must have been poor since she appears to have suffered malnutrition at some time in her youth.

10. The most logical cause of death is childbirth since the other problems did not appear life threatening. Also, the fact that she was buried with the baboon might symbolize her baby and the fact that this is how she died.

## Chemical/Embalming and X-Ray (page 135)

1. The mummy had 10 times less than humans today.

2. Lead poisoning and tooth decay were less common; other hazards such as food poisoning and parasite infestation were more common; some things such as tuberculosis, arthritis, and hardening of the arteries are about the same. Death in childbirth was probably more common, but doctors had good knowledge and skill for setting broken bones.

2. The mummy is 35-40 years old according to analysis of the skeleton.

3. Before death this person gave birth. This could have been the cause of death.

4. The x-rays tell us that doctors knew how to properly set a broken leg. They knew how to preserve and embalm bodies and set bones, which implies a fairly high level of skill and knowledge in some areas.

5. The baboon might be a symbol of the baby. (Accept reasonable answers.)

6. Upper class due to thorough mummification.

7. The baboon mummy and enlarged pelvic region indicate that the woman may have died in childbirth, a risky and often fatal event.

# Answer Key *(cont.)*

## Dental and Skull (page 136)

1. A dentist might be impressed with how straight the teeth were and that there are no cavities but might not be impressed that they were ground down from grit and sand.

2. The lack of decay could be attributed to not eating processed, refined, or overly sugary foods.

3. The sand found in the teeth was probably the result of dry, windy weather and unclean eating conditions.

4. Food was prepared under fairly unclean circumstances. Bread was made by grinding the grain in a stone bowl. This allowed particles of stone to get into the bread.

5. The mummy has a larger jaw, cheekbones, and eye sockets than humans today.

6. The age can be determined by the size of the skull, but the sex was not able to be determined.

7. No.

## Lung and Parasites (page 137)

1. The mummy had a minor case of tuberculosis at some time.

2. It was windy and sandy, so people probably inhaled a certain amount of grit. People also inhaled smoke from fires and torches, which coated their lungs with carbon.

3. The air was still cleaner in Ancient Egypt because they did not have machines or vehicles emitting pollution. ˙

4. The person ate a lot of pork that was not preserved or cooked properly and which resulted in parasitic worm eggs being deposited inside the person's body.

5. Yes. The person must have been special and from the upper class because the majority of Ancient Egyptians did not eat much meat.

6. Schisto eggs were found in the blood vessels, probably from drinking and bathing in the Nile River.

7. No. Tuberculosis, food poisoning, or parasite infestation can cause death, but there is no indication that they did in this instance.

## Bone and Heart (page 138)

1. The height of the skeleton and the pelvis show the person was a female. Signs of arthritis indicated the person was probably 35–40 years old when she died.

2. The person was shorter than today's average, probably because of diet and lifestyle. Evolution also seems to be creating larger people over time.

3. The mummy was poor and malnourished as a child.

4. She must somehow have changed to the upper class as she got older because she ate a heavy meat diet as an adult.

5. The meat built up cholesterol, which did not seem a benefit for the rich because her arteries showed signs of narrowing and hardening.

6. Ailments included Harris lines showing starvation as a child, arthritis, and hardened arteries due to a buildup of cholesterol.

7. No. Neither the malnutrition nor the cholesterol were life threatening.

# Cooperative Group Project: Make a Mummy

After reading the information on Egyptian burial practices, have your students make a mummy to display on a table or bulletin board.

## Preparing for the lesson:

1. Gather pictures of mummies to use as examples. The pictures should include the corpse, wrapped mummy, mummy mask, coffins, and sarcophagus.

2. Gather art supplies for drawing and coloring, such as crayons, pencils, erasers, markers, and metallic paint pens.

3. Prepare the butcher paper mummy by cutting five sheets of butcher paper tall enough to cover an adult.

   - On the first sheet, draw in pencil around one of your medium-sized students. (This will be the embalmed corpse.) He or she should lie on the paper and fold his/her arms over his or her chest. Add a few details like where the arms and hands would be for students to use as a guide. Trace over these lines in black marker.

   - Place the second sheet of butcher paper over the first. This sheet will be the linen-wrapped mummy. Draw the outline of the mummy in pencil just a little bit larger than the drawing of the corpse. (Use the first drawing underneath as a guide.) Add in details for the students, and then trace in black marker.

   - Using the second drawing as a guide, place the third piece of butcher paper over it and draw the outline of a mummy-shaped coffin. This coffin should be a little bit larger than the linen-wrapped mummy drawing. Add in a few details for students, such as where the face, arms, and hands would be, and then trace over it in black marker.

   - Using the previous drawing as a guide, place the fourth sheet of butcher paper over it and draw the outer coffin. This coffin should be a bit larger than the first. Add a few details and then trace over it in black marker.

   - The final sheet of butcher paper will be the rectangular sarcophagus which students can decorate with hieroglyphics.

# Cooperative Group Project: Make a Mummy *(cont.)*

4. Prepare the mummy mask by placing a sheet of white butcher paper over the mummy-shaped inner coffin drawing and tracing just the head and wig. The mummy mask should be just a little bit smaller than the inner coffin yet just a little bit larger than the wrapped mummy.

## Teaching the lesson:

1. Divide the class into 5 cooperative groups. Group 1=the embalmed corpse, Group 2=the linen wrapped and jeweled mummy, Group 3=the inner mummy-shaped coffin, Group 4=the outer coffin, and Group 5=the sarcophagus and mummy mask.

2. Distribute the appropriate butcher paper drawing to each group and have them work together to design and color their drawings.

3. As each group finishes, have them carefully cut out their drawing. Once all drawings are completed, join the mummy together at the top of the head by stapling or using clear tape. Make sure each layer of the mummy is securely fastened but can be lifted to reveal the other layers below. (The wrapped mummy should be taped to the corpse. The mummy mask should be taped to the wrapped mummy. The inner coffin should be taped to the mummy mask. The outer coffin should be taped to the inner coffin, and the sarcophagus should be taped to the outer coffin.)

4. Display the mummy by covering around the legs of a table with butcher paper as if it were the stone sarcophagus. Or staple the mummy carefully onto a bulletin board so the layers can be lifted to see what is underneath.

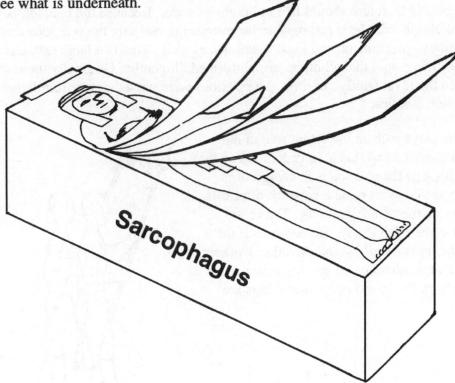

# Ramose the Pharaoh's Vizier

Greetings. I am Ramose, the pharaoh's vizier and number one consultant. As vizier, I oversee all of the workings of Egypt and report back to the pharaoh on the country's state of affairs. The word "pharaoh" literally means "great house," but we use it as another name for "king." The pharaoh is respected and obeyed so that the gods will bless him and Egypt will prosper. Most pharaohs are from groups of rulers that are related by birth or marriage. A pharaoh may either be born to a ruling family or he can marry into a ruling family. Pharaohs by birth are usually the oldest son of the king; pharaohs by marriage are usually men who marry the ruling king's oldest daughter. This family of rulers is known as a dynasty.

Although the pharaoh has a chief queen known as the Great Royal Wife, he also has several other wives comprising the royal harem. The Great Royal Wife is often the king's sister or half sister. There are no laws forbidding such marriages, but it is practiced only among royalty and the gods. Having many wives ensures the pharaoh many children able to take the throne. If a king dies before his son is old enough to rule, the queen rules on the boy's behalf until he comes of age.

The palace is a grand building filled with many servants and beautiful items because we believe our king is also a god and therefore should live in luxurious style. Because the pharaoh is viewed as a god and protector of all the land, he is responsible for overseeing not only the religious functions of Egypt but also the military, government, and legal functions, as well. This is a large task and requires the help of many officials to see to it that all duties are performed diligently. Originally these officials were close relatives to the royal family. In time, the positions were passed down from father to son, forming a network of noble families.

Because religion plays such an important role in our lives, the temples must be well kept in order to keep the gods happy. Although the pharaoh is in charge of caring for the gods, he relies upon a network of priests to do daily tasks on the temple grounds. The most powerful priest is the High Priest. He commands the lesser priests, the temple scribes, and the other workers on the site. The pharaoh relies on me, his vizier, to check with the High Priest and make sure things are running properly.

# Ramose the Pharaoh's Vizier *(cont.)*

Another important function of the pharaoh is to build a strong military. We are not a warlike people by nature and have no need to conquer other lands for food, since the fertile valley provides an ample supply. Although Egypt is well protected from invasion by the desert and the sea, the military carries out many duties necessary to keep Egypt running smoothly. In the Old Kingdom we had no permanent army. Troops were called as needed, and it seems that they did more work in the quarries and mines than they did actual fighting.

By the time of the Middle Kingdom, Egypt had expanded into Nubia. Expeditions were sent to search for gold and other precious goods. The army grew larger and built fortresses along the Nile to subdue Nubia and keep other desert tribes away from the fertile valley. Soldiers used wooden clubs, throw sticks, bows and arrows, and copper-headed spears, daggers, and axes. Although the soldiers carried cowhide shields, no helmets or body armor were worn.

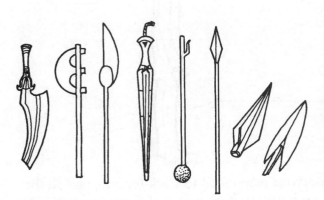

By the New Kingdom, we had expanded farther along the Nile and used new and improved weapons, such as the scimitar, a curved sword. We also now had a large professional army divided into infantry and chariotry. The development of the chariot and the use of leather or bronze protective clothing caused revolutionary changes in war. The military is a very powerful political force in Egypt. It oversees building, mining, and trading expeditions. Although the pharaoh and his sons are ultimately in charge of the army divisions, they are run by a chain of officers. These high military positions offer wealth and power to the holder but are only available to men who can read and write.

The pharaoh must also oversee the legal aspects of the government. He relies on me to make sure the court officials, governors of territories, and the magistrates all perform their duties fairly. We place great emphasis on the rights of individuals. Men and women have equal rights, as do the poor and the slaves. We have many laws that must be followed to maintain this orderly balance, and many of our punishments are harsh. Justice and being treated fairly in front of the law depends on everyone being in the proper place and doing what he/she is supposed to do.

# Ramose the Pharaoh's Vizier *(cont.)*

Since every person in Egypt can own property, strict records are kept regarding property lines and productivity. There are many arguments over boundaries, and often records must be consulted. If a person is caught moving a boundary stone, he can have his ears cut off and even may be taken into slavery. Some landowners refuse to pay their taxes to the pharaoh, and for this they might be beaten.

We also have laws that cover marriage and divorce. Slaves who marry a free person can themselves become free. Men and women have equal rights in marriage, with a certain portion of property and belongings shared as marriage property. Other belongings and property belong to the individual. The oldest son usually inherits the property of his parents upon death, but parents can make other arrangements by writing a will. Children are expected to pay for funeral arrangements for their parents and are responsible for any debts their parents may have left.

Because individual rights are important, people speak before a court on their own behalf. They can present documents or call witnesses. All of the evidence is recorded, and a local magistrate makes a decision. Punishments such as being beaten, locked up, or fined may be carried out immediately. More serious cases are brought to me for sentencing. Only the pharaoh has the power to inflict the death penalty for severe crimes such as perjury, treason, and murder. Although we have no official written code, legal officials can consult our extensive library of past decisions and sentences.

Since all land under the sun belongs to the pharaoh, everyone is required to work for him, and all the products of everyone's labor belong to him. Taxation provides much of the royal family's wealth. The pharaoh needs funds to keep his household running, pay the salaries of the many officials, equip the military, and carry out foreign policy. He controls foreign trade and owns all mines and quarries. Farmers must give portions of their harvest to help build a reserve stock of grain for years when there is a food shortage. So, as you can see, the life of a pharaoh may be luxurious, but it is also filled with many responsibilities in order to keep his people happy and life along the banks of the Nile orderly and prosperous.

146

# Ramose the Pharaoh's Vizier—Vocabulary and Activities

Write the following words on the chalkboard for students to copy on index cards for their picture dictionaries. Remind them to research and write a complete definition, explanation, or example on the lined side and draw a picture on the blank side.

**dynasty**        **pharaoh**        **vizier**

Use some or all of the following activities to reinforce the information presented in *Ramose the Pharaoh's Vizier.*

## If I Were King

Have students write a couplet poem that begins with the phrase, "If I were king, I'd . . . . " Encourage them to write at least two couplets.

> If I were king, I'd rule the land from the sea clear down to Kush,
>
> I'd eat grand food with spices and exotic berries from a bush.
>
> I'd live in a palace filled with things made from glowing gold,
>
> I'd be a kind ruler so my people would love me until I was old.

## Court Case Drama

Divide the class into groups. Assign a magistrate to be the judge. Have students reenact court cases describing the different types of rights and laws in ancient Egypt. Allow students time to prepare their cases with documents and witnesses. Have student groups perform their cases in front of the magistrate and class. Allow the magistrate to decide the case and award an appropriate penalty if needed.

## Make a Poster

Have students draw a picture showing the many different duties and privileges of the pharaoh.

## Vizier Diary

Have students write diary entries describing the day in the life of a vizier. Make sure they include activities from the different branches of government.

## Government Chart
### Pharaoh

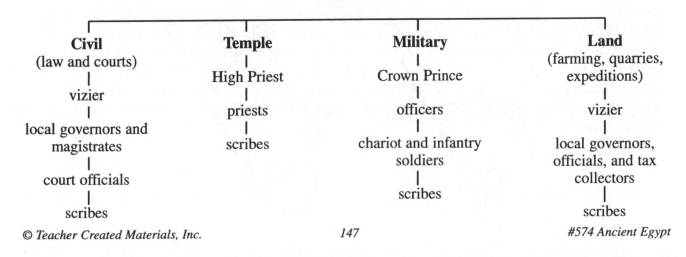

| Civil (law and courts) | Temple | Military | Land (farming, quarries, expeditions) |
|---|---|---|---|
| vizier | High Priest | Crown Prince | vizier |
| local governors and magistrates | priests | officers | local governors, officials, and tax collectors |
| court officials | scribes | chariot and infantry soldiers | scribes |
| scribes | | scribes | |

*Government*

# Make a Double Crown or Headdress

Throughout Egyptian history the pharaohs wore elaborate crowns as symbols of power and authority. All upper-class Egyptians wore elaborate wigs or headdresses. Work as partners to make a crown or headdress for use in a class drama or for your Living History day.

## Materials for the double crown:

- extra-wide aluminum foil (or two sheets of foil taped together)
- red tagboard at least 18" x 24" (45 cm x 60 cm)
- overhead transparency of the Red Crown Pattern (page 150)
- scissors
- transparent tape
- newspaper or tissue paper

## Directions:

1. Wrap and tape a tall foil cylinder around your head. Stuff some crumpled paper into the cylinder.

2. About 10 inches above the forehead (25 cm), crumple the foil together. Use the top portion of the foil and a ball of paper to make the top of the white crown. Remove the crown, add extra tape, and mold the foil to the desired shape. (Spray paint it white, if desired.)

3. Using the overhead transparencies draw a red crown pattern onto red tagboard and cut it out. Fit the crown around your head and adjust the overlap at your forehead. Tape it securely and trim the ear sections.

4. Put on the white crown and then place the red crown over the top of the white. Adjust it and tape it securely. Use a strip of the leftover red tag board to make a curlicue, and tape it onto the crown.

5. Draw and color a cobra head and attach it to the front of the crown.

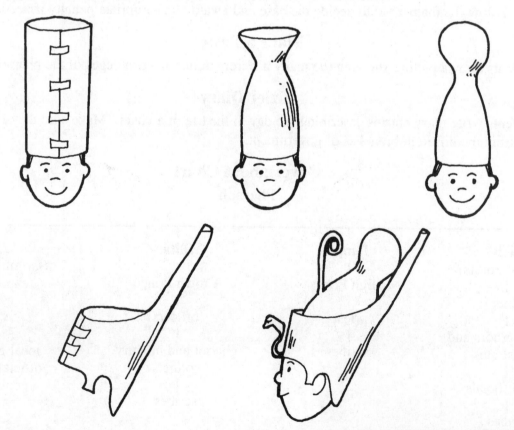

# Make a Double Crown or Headdress *(cont.)*

## Materials for the headdress:

- aluminum foil
- two 12" (30 cm) strips of tagboard, one 24" (60 cm) strip of tagboard
- 2 sheets of light blue 12" x 18" (30 cm x 45 cm) construction paper

- permanent markers or paint pens
- transparent tape or a stapler

## Directions:

1. Wrap the 24" (60 cm) strip of tagboard around your head and fasten it with tape or the stapler. Attach the two 12" (30 cm) to this headband in a crisscross fashion, as shown.

2. Cover this cap with foil and tape it securely. Carefully draw a feather pattern onto the foil cap, using permanent markers or paint pens.

3. Draw wings on the two sheets of light blue construction paper. Decorate the wings and cut them out. Then, tape the wings onto the cap behind the ears and along the top.

4. Draw and decorate a vulture tail and head. Cut the head and tail out and attach them to the headdress.

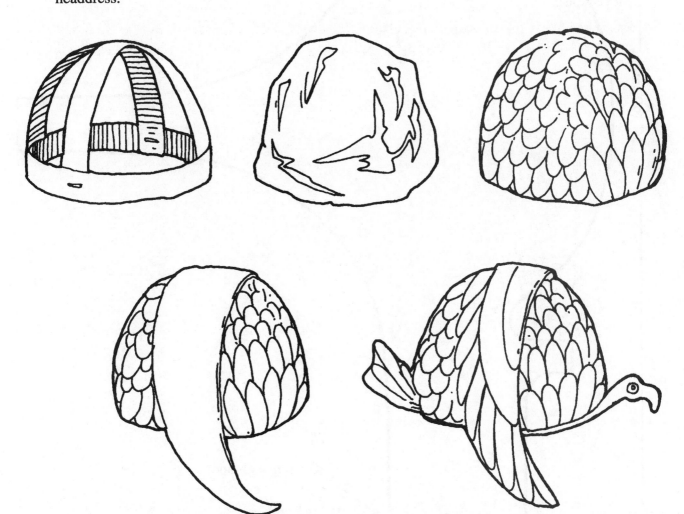

# Red Crown Pattern

Create an overhead transparency of this page. Display it and have students draw the pattern on red tagboard, cut it out, fit it to their heads, and trim it around the ears, as shown.

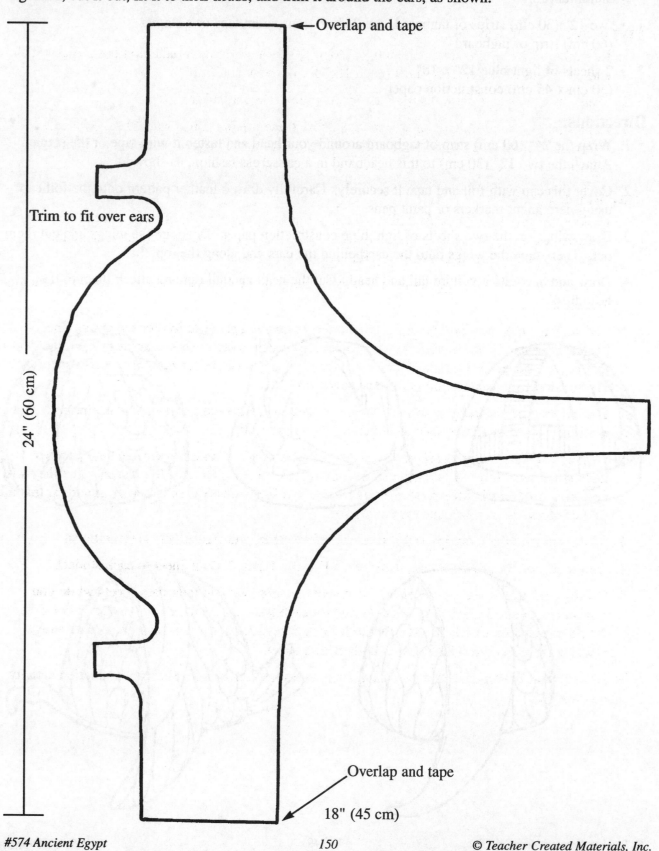

Overlap and tape

Trim to fit over ears

24" (60 cm)

Overlap and tape

18" (45 cm)

# Research Some Famous Pharaohs

Egypt is famous for its many powerful rulers. The following cooperative group project allows students to learn about six of the most famous rulers in an enjoyable and interesting way.

## Preparing for the lesson:

1. Reproduce a Group Presentation Outline (page 152), Presentation Evaluation Form (page 152), and a Famous Pharaoh Data Sheet (page 153) for each student.

2. Create an overhead transparency of the Presentation Evaluation Form.

3. Gather many books containing information about these rulers. Allow students to duplicate information from these and other books. By using reproduced pages, students can highlight needed information and cut and paste from a variety of sources.

## Teaching the lesson:

1. Divide the class into six cooperative groups. Assign each group one of these famous pharaohs to research and report back to the class about: Queen Hatshepsut, King Thutmose III, King Akhenaten, King Tutankhamen, King Ramses, and Queen Cleopatra.

2. Have the student groups gather their research materials snf then distribute the Group Presentation Outlines.

3. Tell students that they will be using this outline to create a presentation for the class. The presentation can be in the form of an informative speech, a dramatic reenactment from the days of that ruler, a travel-back-in-time drama, or whatever they wish, as long as they clearly cover the information from each section of the presentation.

4. Review the outline and give examples for each section. Encourage students to use props, costumes, and visual aids such as pictures, posters, or charts.

5. Display and review the transparency of the "Presentation Evaluation Form" so that students understand what they will be evaluated on during their presentations. Tell students that they will be taking notes during the presentations for use in a future activity, so it is very important that all of the information is presented and recorded.

6. Allow groups time to assign tasks, research information, and create their presentations.

7. On the day of the presentations, distribute a Famous Pharaoh Data Sheet to each student.

8. During each of the six presentations, have students take notes on their data sheets while you complete a "Presentation Evaluation Form" for each speaker. At the end of each presentation, have students in the audience review the information gathered during the speech. Encourage students to add missing information to their data sheets.

9. As an extension, have students use their data sheets to complete the Pharaoh Evaluation activity on page 155.

# Group Presentation Outline

Person(s)
responsible
for
information
and
presentation:

**Pharaoh:**_____

**Introduction**—background information to get the audience interested (joke, dramatization, question, trivia, etc.) _____

_____

_____

**Dates**/kingdom he/she ruled? _____

_____

_____

**Family Life**—married? children? _____

_____

_____

**Domestic Policy**—improvements for Egypt? _____

_____

_____

**Foreign Policy**—trade? expeditions? conquest? _____

_____

_____

**Most Famous Achievement** _____

_____

_____

**Conclusion**—summarize points and give a closing statement that includes an opinion about this ruler. _____

_____

_____

# Presentation Evaluation Form

Name of Presenter _____

☐ Voice Expression _____

☐ Clear and Complete Sentences _____

☐ Eye Contact with Audience _____

☐ Hand Gestures _____

☐ Use of Visual Aids _____

☐ Prepared and Rehearsed _____

☐ Knowledge of Subject _____

_____

Best Part of Presentation _____

_____

Suggestions for Improvement _____

_____

☒ = Excellent; no improvement needed

✔ = O.K.

✳ = Problem area; needs improvement

Grade ☐

# Famous Pharaohs Data Sheet

## Queen Hatshepsut

Family _____

_____

Domestic Policy _____

_____

Foreign Policy _____

_____

Famous for _____

_____

## King Thutmose III

Family _____

_____

Domestic Policy _____

_____

Foreign Policy _____

_____

Famous for _____

_____

## King Akhenaten

Family _____

_____

Domestic Policy _____

_____

Foreign Policy _____

_____

Famous for _____

_____

## King Tutankhamen

Family _____

_____

Domestic Policy _____

_____

Foreign Policy _____

_____

Famous for _____

_____

## King Ramses

Family _____

_____

Domestic Policy _____

_____

Foreign Policy _____

_____

Famous for _____

_____

## Queen Cleopatra

Family _____

_____

Domestic Policy _____

_____

Foreign Policy _____

_____

Famous for _____

_____

# Pharaoh Evaluation

Using your completed "Famous Pharaohs Data Sheet" (page 154), evaluate the **facts** for each and then form an **opinion** about them. Rank the rulers and then write a paragraph about who you believe was the best and worst and the reasons why. Be sure to back up your opinion with as many facts as possible.

## Rank the Rulers

Write the names of the rulers in the order of importance based on who you think was overall the best (1) and worst (6) ruler of Egypt.

1. _____   2. _____   3. _____

4. _____   5. _____   6. _____

The best pharaoh was _____ because

_____

_____

_____

_____

_____

_____

_____

The worst pharaoh was _____ because

_____

_____

_____

_____

_____

_____

_____

_____

# Howard Carter's Incredible Discovery

Compared to other rulers of Ancient Egypt who built great monuments, led armies into battle, or promoted religious change, King Tutankhamen was not very important. He was still just a boy when he became pharaoh during the middle of the fourteenth Century B.C. He died at age 18 or 19, after a reign of only a few years. His mummy rested in peace for 3,000 years. Its discovery by English archaeologist Howard Carter in A.D. 1922 caused much more uproar, excitement, and change than did either his life or death.

Howard Carter was born in 1874. He worked as a draftsman and illustrator for the Antiquities Service. His dedicated work led to his promotion to Chief Inspector of Upper Egypt in 1899. While working in Egypt he decided to pursue his main hobby, painting. In 1903 he left the Antiquities Service and opened a small shop in Luxor (Thebes) to sell his paintings.

At this same time, Lord Carnarvon of England had been given permission from the Egyptian government to excavate an area in the Valley of the Kings. This was well known as a burial site for many of Egypt's pharaohs and noblemen. Carnarvon quickly realized that he lacked the expertise and knowledge to excavate properly. One day he visited Carter's shop, and there began one of the most famous partnerships in the history of Egyptology. In 1907, Carter started working for Lord Carnarvon. Carter traced the ancestors of the pharaohs and discovered that one of the kings' tombs had yet to be found. Although he found six royal tombs over a period of time, he still could not locate the tomb of the missing pharaoh, Tutankhamen. Carter was determined to find it. In 1922 Carter was forced to visit Lord Carnarvon in England to plead for more money. Reluctantly, Lord Carnarvon agreed to finance one more season of excavation by the English archaeologist Howard Carter.

Carter and his fellow archaeologists had little time for their work in the Valley of the Kings. From April to October the desert was scorching, and by mid-December the tourist season began. Therefore, Carter had less than two months to find the elusive tomb of Tutankhamen. Carter decided to try an area that had never been thought of before. He felt it was possible that the hidden tomb could actually exist under the rubble from the already unearthed tomb of Ramses VI, a popular tourist attraction. No one had ever thought of looking under the dirt and rock that had been left when the tomb of Ramses was excavated years before.

After clearing away the piles of dirt and rock, Carter's workers soon found the remains of houses used by the builders of Ramses' tomb. Although this discouraged Carter, he told the workers to continue digging in case they had missed something. By early November, one of the diggers hit something. It appeared to be the top step of a flight of stairs buried in the sand. With great excitement and care, the area was cleared and revealed a staircase of 16 steps leading to a blocked doorway.

# Howard Carter's Incredible Discovery *(cont.)*

Carter recorded in his journal: "November 4, 1922—Hardly had I arrived on the work site than the unusual silence made me realize that something out of the ordinary had happened, and I was greeted by the announcement that a step cut in the rock had been discovered." On November 26, 1922, he wrote, "Today was the day of days, the most wonderful I have ever lived through and certainly one whose like I can never hope to see again." Carter then sent a congratulatory cable to Lord Carnarvon, asking him to join the excavation into the tomb.

Carnarvon immediately set sail to Egypt, accompanied by his daughter, Lady Herbert. Seventeen days after discovering the tomb, Carter, Lord Carnarvon, his daughter, and the Inspector of the Antiquities Service removed the sealed door. At the end of a long, dark passage filled with rubble they found yet another door. Excitement was at fever pitch as they cleared away debris at the base of the door to reveal a seal impression. It was the tomb of Tutankhamen.

The time had come to inspect the tomb. Carter describes this intense moment of discovery in his journal. "Slowly, desperately slowly, it seemed to us, the remains of the passage debris that had encumbered the lower part of the door was removed, until at last we had the whole door before us. The decisive moment had arrived. With trembling hands, I made a tiny breach in the upper left-hand corner. Candle tests were applied as a precaution against foul gases and then, widening the hole a little, I inserted the candle and peered in. At first I could see nothing, the hot air escaping from the chamber causing the candle flame to flicker but presently, as my eyes grew accustomed to the light, details of the room within emerged slowly form the mist; strange animals, statues, and gold—everywhere the glint of gold. For the moment I was struck dumb with amazement, and when Lord Carnarvon, unable to stand the suspense any longer, inquired anxiously, 'Can you see anything?', it was all I could do to get out the words, 'Yes, wonderful things!'"

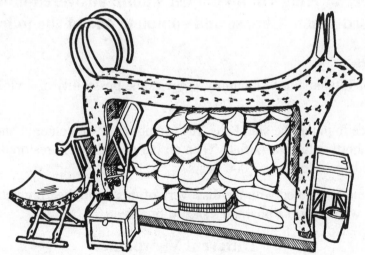

Once through the door they couldn't believe their eyes. The room was piled high with amazing treasures of furniture and items to make the king comfortable in his afterlife. Against the wall facing the door stood three gigantic carved and gilded wooden beds. Twenty to thirty stacked white wooden boxes contained mummified legs of mutton, ducks, and venison. Under another bed was the king's throne, ornately decorated with gold and precious stones. Four gold- and gem-encrusted chariots stood against another wall. Another box held roses, still beautiful after 3,000 years. Two life-size statues of King Tutankhamen guarded another door. Howard Carter was convinced that this passage would lead to the burial chamber and the king's mummified body.

# Howard Carter's Incredible Discovery *(cont.)*

They carefully removed and recorded each item from this first room, known as the antechamber, and sent them away for safe keeping. Once the room was cleared, the next doorway was opened. Inside they found a wall of gold. Beyond the wall they discovered several huge wooden shrines, a stone sarcophagus, and three coffins in the image of Tut. The last of these was made of solid gold and contained the now-famous mummy mask thought to look like the king when he was alive. Inside was the mummified body of Tutankhamen. Wrapped up with the mummified body, between 13 different layers of linens, were 143 pieces of jewelry and amulets.

Eventually the burial chamber, treasury, and annex items were also removed and recorded. It took at least ten years for Howard Carter and his associates to clear the entire tomb and make painstaking records of the different discoveries. Throughout the excavation the public showed great interest in this new archaeological find. Each week the London Illustrated News printed articles about the different treasures removed from the tomb. The world was caught up in the frenzy of the discovery. New fashions and home decor reflected the Egyptian style. Recently, many of the items found have traveled the world to be put on display for others to see. Throngs of people everywhere stream to see these fabulous treasures from the ancient past.

**The discovery of King Tutankhamen's tomb answered many questions, but it also raised some. Choose and complete one of the following activities.**

## King Tut Mysteries

- Modern x-rays of Tutankhamen's mummy suggests the possibility of a violent death. Tell the true story of his death.

- Based on evidence found at the site, King Tut's tomb was twice entered and carelessly plundered for minor items shortly after the burial. Then all burial seals were restored. Why did the tomb survive untouched again for over 3,000 years?

- Many of the people associated with the discovery of this tomb died prematurely. Tell about the "curse" on those who disturb a pharaoh's sacred final rest.

## Different Viewpoint

Imagine you were Howard Carter, Lord Carnarvon, Lady Herbert, or one of the workers. Write a journal entry describing the discovery of the tomb and the contents inside from your perspective.

# The Tomb of Tutankhamen

On this page you will find a floor plan and brief description of the various rooms of King Tut's tomb. Using the information and terms on this page write your own description of the tomb.

**The annex** was crammed full of beautiful objects.

**The burial chamber** contained four shrines (one inside the other), each one covered in gold leaf. Between the outer shrine and the temple wall there was only a narrow passage.

**The sarcophagus** was found inside the shrines, and holding the body of the king.

**The antechamber** held furniture, boxes, and a host of other articles all the way to the ceiling.

**The treasury** contained the most valuable jewels and objects in the tomb. Its entrance was guarded by a statue of Anubis, crouching like a guard dog.

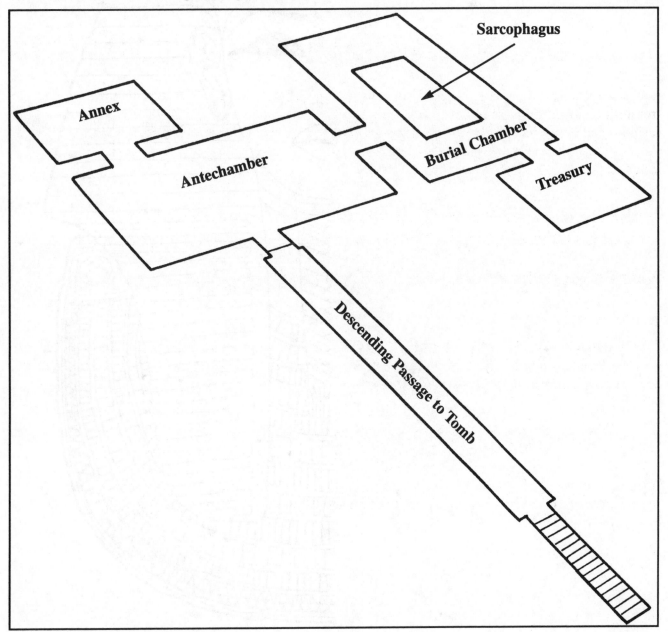

# King Tut's Mummy Mask

Draw the other half of the mummy mask. Then, outline the mask with permanent black marker and color it with markers and paint pens. Cut out your mask and glue it onto black construction paper to display. Write your name on the back.

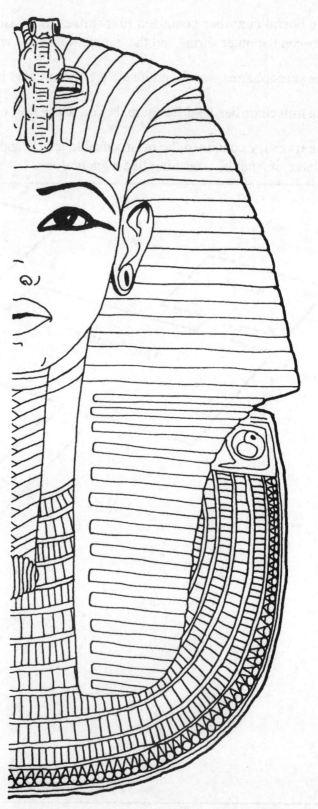

# Could It Be Ramses?

Recently, a new discovery was found in the Valley of the Kings, uncovering a vast network of burial chambers. These chambers are believed to have once contained 50 of the sons of Ramses II, one of Egypt's most famous pharaohs and rulers. Kent Weeks, the archaeologist who made the discovery, says that three different Egyptologists claim that it is probably the greatest archaeological find in Egypt during this century. The tomb site is only about 200 feet (60 m) from King Tutankhamen's, across the Nile River from Luxor. The site had been explored decades ago, but not much was found. Some of its chambers were filled with debris removed from the King Tut excavation. Egyptologists had given up on further excavation into the area and were going forward with plans to build a parking lot over the site.

However, Dr. Kent Weeks was not prepared to give in so easily. In 1988 he embarked on one final exploration of the old dumping ground. He opened a door blocked by rubble for thousands of years and happened upon a corridor containing several doors and a statue of Osiris, the god of the afterlife. Further investigation showed that the site contained a complex of at least 62 underground chambers, probably intended for the sons of Ramses. Among those identified was his first-born. A mural in the tomb portrays him standing next to his father as he points the way to his afterlife. Three other sons are specifically mentioned in the inscriptions. Weeks expects that all of the 50 sons whose tomb sites were previously unknown are here. Evidence of stairways and some collapsed columns suggest that there might be a lower level containing 40 or more chambers where mummies may still be entombed.

Unfortunately, the complex of underground rooms is filled with rubble and debris from past flooding, in some areas filling the rooms to within a few inches from the ceiling. Weeks believes excavation will probably not reveal priceless treasures like those from King Tut's tomb. But it has proven rich with carvings, inscriptions, paintings, hieroglyphics, and artifacts that promise to tell historians an enormous amount about life during the reign of its most important and long-lived kings.

The newly discovered tomb also presents scholars with all sorts of puzzles to ponder. The design of the tomb itself is very different from most found in the Valley of the Kings. This one is more like an octopus, its main body sprouting many tentacles. It is also unusual in that archaeologists had never before discovered a multiple burial of a pharaoh's children. Further studies and excavations may reveal when the tomb was built, the extent and contents of the entire tomb, and how many of Ramses II's children may have been buried there. Will this discovery prove to be the biggest of the century, surpassing even that of Howard Carter in 1922? Only time and hard work will tell.

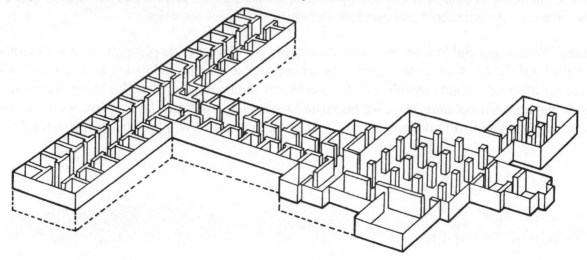

# Shaan the Nobleman's Wife

| **Narrators 1–10** | **Shaan,** the wife | **Khanot,** her husband |
| **Hepsha,** their daughter | **Temnest,** their son | **Myceen,** the head cook |
| **Hanah,** the head servant | **Akhen,** a kitchen servant | **Mayat** and **Kempa,** dressing servants |

**Narrator 1:** Many villages in present-day Egypt are built on the sites of ancient ones. Over the centuries, as one house fell down, another was built on top of it. Whole villages have been lost in this way. Therefore, there is little archaeological record of the earliest villages and the lifestyle of the people. But much evidence of village life has been found in temporary areas built for families of craftsmen and officials working on the royal tombs and pyramids, as well as from artifacts and paintings inside the tombs themselves.

**Narrator 2:** Villages were established along the banks of the Nile and were surrounded by a large brick wall and gate for security. The villages for workers were clustered near the larger towns and developed in an unplanned way, with two- and three-story houses joined together. A network of narrow, winding streets divided the blocks of houses. Drains kept the streets from getting too muddy. These ordinary houses had an entrance area leading to a living room, which had a low mud-brick platform for eating and sleeping. Then there were smaller rooms for storage and a kitchen roofed with branches to let out smoke. These villages probably looked much like those built on the same sites in Egypt today.

**Narrator 3:** Overlooking the rest of the town was the grand palace of the pharaoh. Near the palace would be the spacious homes of the wealthy nobles and officials. Take a moment to travel back in time and visit the home of such a wealthy nobleman. Today Shaan, the nobleman's wife, is planning a party to entertain some of her husband's visiting business associates.

**Shaan:** Welcome to my home. Today the estate is a hive of activity since a grand party is planned for this evening. Our life is not as rich and splendid as life in the Royal Palace, but we are fortunate to live better than the majority of Egyptians. My husband is an important merchant for the pharaoh. He imports wood for building projects, especially the valuable cedar from Lebanon. This morning he will be consulting with some visitors who plan to buy his cedar for building homes for the nobility in Thebes.

**Khanot:** In honor of their visit and to help strike a good bargain, I have asked my wife to plan this party. She runs the household and oversees all family and social activities.

**Shaan:** Women and children are very fortunate in Egypt. Unlike other places, we are well protected and have legal rights. A wife can expect to be treated well and respected by her husband and children. I share my husband's home, wealth, and, eventually, his tomb and afterlife. Our two children are outside playing. Khanot must leave for his business meeting, and I must make plans with our head servant. The children will give you a tour of our estate, and then I will tell you the plans for the party.

# Shaan the Nobleman's Wife *(cont.)*

**Temnest:** My sister and I would be glad to show you around. From a very early age, Egyptian children are trained in good manners and social behavior. We are taught self-control and common sense to help keep order in our daily lives. Later today, when my father returns, he will take us hunting with his guests. He is proud of my sister and me and expects us to help entertain tonight at the party.

**Narrator 4:** According to tomb paintings, children generally had happy childhoods. Unlike practices in later civilizations, girls seemed to be as valued and loved as boys. Children and their families appear to have enjoyed many leisure activities together, such as hunting, playing music, or playing board games like **senet**. Not all cultures regarded children so highly.

**Narrator 5:** Boys played many games that tested their strength and skill. Such games included a type of leapfrog called khazza lawizza that is still played today. They also enjoyed wrestling, swimming, running, and target practice with a javelin or bow and arrow. Both girls and boys enjoyed ball games and games with tops, marbles, and knucklebones, an early form of dice. Girls danced and played with wooden dolls or wooden animals with moving parts.

**Hepsha:** Our home stands on a large estate surrounded by a high walls. At the entry there is a gateway and the gatekeeper's lodge. As we move to the main house, you will see our family shrine for daily worship. This pathway leads to the house, which was built around a central hall.

**Temnest:** When the mud-brick walls were built, they were plastered and whitewashed outside. Inside, the floors are covered in large tiles painted in bright colors. Large wooden doors separate the rooms, and murals of gardens and pools decorate the walls. The interior is painted in soft colors with the tall columns in red and the rafters in pink. Running along the painted ceiling is a frieze—a design of fruit and flowers.

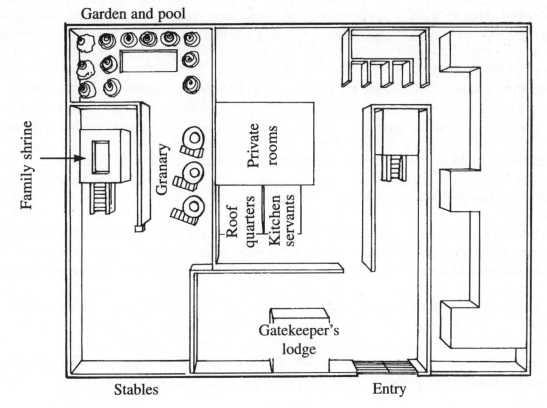

# Shaan the Nobleman's Wife *(cont.)*

**Hepsha:** Apart from the central hall for entertaining, we have a smaller reception room, family room, bedrooms, and a modern bathroom with stone-lined walls and floors and a lavatory. These stairs lead up to the roof quarters, which offer a cool breeze, shade, and a beautiful view of the grounds. From up here you can see why Myceen, our head cook, is happy with our kitchen and storage bins with ample space for grains and other food crops. Across from the family shrine you can see our garden and pool surrounded by trees and shrubs. The pool is filled with waters from the Nile that flow here through a small canal. There are ducks, fish, and lilies growing in it. This is one of our family's favorite spots to relax together after a long day of work.

**Temnest:** You can also see the rooms for our servants and workers, the stables, and sheds for our animals. Come back inside, and we will show you some of our treasured possessions before Mother tells you the great plans for tonight. In addition to the usual beds, headrests, and stools, we also have some delightful chairs with animal-shaped legs. Many of our chairs and tables are inlaid with ivory and ebony.

**Hepsha:** Here are a painting of Bes and the niches carved into the wall to hold our offerings and statues of family and work-related gods. Religion dominates our life, much of which is serious and solemn. But we also like fun and joy in our lives, which is why we look forward to planning parties.

**Shaan:** Children, run along now and ready yourselves for the hunt. Father will be home soon with our guests, and they will want to leave promptly. As you can see, the kitchen is alive with activity. Here is Myceen and her helpers, who will review tonight's menu.

**Myceen:** The Mistress has decided upon roast ox and gazelle as the main course. We will also serve fish and waterfowl. With luck, the Master will bring us more birds from his hunting trip. Then we can quickly pluck and cook them so that our guests can eat their "catches" from the afternoon's hunt.

**Akhen:** For vegetables we have onions, leeks, cucumbers, radishes, lettuce, and all kinds of beans served with an oil and vinegar dressing. Although we do not have an abundance of fresh fruit because of our climate, we will serve a variety of figs, dates, grapes, raisins, melons, and pomegranates. We will also serve a wide selection of wines, some which have been imported from oversees. The Master has spared no expense for this party!

# Shaan the Nobleman's Wife *(cont.)*

**Narrator 6:** Of course, not all Egyptians ate this well. The usual diet for common people included wheat or barley bread, dried fish, and vegetables. Various beans and lentils were also important and provided necessary protein. Meat was very expensive and eaten only on special occasions like festivals. Water and beer made from barley were the beverages of the poor.

**Myceen:** The preparation of the food is well in hand. We have no worry that any guest will go home hungry. Of course, the greatest compliment to a host is if guests are carried home in their **litters**, too full to walk on their own. While I get on with my work, perhaps you can join Hanah and the Mistress as they discuss plans for tonight's entertainment.

**Hanah:** Music will be provided by a small orchestra of women playing lutes, lyres, reed pipes, and even some harps. I have also arranged for some tambourine and castanet players. Dancing girls will provide the main entertainment, but I also have a surprise! An acrobatic troupe is in town, along with other acts, such as a fire swallower. I had to deal shrewdly to get them on such short notice, but they have agreed to attend.

**Shaan:** You truly are a marvel, Hanah. I don't know what our family would do without you. Look at the time. I must go and prepare my clothing for the evening. It will not be long before our first guests will be arriving. Word of our party has spread throughout the neighborhood, and already a group of people have collected outside to see the guests arrive. I hope Khanot, the children, and the visitors from Thebes are having a successful hunt and will return soon.

**Narrator 7:** Out on the marsh, Khanot and the others sailed through the thickets on skiffs made from papyrus. At the prow of the boat stood the men with throwing sticks. Some of these sticks were shaped like snakes to magically "bite" into the birds. Others resembled boomerangs. As they approached a bird, they would throw the stick to stun it. Then they could haul it into the boat and club it to death. The hunt and the morning meetings pleased the guests, and all returned to the estate happily ready to prepare themselves for the evening's festivities. They began by bathing and applying lotus-scented creams and oils to keep their skin supple in the hot, dry climate. Two of Shaan's servants helped her dress for this special evening.

**Mayat:** I see you have selected your fine linen undergarment for this evening. Its long, straight shape will set off your pleated and fringed robe nicely. Stand still while I wrap it around your waist and pull the top corners over your shoulders. I must tie the knot across your chest tight so it will stay in place throughout the party.

# Shaan the Nobleman's Wife *(cont.)*

**Narrator 8:** Since the climate in Egypt was hot, people needed light, loose, and easily cleaned clothing. Linen from flax provided such cloth. Most people wore simple sheaths made from undyed linen sometimes decorated by pleating. Only the rich could afford brightly colored cloth or high-grade linen that was almost transparent.

**Kempa:** Here are your red leather sandals. These are a better choice for a special evening than your woven reed ones. I have also put the finishing touches on your plaited wig. It is made from the best quality hair and vegetable fibers, with each strand attached to the netting base with wax. Usually you like to wear combs of ivory or metal hairpins, but for tonight I thought it might look prettier to add a few gold spangles instead. Once your wig is in place, I will tie a ribbon around your head and add some flowers picked from our garden.

**Narrator 9:** Only the wealthy could afford such extravagant wigs. Most Egyptians wore a decorated headband or a cloth headdress to protect themselves from the sun.

**Mayat:** Now for your cosmetics and jewelry. Close your eyes while I line your upper eyelid with black **kohl**. Now another line along your lower lid. There. I'll extend this line to make your eyes look larger. Not only does this look pretty, but it will also help reduce the glare from the desert sun. On your eyelids we will apply a layer of ground green malachite.

**Kempa:** Here, Mistress, take your bronze mirror to apply your lipstick made from red ocher and resin. Perhaps you would like to color your cheeks a bit also. And for such a special occasion as this, I'm sure you will want to use some red henna to decorate your fingernails, toenails, and palms of your hands.

**Mayat:** I have selected your favorite collar of red, blue, and yellow stones strung together to look like flowers. It is a bit heavy, so we will need to support it in back with a pendant. You are lucky that it is now fashionable to pierce ears. Here are some button-shaped studs that match your collar. All you need now are your gold bracelets, armlets, and anklets.

**Narrator 10:** All Egyptians, rich and poor, enjoyed adornments of makeup and jewelry. Jewelry served two purposes—as decoration and as protection from evil spirits. Men also wore eye makeup, wigs, and jewelry. They usually wore a knee-length kilt called a **shenti** knotted at the waist. Sometimes they added a sleeved shirtlike garment. Wealthy men also wore pleated robes. Of course, since Egypt was very hot, many people wore few clothes. Servants and men working in the fields wore little more than a loincloth. Children usually wore no clothes at all and had their heads shaved, except for single long braids on the right sides of their heads called "the lock of youth." On special occasions, the children were dressed in fine linen like their parents.

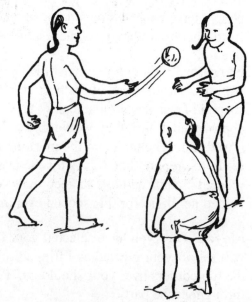

# Shaan the Nobleman's Wife *(cont.)*

**Kempa:** You look lovely, Mistress. I will check on the children and our guests. I'm sure everyone will be arriving soon in their litters or chariots. I can't wait to see the brightly colored clothes and jewelry they'll wear for the evening! Ah, here comes Hanah. I'm sure she wants to finalize the schedule for tonight.

**Hanah:** You look beautiful, the perfect hostess for the evening. Everything is ready, and people are waiting. Our guests from Thebes are seated in the central hall with the Master. The children are reciting poetry for them while we wait for the other guests. I have arranged for each guest to be presented with flowers as they enter the hall. Cones of scented wax **pomade** are also available to place atop their wigs, if they desire. The pomade will gradually melt throughout the warm evening, drenching the wigs with lovely aroma.

**Shaan:** Thank all of you for your help. Let's go enjoy our guests and this beautiful evening.

**Hanah:** The hosts have thought of everything. Our Master has made sure there is a plentiful supply of wine and the room is full of laughter and noise. Once everyone arrives, Khanot will make a speech to welcome his guests, especially his business associates from Thebes. Then the feast and entertainment will begin. Time passes quickly at such festive events.

**Shaan:** It is very late, but I have thoroughly enjoyed myself. Giving a successful party is satisfying but also very tiring. I wasn't sorry to see the last guest leave. I will be happy to take off this heavy jewelry and wig.

**Khanot:** Our visitors from Thebes have retired, and our deal is set. Thank you, my wife, for a lovely and profitable evening. Without your help I never could have completed such successful negotiations. Our children are safely asleep in their beds, and the two of us can now relax and reflect on this busy and happy day before we retire for the night.

# Shaan the Nobleman's Wife—Vocabulary and Comprehension

Write the following words on the chalkboard for students to copy on index cards for their picture dictionary. Tell students to write each word on a card. Remind them to research and write a complete definition, explanation, or example and draw a picture.

**shenti**        **litter**        **kohl**        **senet**        **pomade**

Use some or all of the following questions for whole-class discussion, small-group work, or individual written assessment. Allow students to refer to *Shaan the Nobleman's Wife* to answer them.

1. How did the wealthy nobles live differently from most common Egyptians? Include examples of food, shelter, and clothing. *(The wealthy lived in large homes with more rooms and more furniture. They ate a wider variety of food and more meat than common Egyptians. Their clothing was much finer and fancier; sometimes they wore colored cloth; and they wore much more elaborate jewelry and wigs.)*

2. Describe the different roles of the husband and wife within the family. *(The husband was responsible for earning a living by working in some trade. The wife was responsible for running the household and raising the children.)*

3. Do you think most children were treated well in Egypt? Why or why not? *(Accept reasonable answers.)*

4. Name three ways this Egyptian home is similar to your own. Name three ways it is different. *(Accept reasonable answers.)*

5. What did wealthy Egyptians eat and drink? *(They ate meats, such as roasted ox, gazelle, and water fowl, as well as fish. They ate vegetables, such as onions, leeks, cucumbers, radishes, lettuce, and beans. They ate fruits, such as figs, dates, grapes, raisins, melons, and pomegranates. They drank wine and beer and ate good bread.)*

6. What did Egyptians do for fun? *(They hunted, listened to music, danced, and played games like senet for fun.)*

# Climb the Social Pyramid

Based on what you have learned about Ancient Egyptian society, write in the proper position of the social pyramid the different occupations listed at the bottom of the page.

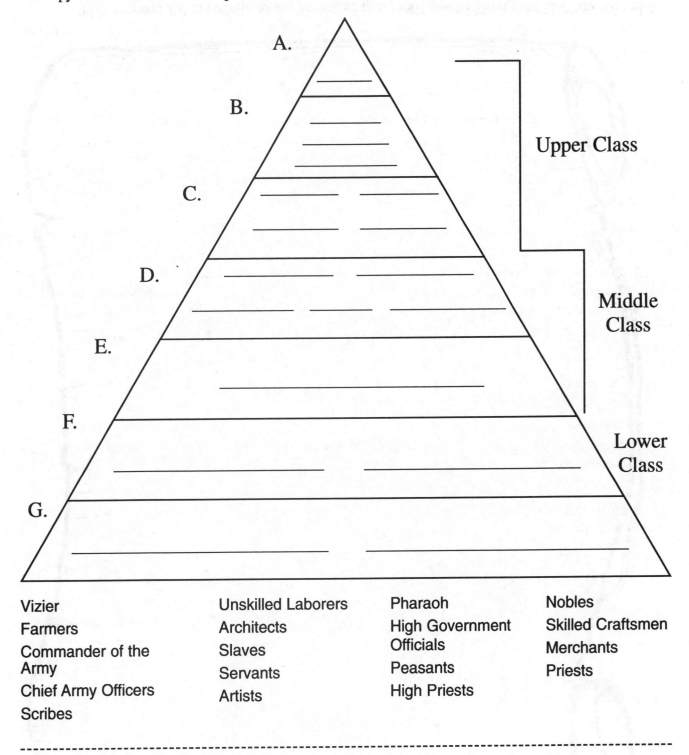

A.

B.

C.

Upper Class

D.

Middle Class

E.

F.

Lower Class

G.

| | | | |
|---|---|---|---|
| Vizier | Unskilled Laborers | Pharaoh | Nobles |
| Farmers | Architects | High Government Officials | Skilled Craftsmen |
| Commander of the Army | Slaves | | Merchants |
| Chief Army Officers | Servants | Peasants | Priests |
| Scribes | Artists | High Priests | |

- - - - - - - - - - - - - - - - - - - - - - - - - - - - - - - - - - - - - - - - - - - - - - - - - - - - - - - -

**\*Fold up answers before reproducing for students.**

A. Pharaoh; B. Vizier, High Priest, Chief Commander of the Army; C. High Government Officials, Priests, Army Officers, Nobles; D. Scribes, Skilled Craftsmen, Architects, Artists, Merchants; E. Farmers; F. Unskilled Laborers, Peasants; G. Slaves, Servants

# Dear Diary

Use the papyrus sheet below to describe a day in your life as a worker from the middle or lower class in Ancient Egypt. Explain your daily duties, where you live, your family life, how you like or dislike your job, why you have this job, and your feelings toward the privileged upper class.

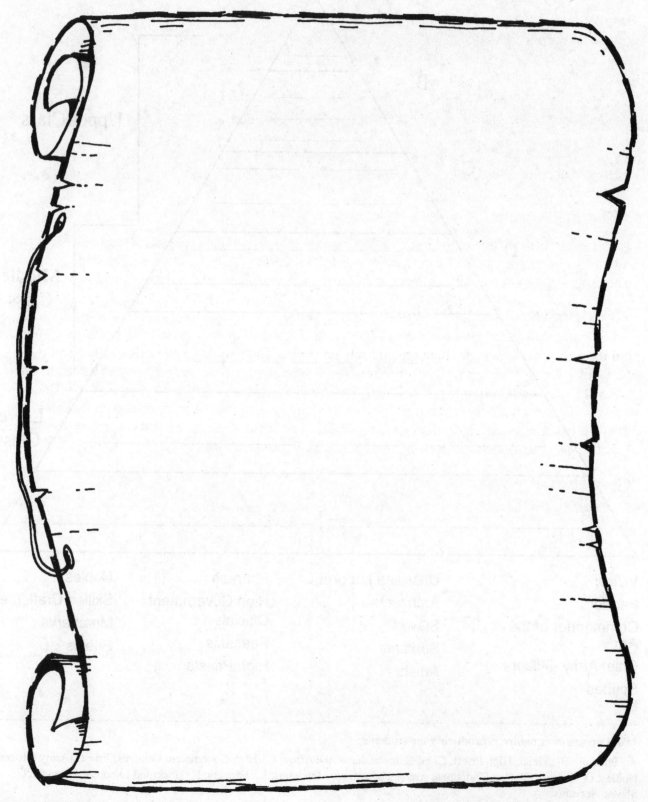

# Cities and Homes

Allow students an opportunity to show their understanding of how the Ancient Egyptians lived by assigning one or both of these activities.

## Draw a City Map

Have students draw, color, and label a map of a typical city in Ancient Egypt. Be sure to have student include the following items on their maps:

- a name for their city
- a wall around the majority of the town
- the pharaoh's palace
- farmland near the Nile trading area near the docks
- temple grounds

- homes of workers and craftsmen
- homes of nobles and officials
- Nile River
- an outdoor market and for irrigation

Maps can be made individually, in partners, or in small groups. Have students share their maps and explain why items are located where they are. The Houghton Mifflin Social Studies series *A Message of Ancient Days* has an excellent example in their Minipedia section on pages 492 and 493.

## Draw Home and Property Plans

Have students imagine they have a bird's-eye view of an Egyptian estate and their own home and yard. Tell them to further imagine there are no roofs on the buildings so they can see into them and tell where the various rooms, stairs, hallways, etc., are. Have them draw the egyptian home and estate grounds on half a piece of construction paper and their own home and grounds on the other half. Have students label the different items in each drawing. Then, on the back of the paper have students list all of the ways the two homes are alike. In another column, have them list all of the ways that they are different. Ask volunteers to share their drawings and lists with the class.

Egyptian Estate                              My Home

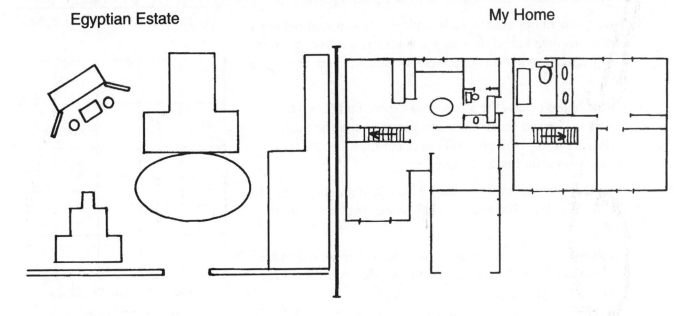

# Make a Senet Game

Senet was a popular board game in ancient Egypt. It is played on a square board with 25 squares called "oyoon," or eyes. The two players each have 12 playing pieces called "kelbs." The object is to capture your opponent's kelbs. The player with the highest number of kelbs at the end of the game is the winner.

## Making the Playing Board and Kelbs:

1. Using a square sheet of heavy tagboard and a ruler, measure and draw 25 squares, five across and five down. Draw an X in the center square.

2. Gather 12 identical playing pieces for each player. These can be shells, checkers, stones, coins, or other objects that will fit in a square.

## Placing the Kelbs:

1. Roll dice, flip a coin, or draw cards to see who places pieces first.

2. The first player sets 2 kelbs on the board in any square except the center one. (There is an advantage to placing kelbs on the outside edge.)

3. The second player then sets 2 kelbs on the board. Repeat this process until all squares except the center are covered.

## Playing the Game:

1. Roll dice, flip a coin, or draw cards to see who moves first.

2. Kelbs can move forward, backward, or sideways, but not diagonally. Kelbs cannot jump over other kelbs. In one turn, a player can move only one kelb one space. The player who moves first must move a kelb into the center square.

3. To capture an opponent's kelb, a player must trap it between two of his own kelbs. If a player voluntarily moves his own kelb between two of his opponent's kelbs, his kelb cannot be taken.

4. As the board clears, the game grows more complex. If a player is blocked on all sides and cannot move, he must forfeit his turn. However, his opponent must open a space for the player on his next move.

5. If a player captures a kelb, he/she may take another turn—if and ONLY IF in that next turn he/she can capture another kelb.

6. Play continues in this manner until one player cannot move his kelbs, refuses to move his kelbs, or when all of his kelbs have been captured.

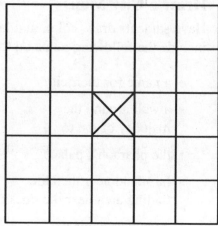

Playing Board

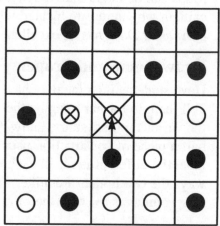

Ⓧ =captured on first move

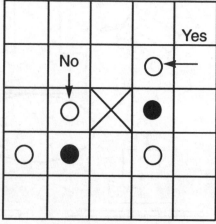

How to capture kelbs

# Persuasive Writing

Evaluate your students' understanding of life in Ancient Egypt by assigning a persuasive writing composition.

## Preparing for the lesson:

1. Reproduce a "Persuasive Writing Organizer" (page 174) and "Editing Checklist" (page 25) for each student.

2. Create overhead transparencies of the "Writing Process" (page 24) and the "Persuasive Writing Organizer."

## Teaching the lesson:

1. Discuss with the class what it must have been like to be a child in Ancient Egypt. List on the board responses to these categories: school, home, games, and family life.

2. Tell students that they will write a persuasive composition about which would be a better life for a child—living today or living in Ancient Egypt. Display and review the "Writing Process" transparency.

3. Give a "Persuasive Writing Organizer" to each student. Tell students they will use this page for their prewriting stage. Display the transparency of the "Persuasive Writing Organizer" and explain how they should use it to plan and write their compositions.

   - Introduction: The introduction should give some background information to get the reader interested. It should tell which side of the issue the writer is taking. The introduction should also tell the three main reasons the writer is using to persuade or convince the reader that his/her position is best.

   - Body: The body of the composition should clearly state the three reasons the writer believes the way he or she does. For each reason, there should be at least three supporting details or examples. Each reason and its supporting details should be a separate paragraph.

   - Conclusion: The conclusion should summarize the reasons for the writer's position. It also needs to include a convincing and persuasive closing statement.

4. Allow time for students to complete rough drafts of their compositions.

5. Distribute an "Editing Checklist" to each student and review how they should use it to improve their compositions.

6. When students have completed the final drafts of their compositions, have them share compositions. Note which position was the most popular. Ask whether anyone who took the opposite position was persuaded to change his or her mind after hearing the compositions.

7. As an extension to the writing activity, students could give persuasive speeches or divide into groups based on their positions and participate in a debate.

# Persuasive Writing Organizer

Introduction (Background information, issue, position on the issue, and three main reasons for your position)

_____

_____

| REASON #1 | SUPPORTING DETAILS: |
|---|---|
|  | _____ |
|  | _____ |
| REASON #2 | SUPPORTING DETAILS: |
|  | _____ |
|  | _____ |
| REASON #3 | SUPPORTING DETAILS: |
|  | _____ |
|  | _____ |

CONCLUSION (summarize your reasons, give a convincing closing statement)

_____

_____

_____

# Trends of the Times

Guests arriving at Shaan's party would have looked splendid. The Ancient Egyptians loved beauty and fashion. Use the information from the story and these pages to draw a picture of two guests as they arrive for the special evening. Use a variety of colors to create an authentic illustration.

- Women wore long sheath dresses. Wealthy women's sheaths were often finely pleated or woven with threads of gold.

- Men wore linen kilts called shentis that were wrapped around their waists and secured with elaborate knots. They would fall in narrow pleats.

- Men and women wore open sandals made from reed or leather and secured with a thong between the toes.

- Men and women wore elaborate headdresses or wigs made from real hair and vegetable fibers.

- Cones or pomades of sweet lotus or lily-scented animal fat or beeswax were worn on top of wigs so that they would melt and release their scent.

- Common Egyptians wore cloth headdresses or headbands.

- Scented oils and creams were applied to protect the skin from the hot desert climate.

- Women plucked their eyebrows and painted a new exaggerated shape in black kohl.

- Men and women used kohl to paint black lines around the eyes to reduce the sun's glare.

# Trends of the Times *(cont.)*

- Malachite (a green copper ore) was ground into powder and used to paint the eyelids. Only the very rich could afford blue lapis lazuli for their eyes.

- Cheeks and lips were colored red, using ochre mixed with animals fat. On special occasions red henna was used to decorate fingernails, toenails, palms of the hands, and soles of the feet.

- Men and women pierced their ears and wore large earrings or ear studs. They wore silver and/or gold rings on many fingers.

- Collars of gold and precious gems were fashionable. They were usually tied in position at the back of the neck.

- Metal bracelets were popular and were worn above the elbow and on wrists and ankles. Bracelets were also made from stones strung together on wire.

- Sometimes long pendants were worn. Others wore necklaces of stones and beads strung in elaborate patterns.

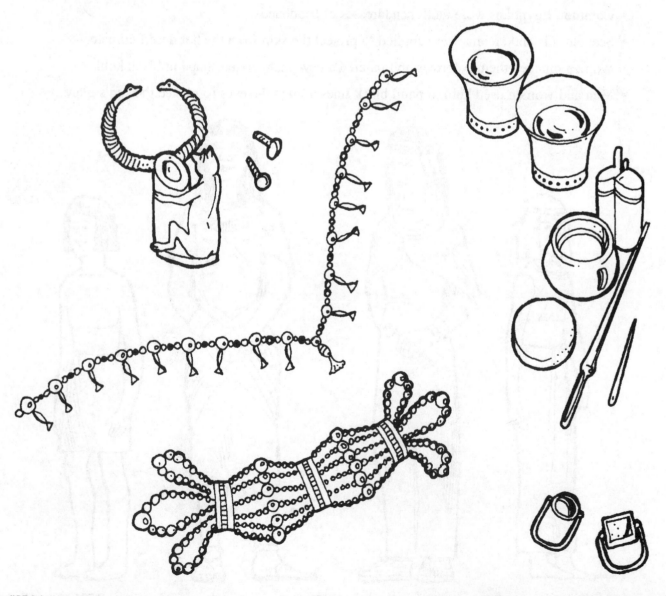

176

# Make a Cloth Headdress

For celebrations, no Egyptian would be without a wig, headdress, or jewelry. Follow the directions below to make a headdress like the one King Tut wears on his mummy mask.

1. Get a square of fabric at least 28" x 28" (70 cm x 70 cm). Use plain or printed material or decorate the fabric with paints and plastic gems. (Silky smooth fabrics do not hold their shape well.)

2. Hold the fabric in front of your face so that you are looking at the front side. Wrap the fabric around your head so that it covers your face. Tie two corners of the cloth securely behind your head.

3. Lift the front of the cloth and carefully pull it back over your head.

4. Straighten the "points" at your temples and lay the corners over your shoulders.

front side

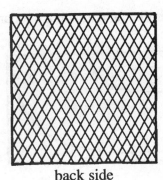
back side

# Make an Egyptian Collar

No Ancient Egyptian party outfit would be complete without lots of big jewelry. Follow the directions below to make an Egyptian collar out of paper. You could also use cloth.

1. Research in your library to find sample collars and examples of Egyptian designs. *Egyptian Designs* by Catherine Calhoun is an excellent source.

2. Fold a 12" x 18" (30 cm x 45 cm) piece of yellow or gold construction paper in half lengthwise.

3. Draw a collar shape on one side and cut it out. You will have a doughnut-shaped collar.

4. Cut a slit in the back so you can put the collar around your neck. Adjust the neck opening so that it is comfortable.

5. Using a black marker, draw a series of thin and thick bands around the collar. In each band draw a Egyptian design or pattern in black marker. Once you have filled the entire collar with patterns, color the designs with markers or paint pens to represent precious stones or inlay.

6. Put the collar around your neck and tape the edges together so it stays on.

7. To make an Egyptian necklace, cut a thinner collar, and attach a pendant or amulet shape to hang from the front of it.

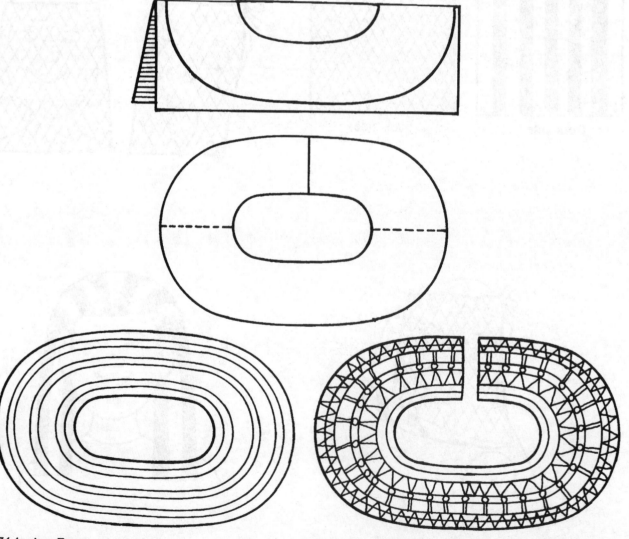

178

# Living History—A Day in Ancient Egypt

With the class, re-create a day in the life of the Ancient Egyptians. Begin to plan for this day at least two weeks in advance. You may wish to team with another class or an entire grade level to share in this special day. Parents may also enjoy participating in all or some of the activities. After you have decided on a schedule of events, you may wish to write a letter home to parents inviting them to participate. Photocopy pages 180–182 for each student and have students take them home at least one week ahead of time. Have students return the bottom part of 180 signed by parents so you know what items each will provide.

## Suggested Activities to Schedule During the Day

1. Students bring their food items for the feast.

2. Students dress as Egyptians (see pages 181-182 for suggestions and guidelines).

3. Reenactment of an Egyptian funeral procession

4. Pyramid Building Competition (See page 51.)

5. Senet Tournament (See page 172.)

6. Prepare and eat an authentic feast while listening to Egyptian music.

7. Watch a movie about Egypt.

8. Performance of an Egyptian dance to Egyptian music

9. Dramatization of an Egyptian myth (Have students write and perform their own plays or one of the Moments in Time in the unit.)

10. Divide students into groups to work on unit activities you may not have done or want to repeat:

    Gifts of the Nile (page 28)

    Make a Personal Cartouche (page 96)

    Make a Scarab Seal Stamp (page 97)

    Build Temple Workshops (page 106)

    Mathematical Grid Egyptian Portraits (pages 107 and 108)

    Make a Relief Carving (page 109)

    Make Clay Coil Pottery (page 110)

    Egyptian Paste/Faience Amulets or Shabti Sculptures (page 112)

    Cooperative Group Project: Make a Mummy (pages 142 and 143)

# Living History—A Day in Ancient Egypt *(cont.)*

## Egyptian Feast Menu

White and Red Grape Juice

Egyptian or Pita Bread

Grapes and Melon

Paper Cups

Green Salad

Dried Fruits

Paper Plates

Napkins

Bean Salad

Dried Jerky Meats

Plastic Utensils

## Egyptian Bread (makes 4 small loaves)

3 ½ cups (833 mL) whole-wheat flour

2 cups (472 mL) water

1 teaspoon (5 mL) salt

1. Put the flour and salt in a very large bowl. Add the water slowly, mixing well.
2. Knead the dough on a floured surface. Add a little more flour if it is too sticky.
3. Divide the dough into four pieces. Shape each piece into a round disk.
4. Place the dough on a greased cookie sheet and cover it with a cloth overnight.
5. The next day, bake the dough for 30 minutes at 350° F (180° C), or until golden brown.

## Bean Salad
### (makes 8 servings)

**Dressing**

1 clove minced garlic

½ teaspoon (2.5 mL) dry mustard

½ teaspoon (2.5 mL) basil

½ teaspoon (2.5 mL) oregano

¼ teaspoon (1.25 mL) rosemary

1 tablespoon (15 mL) minced parsley

½ cup (118 mL) olive oil

¼ cup (60 mL) wine vinegar

**Salad**

2 cups (472 mL) canned green beans, drained

1 cup (236 mL) canned garbanzo beans, drained

1 cup (236 mL) canned red kidney beans, drained

1 medium onion, thinly sliced

1. Combine the salad ingredients in a large bowl.
2. Combine dressing ingredients; pour them over the salad.
3. Mix the salad thoroughly; refrigerate it at least one hour before serving.

# Living History—A Day in Ancient Egypt *(cont.)*

## Egyptian Clothing and Music

Egyptians loved to dress up and give a party! Use the directions throughout the unit to make a party costume for your Day in Ancient Egypt. Here are some suggestions:

**Hair**—Braid your hair into tiny braids overnight. Take out the braids the next day and fluff your hair to make it full. Wear flowers or a headband in your hair. Make and wear a crown or headdress (pages 148 and 177).

**Make-up**—Men and women wore elaborate makeup. Use a black eye pencil to line above and below your lids. Bring the lines together at the corner of your eyes and extend the line to your temples. Use the black pencil to exaggerate your eyebrows. Color your eyelids with blue and/or green eye shadow. Put a little blush on your cheeks and a little lipstick on your lips. Paint your fingernails and toenails with red nail polish. Draw Egyptian symbols on the palms of your hands with a red marker.

**Jewelry**—Men and women wore lots of metal jewelry with precious stones. Pile on the earrings, bracelets, arm bands, anklets, rings, and necklaces. Make and wear a collar or necklace (page 178).

**Clothing**—See page 182.

**Sandals**—A sandal that comes up between the toes is most authentic, but any type will be fine. Check school policy to see if other shoes must be brought for outdoor activities.

**Music**—The Egyptians loved to listen to fine music during their parties. You may wish to bring cassette tapes with Egyptian folk music, music from the Middle East, or any music tapes with the instruments associated with specific Egyptian gods. For Osiris, god of the Underworld, choose flutes and bells. Isis, his wife and goddess of healing and fertility, is represented by a rattle. Thoth, the moon god and god of scribes, is associated with the harp or lyre. Other instruments used by Ancient Egyptians include castanets, tambourines, and drums.

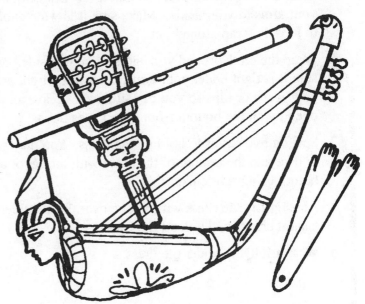

# Living History—A Day in Ancient Egypt *(cont.)*

## Make a Shenti

To a make a shenti you will need a piece of white cloth or twin sized sheet.  No sewing is required, although you may want a large safety pin to secure the shenti at the waist.  Wear a solid white t-shirt with your shenti and shorts underneath it.

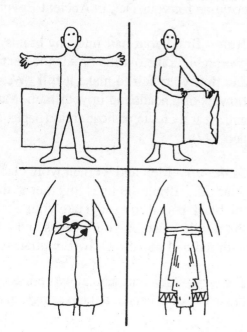

1.  Get a piece of cloth that is as wide as your arms and long enough to reach from your waist to mid-calf.

2.  Place the cloth around your waist.  Using your right hand, grab one end of the cloth and bring it over to your left side as if to tie.  Using your left hand, grab the cloth mid-way on the top allowing the end to dangle free.

3.  Still holding the cloth in these places, twist the cloth left side over the right side to form two rabbit ears.  Pull these two rabbit ears tightly.

4.  Holding onto the rabbit ears, roll over the front of the shenti a couple of times to secure the knot in place.  You now have a shenti with a pleated front.

5.  If desired, paint the bottom edge of the shenti with an Egyptian border using fabric paints.

## Make a Sheath Dress

To make the dress will need a piece of white cloth or a twin sized sheet.  You may choose to sew the dress by hand with a whip stitch, safety pin it together, or use a sewing machine.

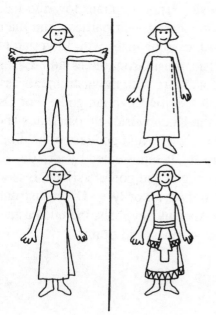

1.  Measure and cut the cloth so that it reaches from under your arms to your ankle.  Make sure it is wide enough to loosely wrap around you.

2.  Wrap the cloth around you and sew up one side.  Make sure it is tight under your arms, but not too tight around your waist or hips so you can sit down.  Leave an opening on the bottom from your knees down.

3.  Sew on two straps to hold up the dress.  You may want to decorate the bottom of the dress with an Egyptian border using fabric paints.

4.  Accompany the dress with a robe over the shoulders or a short shenti tied around the waist.

5.  Wear a full slip under the dress.

# Ancient Egypt—Assessment

## Multiple Choice

On the blanks, write the letter of the answer that correctly completes each statement.

_____ 1. Egypt is on the continent of

      a. South America     b. Africa     c. Asia     d. Europe

_____ 2. Each year, farmers measured the height of the Nile flooding using a

      a. measuring stick     b. shaduf     c. Nilometer     d. papyrus reed

_____ 3. The name of the Egyptian writing system is

      a. hieroglyphics     b. cuneiform     c. script     d. tally marks

_____ 4. A famous scholar unlocked the mystery of Egyptian writing by decoding

      a. a papyrus scroll     b. the Rosetta Stone     c. a cave painting
      d. Tut's tomb

_____ 5. Instead of pyramids, many pharaohs were buried in tombs located in

      a. Memphis     b. the Nile delta     c. Cairo     d. the Valley of the Kings

_____ 6. The Egyptian practice of worshiping many different gods is

      a. deism     b. monotheism     c. atheism     d. polytheism

_____ 7. The collection of poems, spells, and incantations used by Egyptians to move on to a happy afterlife is the

      a. *Book of the Dead*     b. Arabian Nights     c. Rosetta Stone
      d. papyrus scroll library

_____ 8. Although the pharaoh was most powerful, the person he relied on to oversee his kingdom was the

      a. scribe     b. magistrate     c. priest     d. vizier

_____ 9. A farmer, a merchant, and an artist were all part of the

      a. upper class     b. middle class     c. lower class     d. royal family

_____ 10. The Head Priest, Chief Commander of the Army, High Officials, and Nobles belonged to the

      a. upper class     b. middle class     c. lower class     d. royal family

# Ancient Egypt—Assessment *(cont.)*

## Matching

Read each description. Choose the correct response from the vocabulary below. Then write the letter for your response in the blank.

_____ 1. This is the Egyptian form of heaven. Egyptians believed that after they died they could have a happy afterlife in this place that was very similar to Egypt but without any sorrows.

_____ 2. These included papyrus goods, building stones, and grains.

_____ 3. This was the largest building of its kind ever built. It was built by King Khufu.

_____ 4. These were small mummy-like statues sculpted out of Egyptian paste. They were buried with the dead to work as servants in the fields during the afterlife.

_____ 5. This is the season when the Nile floods to its highest level. During this season the farmers help with building and trade expeditions since they cannot work in their fields.

_____ 6. This simple machine was like a lever. It was used to help the farmers irrigate their crops by raising water from the Nile into their canals.

_____ 7. These were the three spirits of the dead. One was like the person's shadow. Another had a body of a bird so that it could fly out of the tomb and visit its relatives. The other spirit went through to the Underworld to pass the Weighing of the Heart test.

_____ 8. This is the season when the waters of the Nile begin to recede. This is the time for planting seeds and planning for crops.

_____ 9. This is a giant statue of a lion with the head of King Khafre. It was built to guard the dead in Giza and overlook the great pyramids.

_____ 10. These included cedar from Lebanon, olive oil from Crete, and gold and precious gems form Nubia.

_____ 11. This was a type of jewelry that was worn as a protection against evil spirits. Sometimes it was made in the shape of an ankh or a scarab beetle.

_____ 12. This is the season when all of the crops were picked. Usually there was a great festival to celebrate the year's plentiful bounty.

## Vocabulary Terms

a. shabti

b. amulet

c. sphinx

d. Great Pyramid of Giza

e. exports

f. imports

g. ba, ka, akh

h. shaduf

i. Field of Reeds

j. shait (inundation)

k. piruit (emergence)

l. shemu (harvest)

# Ancient Egypt—Assessment *(cont.)*

## Fill in the Blanks

Use the terms at the top of this page to fill in the blanks.

### Terms

| | |
|---|---|
| **myths** | **pharaoh** |
| **barter** | **mummified** |
| **flax** | **papyrus** |
| **shrine** | **sarcophagus** |
| **canopic jars** | **scribe** |

1. _____ was one of the most important crops in Egypt. It grew in the waters of the Nile and could be made into paper, sandals, and mats.

2. Because of Egypt's hot climate, most clothing needed to be light and cool. _____ provided such clothing and was woven into cloth and other household products.

3. The Egyptians did not have coins or money to purchase goods. Instead they would _____ for goods by trading one type of item for another.

4. All of the high-ranking jobs in Egypt required reading and writing. By becoming a_____, a boy could learn how to read and write, thereby allowing him an opportunity to raise his position in society.

5. Most people did not go into the Temple to worship. Instead, they had a family or village _____ where they could give offerings to the gods and worship.

6. The Egyptians told many stories and legends to help explain the different roles of the gods and why certain things were the way they were. One of the most famous _____ tells about how Osiris became the King of the Underworld.

7. The Egyptians believed in a happy afterlife after they died. But, in order to have this afterlife it was important to preserve the body. The Egyptians _____ their dead so that the person's spirits would be able to recognize the body and return to the tomb.

8. Part of preserving the body involved saving some of the internal organs. These organs were placed in _____ shaped like the animal heads of different gods.

9. After being wrapped in linen and placed in coffins, the dead body would finally be placed in a _____ or large stone coffin.

10. The _____ was the king of Egypt. He was also considered to be a god on Earth to the Egyptians.

# Ancient Egypt—Assessment *(cont.)*

### Essay

Use another sheet of paper to answer the following questions. Be as detailed and specific as possible.

1. Why did most people in Egypt settle along the banks of the Nile? Name at least three "gifts" the Nile had to offer.

2. How did the Nile provide opportunities for trade with other lands?

3. What were the pyramids? Describe why they were built, who actually did the labor in building them, and why later Egyptians decided to no longer build pyramids.

4. Who went to school? List at least two ways that school in ancient Egypt was different from school today. List at least two ways that school was similar to today.

5. Why was it beneficial to become a scribe?

6. How did most Egyptians worship?

7. Who were the only people allowed into the temples? Why?

8. Name any three Egyptian gods. Describe what they looked like and their functions.

9. Why did the Egyptians mummify their dead?

10. What is the Weighing of the Heart ceremony?

11. Describe the Ancient Egyptian government structure and the roles of the pharaoh, vizier, magistrates (judges), Head Priest, and Commander of the Army.

12. What was life like for Egyptian families? Describe the roles of the father, mother, son, and daughter.

# Ancient Egypt Assessment—Answer Key

**Multiple Choice** (page 183)

1. b, 2. c, 3. a, 4. b, 5. d, 6. d, 7. a, 8. d, 9. b, 10. a

**Matching** (page 184)

1. i, 2. e, 3. d, 4. a, 5. j, 6. h, 7. g, 8. k, 9. c, 10. f, 11. b, 12. 1

**Fill in the Blanks** (page 185)

1. papyrus, 2. flax, 3. barter, 4. scribe, 5. shrine, 6. myths, 7. mummified, 8. canopic jars, 9. sarcophagus, 10. pharaoh

**Essay** (page 186)

1. People settled along the Nile because it was the only fertile area within a large desert. The Nile provided many things, including water for crops, fertile soil after the flooding, papyrus, fish and water fowl to eat, a mode of transportation for trade, and a way to transport huge building stones to build the pyramids.

2. The Nile stretched from the Mediterranean Sea south into Nubia and Kush, allowing access to lands in the south as well as land touched by the Mediterranean Sea.

3. The pyramids were huge tombs made from stone, built for the pharaohs as their stairway to heaven. The pyramids were built by slaves and farmers during the flooding of the Nile. Egyptians discovered that building pyramids was very costly, took many years and many workers, and were easily robbed and plundered. Eventually, tombs were carved into the cliffs at the Valley of the Kings instead of building pyramids.

4. Only boys who could afford the tuition or were sponsored could attend school. (Accept reasonable answers for the rest of the question.)

5. Scribes did not have to help with building projects or work in the fields. Only a scribe could advance his position in society because he could read and write.

6. Most Egyptians were not allowed in the temples, so they worshiped at family or local village shrines. Sometimes the village would participate in a religious festival.

7. Only the priests were allowed into the temples because they went through special cleansing rituals to purify themselves before seeing the gods.

8. (Accept reasonable answers.)

9. The Egyptians believed the only way they could have a happy afterlife was if the spirit could recognize the body to return to it, and mummification preserved the body.

10. The Weighing of the Heart ceremony took place in the Underworld to judge whether or not the person was worthy of a happy afterlife. The heart was weighed against the feather of truth. If it was lighter, the person went on to the Field of Reeds. If it was heavy, it was devoured by a monster named Ammit.

11. The head of the government was the pharaoh, responsible for all of Egypt. The vizier reported to the pharaoh about what was happening in the courts, expeditions, building projects, and most other things. The magistrates ran the court system and enforced the laws. The Head Priest was in charge of the temples, religion, and scribes. The Commander of the Army, usually one of the pharaoh's sons, was in charge of exploration of, expeditions to, and conquering of other lands.

12. The Egyptian family was a strong and important unit. Fathers worked to support the family. Mothers ran the household and raised the children. Boys went to school or learned a trade from their fathers. Girls were taught at home how to run the house and be a good wife. Children were taught manners and respect. Women and children were treated well and respected. Families enjoyed playing together.

# Literature Connection Planning Guide

# Using Literature

The literature lessons are arranged so that they correspond to sections in the book. You may wish to incorporate one or more of the suggestions below into the format you follow.

- Prereading Activity—Discuss past chapters, predict future events, and/or connect the story to other classroom activities.

- Read the Section—Choose a reading strategy (see number 6 below).

- Vocabulary Activity—See the suggestions for activities (page 191) and words for each section (pages 194, 199, 204, 211, 214).

- Comprehension Activities and Questions—See the suggestions for activities (page 192) and questions for each section (pages 194, 199, 204, 211, 214).

- Written Language Activities

- Hands-On Activities

## Preparing to Teach the Literature Lessons

1. Have students make a literature journal by stapling writing paper between construction paper covers before starting the lessons. This provides a way for them to keep a record of their responses to comprehension questions, definitions for vocabulary words, and thoughts and feelings about the story as they read it. Have students decorate the front covers with the title of the book, their names, and appropriate illustrations.

2. Preview the story and make notes in your copy of the book. This allows you to easily find vocabulary words, descriptions, figurative language, and sections covered by the comprehension questions.

3. Get an overview of the activities for the literature unit so you can gather the materials you need ahead of time. Decide how much time you want to schedule for each activity.

4. Make overhead transparencies of the vocabulary lists and comprehension questions (pages 194, 199, 204, 211, 214) and reproduce them for students as you begin each section. Discuss the vocabulary with students. Ask them whether they already know the meanings of any of the words. Ask students to pay close attention while reading to see whether they can use context clues to determine the meanings of unfamiliar words. Then, discuss the comprehension questions with students. Ask volunteers to help you determine key words in the questions. Underline the key words on the transparencies.

5. Make an overhead transparency of the Story Plot Outline (page 125) to use as students are reading the book. You may wish to reproduce this outline for students to fill in.

6. Reading Strategies—Vary the strategies you use so students get practice with each.

- Round Robin Reading—Students orally read in groups, taking turns around the table.

- Popcorn Reading—Read orally as a class, allowing students to call on other students.

- Partner Reading—Students pair up and read orally to each other.

- Teacher Reading—Teacher reads aloud to the class.

- Silent Reading—Students read individually and silently.

# Background Information

## About the Author

Eloise Jarvis McGraw is a multitalented woman who has always loved writing and the arts. Born in Houston, Texas, in 1915, she began writing when she was about eight years old. In 1937 she received a Bachelor of Arts degree from Principia College. She pursued graduate work in painting and sculpting and became an instructor of portrait and figure painting. But her greater love was always writing. In 1940 she married another writer of children's books, William Corbin McGraw.

Together the McGraws began traveling and recording information for their books. Their trip to France in 1985 provided an inspiration for Eloise McGraw's book *The Striped Ships*, a novel about the Norman Invasion of England. The McGraws' extensive travels throughout Egypt provided inspiration and information for her books *The Golden Goblet* and two other books on Egypt—*Mara, Daughter of the Nile* and *Pharaoh*.

Eloise Jarvis McGraw

McGraw was awarded the Lewis Carroll Shelf Award in 1963, and many of her books have achieved important recognition. *Crown Fire* was an honor book at the New York Herald-Tribune Children's Book Festival, and *Moccasin Trail* and *The Golden Goblet* were runners-up for the prestigious Newbery Award.

## Book Summary

Young Ranofer is the son of a famous goldsmith who makes fine jewelry for the royal family. Ranofer happily begins learning his father's trade when fate takes an ugly turn. Unknown to Ranofer, his father has another son, Gebu, who was born to his first wife, an evil and unkind woman. When Ranofer's father dies, Ranofer is forced to live with his cruel half brother.

Ranofer's dream to become an apprentice to the great goldsmith Zau is dashed. Gebu beats him and feeds him only the crumbs left over from his own meals. He breaks Ranofer's heart by refusing to pay the apprentice fee for the goldsmith shop and instead forcing Ranofer to work as a laborer sweeping up after the gold workers and running errands for a pittance.

Ranofer discovers that Gebu is using him to steal small portions of gold dust from the shop. When Ranofer confronts his brother, Gebu moves him to apprentice at a stone-cutter's shop. When Ranofer discovers a golden goblet in his brother's room, he learns that Gebu is stealing from the pharaoh's tombs, a crime punishable by death. How can Ranofer turn in his brother without being punished for the crime himself?

With two good friends, Ranofer follows Gebu to the Valley of the Kings to get firsthand proof that Gebu is robbing the tomb. Ranofer then reports the crime and Gebu to the queen. The queen tests Ranofer to make sure he is telling the truth and then rewards him with a donkey and an apprenticeship to Zau's goldsmith shop. Gebu is captured and punished, and justice is served.

# Vocabulary Activities

Help your students learn and retain the vocabulary suggested for each section of the story by providing them with interesting vocabulary activities, such as those suggested below.

1. Have students write each word in their journals. Then, have them find the word in the story and look up the definitions in dictionaries. Have students write in their journals the definitions that match the uses of the words in the book.

2. Have students work in groups to make vocabulary flash cards by writing the sentences from the book that contain the vocabulary words on one side of some index cards and the meanings of the words on the other side. Have students quiz each other about the definitions of the words. Cards can also be used by individual students to test themselves.

3. Have individuals make illustrated vocabulary dictionaries by writing the words and definitions on large index cards along with illustrations. As words are added while reading the book, students rearrange the cards so that the words are in alphabetical order. After students have finished the book, bind the cards together, using a hole-puncher and yarn.

4. Have students make a synonym-antonym chart in their journals. As they write down their vocabulary words and the sentences from the book, have them also write synonyms that could be substituted in the sentences without changing the meanings. Then, have them write antonyms that change the meanings of the sentences when they are substituted for the vocabulary words.

5. Tell students to make parts of speech charts in the journals. The headings should include *Noun, Verb, Adjective,* and *Adverb.* Ask students to write the sentence from the book with the vocabulary word highlighted under the appropriate heading.

6. Have students use the vocabulary words to write poems or summaries about the chapters in that section. Highlight the vocabulary words and display some of the best poems or summaries.

7. Challenge students to work in pairs and use graph paper to make vocabulary crossword puzzles. Reproduce some of the best puzzles to distribute to the class.

8. Have a classroom vocabulary bee (similar to a spelling bee). Students play individually or in teams. Students should spell the words and give the correct definitions after you read aloud the sentences from the book that contain the appropriate vocabulary words.

9. Play vocabulary hide-and-seek by having students work in groups to write the sentences from the book that contain the vocabulary words on one set of index cards and the definitions of the vocabulary words on another set of index cards. Give one group a designated area to hide their cards and have another group try to find the cards, matching the words with their definitions.

10. Have students play vocabulary charades by acting out each vocabulary word.

11. Write a vocabulary word of the day on the chalkboard before students enter the classroom. When students arrive, discuss the meaning of the word. Ask students to correctly use the word as frequently as possible throughout the day. Make a tally mark next to the word each time a student uses it correctly.

# Comprehension Activities

Help your students better understand the story by using the comprehension questions suggested for each section and one or more of the activities suggested below.

1.  Have students answer some or all of the questions, using complete sentences, in their literature journals. Invite students to discuss their answers.

2.  Play comprehension hot seat. Have one student come to the front of the class to portray one of the characters from the book. Have the rest of the students ask appropriate questions from the list, along with questions of their own. The student in the hot seat should respond to the questions as if he/she were that character. Tell students to think carefully about how the character would talk, feel, move, etc. Evaluate students' ability to respond correctly, based on their assumed identity. Have students take turns being in the hot seat and pretending to be other characters.

3.  Have students make comprehension comic strips that show scenes from the story that answer one or more of the questions.

4.  Have students make illustrated posters or dioramas to answer one or more questions.

5.  Play hide-and-seek by writing the questions on one set of index cards and the answers on another set. Hide the cards and have students find them, matching the questions with the correct answers.

6.  Divide the class into groups. Ask each group to dramatize the answer to a question.

7.  Have students write dialogues between characters from the story, answering one or all of the questions. Invite volunteers to read their dialogues to the class.

8.  Play comprehension Jeopardy by dividing the class into two teams. Have each team write questions for that section of the book or any previous sections. Write the student-created questions (worth 5 points) and the comprehension questions (worth 10 points) on strips of paper. Put the strips in a container. Have each team take turns drawing out a question and then discussing and answering it. (Do not let them know ahead of time who will be called on to answer for the team; that way everyone on the team must participate.) The team with the most points wins.

9.  Play Cooperative Group Battle by dividing the class into groups of four. Assign each person in the group a number from 1–4. Give each group pieces of scratch paper to write their answers. Have them write their group's name at the top of each piece of paper. Using the questions from the list, assign each question a point value based on its difficulty. To play the game, read aloud the question and its value. Allow the groups to quietly discuss their answer for about one minute. Call "time" and tell the class which person (1, 2, 3, or 4) in the group is to write the answer. There is to be no talking while the person is writing. Allow 1–2 minutes to write their answers and deliver them to you. The paper must be in your hands before the time is up, or the team receives no points. Read the answers and give all or partial points for their responses. Continue until all questions have been answered. Assign writers in a random order so that all students must participate on each question.

# Before Reading the Book

Before you begin reading *The Golden Goblet* with your students, choose some of these prereading activities to stimulate their interest and enhance their comprehension.

1. Have students examine the front cover title and picture. Discuss and predict what the story might be about based on the information found on the cover.

2. Write "Ancient Egypt" on the board along with these categories: geography, economy, architecture, education, art, religion, government, society, and family. Have students brainstorm all of the information they already know about Egypt and write it on the board. If you are reading the book before teaching the social studies portion of this unit, you may need to coach students to come up with information for each category.

3. Inform students that this is a fiction book based on historical places and facts, such as events, culture, legal rights, and artifacts discovered in Ancient Egypt. Discuss other historical fiction books as examples. Tell students that throughout the story you will be noting actual places and historical elements of Ancient Egypt to lend the story authenticity.

4. Tell students that all stories have a problem and obstacles that must be overcome to solve the problem. Divide the class into five groups. Assign each group one of the questions below. Have each group discuss its question and then share its response with the rest of the class.

   a. What would it be like if you had an afterlife in which you could visit your family and friends after you died? What positive and negative effects might this have on them?

   b. What would it be like if most boys and girls did not go to school? What would you do all day instead? Be realistic.

   c. How would you feel if you were forced to live with someone who was cruel to you and would not let you make any choices for yourself? What would you do? What would you do if the law approved this kind of treatment of you?

   d. Describe how your life would be different if you were forced to quit school and earn a living to support yourself. What kind of job could you get with your present education and skills? What kind of lifestyle would you have with only the money you earn?

   e. What would you do if you discovered someone was using you to commit a crime? What would you do if you learned that you would be punished severely if you turned in that person?

5. Begin a "Story Plot Outline" for the book by using an overhead transparency made from page 125. As you read each section, refer to this outline to fill in the developing plot. This is a good way to review the section students have just read.

# Vocabulary

| Chapter 1 | Chapter 2 | Chapter 3 |
|---|---|---|
| crucible | papyrus | jubilant |
| apprentice | negligently | murmured |
| exasperated | vindictively | bungling |
| scant | reproach | blissful |
| aghast | pharaoh | |

## Comprehension Questions

1. How is Ranofer's job as a laborer in the gold shop different from working as an apprentice? (Chapter 1)

_____

_____

2. Why does Gebu allow Ranofer to work in the gold shop? (Chapter 1)

_____

_____

3. Name the two new friends of Ranofer. How did he meet these new friends? (Chapter 2)

_____

_____

4. What happens when Ranofer tells Gebu he knows what is going on with the wineskin? What would you have done if you were Ranofer? (Chapter 2)

_____

_____

5. Pretend you are Ranofer. What do you know how to do that most boys your age today do not know how to do? Name three things boys Ranofer's age do today that he is not able to do. (Chapter 3)

_____

_____

6. What important job did Rekh entrust to Ranofer? How did Ranofer complete it? (Chapter 3)

_____

_____

7. What did Gebu do when Ranofer did not come home with the wineskin from Ibni? What other options did Ranofer have? (Chapter 3)

_____

_____

# Character Web

As you read Chapters 1–3, discuss the workings of the gold shop and the main characters of the story. Use the web below to describe the characters and their relationships to each other. Identify the "good" characters and the "evil" characters of the story. As you read further chapters, add characters important to the plot of the story.

## FRIENDS

Heqet_____

_____

_____

Ancient _____

_____

_____

## EMEMIES

Gebu _____

_____

_____

Ibni _____

_____

Setma_____

_____

Wenamon _____

_____

**RANOFER** _____

_____

_____

_____

## GOLDSMITHS

Zau _____

Rekh _____

Sata _____

# Write a Monologue or Dialogue

Students enjoy writing conversations between characters. This lesson will help students learn how to write effective monologues and dialogues.

## Preparing for the lesson:

1. Reproduce Write a Monologue or Dialogue (page 197) for students.

2. Gather an overhead projector and three different colors of overhead pens or a chalkboard and three different colors of chalk.

3. (Optional) Make large name tags for the characters: Gebu, Setma, and Wenamon.

## Teaching the lesson:

1. After reading Chapters 1–3, tell students that they are going to write conversations that *could have taken place* in the story but did not. First, you will provide a demonstration.

2. Choose three character students to come to the front of the classroom. Assign a character to each—Gebu, Setma, and Wenamon. Put on name tags, if made.

3. Choose a recorder student for each character. These recorders are to write down only what their character does, not what he says. For example, they should describe facial expressions, gestures, and movement.

4. Tell the characters they are going to reenact the conversation they had when they all went to Gebu's house in Chapter 2. There is no right or wrong conversation, so they can just make up whatever seems most logical. They should take turns talking, talk slowly so you can record their words, and act out their conversation with facial expressions, gestures, and movement.

5. Use one color of pen or chalk to write down what each character says. Leave plenty of room between the words of one character and another.

6. After each character has spoken at least one or two times and you have recorded what was said, stop the conversation. Thank the students and send them back to their seats.

7. Call the class's attention to what you recorded. Tell students that these are the actual words that came out of the characters' mouths. Therefore, these are the words that belong within quotation marks. Add quotation marks to the sentences.

8. Elicit from students that words alone don't tell who is doing the talking or what else is happening as the characters are speaking.

9. Use another color of pen or chalk to show how the speaker's name can be placed before, after, or in the middle of the actual quotation to show who is speaking.

10. As you go through the dialogue lines, have the recorders tell what their character was doing as he spoke. Using the third color of pen or chalk, write that information into the dialogue.

11. Review the three parts of a conversation: the speaker, the speaker's words, and the speaker's actions. Discuss the difference between a monologue (one person speaking) and a dialogue (more than one person speaking).

12. Distribute a copy of page 197 to each student. Allow time for students to write a monologue or dialogue. Ask for volunteers to share their writing with the class.

# Write a Monologue or Dialogue *(cont.)*

Choose one of the situations below to write a monologue or dialogue. Make sure you use a variety of quotation styles and clearly describe the actions and feelings of the characters. Have each character speak at least three times.

---

**Monologue**—one person speaking

**Dialogue**—two or more people speaking

**Examples of Styles:**

*Speaker before* Face angry, *Ranofer said*, "I won't do it! I won't steal for you."

*Speaker after* Ranofer scowled. "I won't do it! I won't steal for you," *he said.*

*Speaker in between* "I won't do it!" *Ranofer said*, angrily. "I won't steal for you." He stomped away.

---

1. Write a monologue showing what Ranofer would say to Gebu if he knew Gebu could not harm him. _____

_____

_____

_____

_____

_____

2. Write a dialogue between Ranofer and Rekh in which Ranofer tells Rekh about the wineskins.

_____

_____

_____

_____

_____

3. Write a dialogue between Ranofer and Heqet in which Ranofer describes his life with Gebu.

_____

_____

_____

_____

_____

_____

# **Similes**

A simile uses the words LIKE or AS to compare two things. Eloise Jarvis McGraw uses many similes to describe the characters and situations in the story. Find each of these similes in your book and explain what each one means.

1. Page 9: He turned the ingot out and tried to lose himself again in his tasks; but the thought of Gebu, like the ache of a tooth, was hard to lose.

   _____

   _____

   _____

2. Page 10: His voice was like the sound of a badly made flute, and sibilant with his Babylonian accent. _____

   _____

   _____

3. Page 16: His shoulder had begun to throb and smart from the goldsmith's touch, like a sleeping devil roused to angry wakefulness, but the greatest pain was in his mind.

   _____

   _____

   _____

4. Page 17: Heavy as a yoke, responsibility settled over Ranofer's mind.

   _____

   _____

5. Page 21: There was a moment's awkward silence, during which Ranofer struggled without much success against the familiar frightened loneliness that had swept in again as through an opened door. _____

   _____

   _____

6. Page 30: Ranofer had seen the pair often hobbling about the streets of the City of the Dead, but their sudden appearance here sent his wits scattering like startled birds.

   _____

   _____

   _____

7. Page 33: He reached the foot of the stairs and stood there winking, his bulk dwarfing the boy, who was thin as a reed. _____

   _____

   _____

# Vocabulary

| Chapter 4 | Chapter 5 | Chapter 6 |
|---|---|---|
| indifferent | joviality | sarcophagi |
| devise | writhing | traitorously |
| distractedly | buoyant | incredulous |
| homely | | |
| bellow | | |
| raucous | | |

## Comprehension Questions

1. Ranofer felt it was either a god or his father's ba who had helped him with his plan. Explain how they could have helped. (Chapter 4)_____

2. Describe how the Egyptians were buried, depending on their social status. (Chapter 4)

3. Do you think Ranofer will be able to trust Heqet? Why or why not? (Chapter 4)

4. Why was robbing a tomb considered such a terrible crime? (Chapter 5)

5. Why does Gebu make Ranofer an apprentice at the stonecutter's shop? What was Ranofer's plan to avoid this? (Chapter 5)_____

6. How is Ranofer treated differently at the stonecutter's shop? Pretend you are Pai. How would you describe your new stonecutter's apprentice? (Chapter 6)

7. What are some of the Egyptian superstitions about the night? (Chapter 6)

# Heqet's Sayings

Heqet has a clever way with words, making a riddle or joke to explain a situation. Explain each of the following sayings. Then, try your hand at writing your own Heqetlike sayings for the situations listed.

1. Page 20: "Aye, well enough, though I do not know my head from my tail in this place, as the cat said when she tumbled into the fowler's net."

   _____

2. Page 46: "It will quiet your rumblings, as the man said when he tossed his right leg to the crocodile."

   _____

3. Page 51: "Simple if you know the trick of it, remarked the vulture as she laid a falcon egg."

   _____

4. Page 64: "I thought I heard a voice, the cow remarked as she stood on the leopard's tail."

   _____

5. Page 66: "Things got a little crowded, as the mole explained when he crawled out of the anthill."

   _____

6. Page 67: "I fear my mind is not on my work, as the worm said when the lark bit its head off."

   _____

7. Page 72: "Never fear. We'll catch him, as the tortoise said to the snail."

   _____

## Now You Try It

1. I was feeling guilty for eating the last bread, remarked the _____

   _____

2. This sure is hard work, as the _____

   _____

3. The gold was too hot to touch, remarked the _____

   _____

4. The thought of Ibni makes my skin crawl, as the _____

   _____

5. It feels good to have a friend to trust, remarked the _____

   _____

# Write a Friendship Poem

Ranofer feels he has a true friend in Heqet.  Think about the qualities you value most in a friend.
Complete the concept web by writing those qualities in their order of importance to you.  On the line
under the web, tell why your #1 quality is so important to have in a friend.

#1   #2   #3   #4

**FRIENDSHIP**

#5   #6   #7   #8

To me, the most important quality in a friend is _____

because _____

_____

_____ .

**Ode to Friendship**

_____

_____

_____

_____

_____

_____

_____

# Culture Clues

Literature can tell you much about a culture and historical time period. Using the first six chapters of the book, work as a group or team to record as many clues as possible for the following categories. Whenever possible, write the page number where you found the clues.

| Food | Clothing | Buildings |
|---|---|---|
| | | |
| Social classes | Geography and climate | Family life |
| | | |
| Superstitions | Gods and religion | Arts and crafts |
| | | |
| Economy, money, and trade | Government leaders and laws | Education and job training |
| | | |

# The Job Debate

In Chapter 5, Ranofer is forced to quit his work at the gold shop and apprentice at the stonecutter's shop. Ranofer is very dismayed at this prospect and tries to reason with Gebu. Divide the class into two groups. Ask one group to take the position of Gebu and offer reasons why Ranofer should work at the stonecutter's shop. Have the other half take the position of Ranofer and offer reasons why he should work at the gold shop.

First, have groups use the book to find and list supporting arguments for their positions. After a designated time, have the groups face each other to form debate teams. Remind students that when it is not their turn to speak, they must be good listeners. Everyone on both teams is allowed a turn to speak.

The debate begins by one team stating its position and telling one well-elaborated reason supporting it. The other team then responds to the first team's comments, but members can only point out faulty logic in the ideas—not make personal attacks or add supporting reasons for their own position. Then the second team tells its position and provides one reason supporting it. The first team gets a chance to respond in turn.

The debate continues in this manner until neither team has any additional reasons to support its position. Poll the class to find out which team presented its case the best and thereby won the debate.

## Superstitions

The Egyptians were very religious and superstitious people. Draw the chart shown below on the chalkboard or a transparency. Have students skim the book to locate examples of Egyptian superstitions. Have students brainstorm superstitions of today. These could be religious superstitions, everyday superstitions, or those that surround holidays, such as Halloween. Discuss the relevance of superstitions to the two cultures. Compare and contrast reasons people believe in superstitions.

As an extension, have some students research further into common superstitions and their origins and report their findings back to the class. Students may be amused at the number and variety of superstitions still practiced today in our very scientific culture.

| **Superstitions in Ancient Egypt** | **Superstitions in the United States Today** |
|---|---|
| khefts—evil spirits | devil and other evil spirits |
| ba—spirits that return from the dead | ghosts—spirits that return from the dead |
| wore amulets for protection | carry rabbit's foot for good luck |
| said names of gods | bad luck omens—black cat, broken mirror |
| didn't say names of mean gods | good omens—find 4-leaf clover, rainbow |

# Vocabulary

| Chapter 7 | Chapter 8 | Chapter 9 |
|---|---|---|
| treacherous | imbecile | dubious |
| torment | dreary | ridicule |
| collided | | concealed |
| belligerent | | exhilarating |
| lithe | | |
| amiable | | |
| jubilant | | |

## Comprehension Questions

1. How do Heqet and Ranofer plan for Ranofer to continue learning the goldsmith trade even though he now works at the stonecutter's shop? (Chapter 7)_____

   _____

   _____

2. What is happening in the spring that requires most of the men in the stonecutter's shop to leave and work elsewhere? (Chapter 7)_____

   _____

   _____

3. Why is Ranofer jubilant to meet Heqet on his midday break? Why do the boys fight? (Chapter 7)_____

   _____

   _____

4. Describe the conversation between Zau and Ranofer. How does this provide foreshadowing for the rest of the story? (Chapter 8) _____

   _____

   _____

5. What makes Ranofer think Gebu is stealing again? What can he do to learn how Gebu is getting rich? (Chapter 9)_____

   _____

   _____

6. Why is Ranofer afraid of the dark? (Chapter 9) _____

   _____

   _____

# Cartoon Dialogue

Use the cartoon format to show how well you understand one of the following scenes from the story:

1. Ranofer, Heqet, and the Ancient during their first lunch and fight.

2. Ranofer, Heqet, and Zau at the Master's gold shop.

3. Ranofer, Heqet, and the Ancient making plans to catch Gebu stealing.

Reread the scene you chose and plan each cartoon box carefully. Make sure your cartoon shows the characters' interactions, dialogue, and emotions with clear dialogue bubbles and colorful pictures.

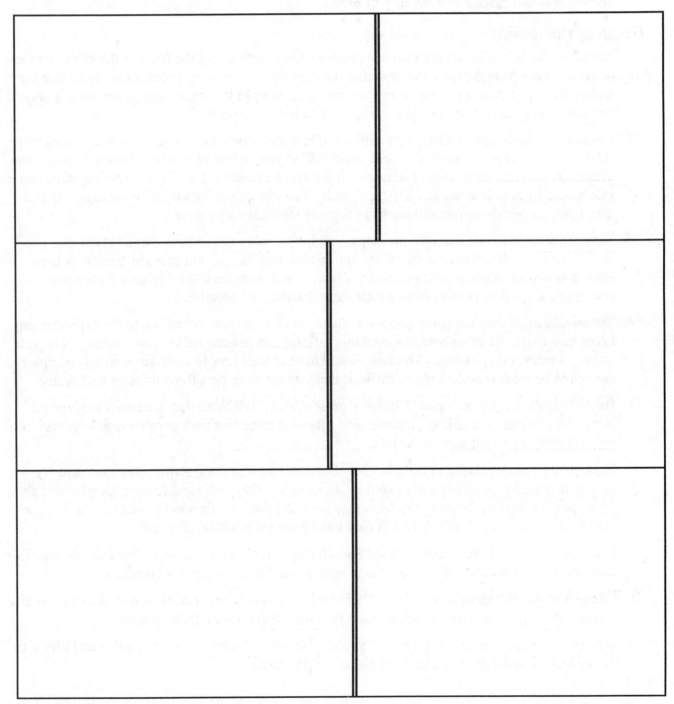

# Can You Explain?

Ranofer seems to know how to do things in the gold shop that most boys today don't. Have students notice that the author is so detailed in her descriptions of the steps for gold making that you can visualize exactly what is happening. Have your students prepare and give a demonstration speech that describes something that they are good at.

## Preparing for the lesson:

1. Gather bread, peanut butter, jelly, knife, and a paper plate for your demonstration.

2. Reproduce a copy of the "Speech Organizer" and "Speech Evaluation Form" (pages 207 and 208) for students and make a transparency of each.

## Teaching the lesson:

1. Introduce the lesson by setting your sandwich-making materials in the front of the class. Review some passages from the book that describe some of the gold-making procedures. Note that the author could not draw a picture or use gestures to help make the steps clear. Therefore, it was important that she be very detailed and specific in her descriptions.

2. Demonstrate to students exactly how difficult it is to describe a task. Ask a volunteer to come to the front of the class. Have the student stand behind you so that he or she cannot influence your actions by pointing or making gestures. Tell the volunteer he or she will describe the steps that go into making a peanut butter and jelly sandwich. You will do only what he or she says, and if the directions are not clear, you will interpret them as logically as possible.

3. Have the student slowly describe the steps; you follow them as you hear them. Make sure you show how some directions can be misinterpreted because they do not provide specific details. Have a new student come forward and try again. Elicit from the class that each time a new student tries, the directions become much more detailed and specific.

4. Tell students that they are going to have a chance to demonstrate something to the class that they know how to do. The task could be cooking, a simple art project, building something, playing a game—whatever they choose. The task should have at least four to eight steps so it is complex enough to be interesting, but not so difficult that it takes more than three minutes to describe.

5. Have students develop and make a how-to presentation. Tell them they will need to show the steps, use gestures, and talk at the same time. Remind them that they need enough information or relevant chat to prevent gaps in the talk.

6. Students may wish to bring in materials for their task and mime the steps rather than actually mixing ingredients or gluing parts together. In this case, they will need to have samples that show the different stages of the task. Students may wish to bring in a finished product of the food or item to share with the class. Tell them they must practice, practice, practice!

7. Using the overhead transparency of the "Speech Organizer" explain how students should organize their speeches. Distribute the organizers to students and assign dates for speeches.

8. Using the overhead transparency of the "Speech Evaluation Form" review it with the class so that students thoroughly understand what you expect from them during their speeches.

9. When the speeches are given, fill out a "Speech Evaluation Form" for each speaker and give it to the student for immediate feedback on his or her presentation.

# Speech Organizer

Name_____ Date of Speech _____

---

**Introduction**—Get the audience interested in your topic with a question, some trivia, a joke, or dramatization. Let the audience know what your speech is going to be about.

_____

_____

_____

_____

_____

---

**Body**—Give a clear description of events or steps; list materials, if necessary; and give supporting details for persuading or informing.

_____

_____

_____

_____

_____

_____

_____

---

**Conclusion**—Summarize or restate your main points. End with a strong closing statement.

_____

_____

_____

_____

---

# Speech Evaluation Form

Speaker

**X** = No changes needed          ✔ = Just okay          ✱ = Problem.  Editor will help make corrections.

Place an evaluation mark in each category, along with some constructive comments.

## Speech Format:

❑  Introduction (background to gain interest) _____

❑  Body (specific supporting details) _____

❑  Conclusion (summary and closing statement) _____

## Speaking Technique:

❑  Voice Expression (volume, speed, and inflection) _____

❑  Sentence Structure (clear and complete sentences, without run-ons) _____

❑  Correct Grammar _____

❑  Eye Contact (look at audience)_____

❑  Appropriate Hand Gestures _____

❑  Visual Aids (props, pictures) _____

❑  Prepared and Rehearsed (smooth delivery) _____

❑  Time Limit (3–5 minutes)_____

Best part of the speech:_____

_____

_____

_____

Suggestions for improvement: _____

_____

_____

_____

Evaluator: _____

# Autobiographical Incident

Ranofer goes with Heqet to Zau's gold shop in hopes of finding a way out of his unhappy situation. Zau tells Ranofer that he must reshape his life into another form. Only then will he consider taking him as a pupil. Although Ranofer is discouraged, this also makes him understand that he can no longer be a victim and must do something himself if he is ever to reach his dream.

Using this scene as an example, have your students think of a time in their lives when they were inspired to do something or change their way of thinking.

## Preparing for the lesson:

1. Create overhead transparencies of "The Writing Process" (page 24) and the "Autobiographical Incident Organizer" (page 21).

2. Reproduce an "Editing Checklist" (page 25) and an "Autobiographical Incident Organizer" for each student.

## Teaching the lesson:

1. Discuss the scene mentioned above, in which Ranofer goes to Zau. Write the word "Inspire" on the chalkboard or overhead. Discuss the meaning of this word and how a person or event might inspire someone to want to change. Provide examples of famous instances of people (in religion, sports, business, etc.) inspired to change their lives.

2. Have students think of a time in their lives when someone or some event has made them want to change their lives or try for new goals. Tell them that they each will be writing a composition describing this inspirational person or event.

3. Display the transparency for "The Writing Process" and discuss the steps with students.

4. Distribute the "Autobiographical Incident Organizer" and tell students to use it for their prewriting. Review the format.

   - Start with an introduction that states the main idea and tells the reader the purpose of the composition.

   - The body of the composition should give plenty of supporting details that are arranged in a logical and sequential order. Elaborate by using descriptive language, such as metaphors, similes, and personification, as well as descriptive examples, adjectives, adverbs, and prepositional phrases.

   - The conclusion should summarize the main idea of the composition and explain why the person or event was so inspiring.

5. Have students use the organizer to begin writing. Distribute the "Editing Checklists" and remind students how to use the checklist to improve their rough drafts.

6. After students have completed their final drafts, have them read aloud to the class their compositions. Compare and contrast the different inspirations for change. How are these people or events different or similar to those that inspired Ranofer?

# Autobiographical Incident Organizer

Ranofer goes with Heqet to Zau's gold shop in hopes of finding a way out of his unhappy situation. Zau tells Ranofer that he must reshape his life into another form. Only then will he consider taking him as a pupil. Although Ranofer is discouraged, this also makes him understand that he can no longer be a victim and must do something himself if he is ever to reach his dream. Since Zau is someone whom Ranofer respects, he has inspired him to take steps to change his life.

Think of a time in your life when someone or some event has inspired you to learn something new, to change your way of doing something, or to strive for a goal. Write a composition about its effect on your life. Use this page to organize your information to be sure the reader will understand what happened, when and where it happened, the reactions and feelings of the people involved, and why this incident is especially memorable to you.

**Introduction/Opening Statement:** Lets the reader know what you are going to talk about.

_____

_____

_____

_____

**Specific Supporting Details/Sequence Statements**: Includes a clear sequence of events, describes when and where the inspiration took place, and gives the reactions and feelings of the people who are involved.

1. _____

2. _____

3. _____

4. _____

5. _____

**Conclusion/Summary Statements:** Wrap up your composition by describing at least three reasons why this incident was especially memorable and inspiring to you. Then give a strong closing statement.

_____

_____

_____

_____

# Vocabulary

| Chapter 10 | Chapter 11 | Chapter 12 |
|---|---|---|
| stealth | astounded | devastatingly |
| ceased | preoccupation | console |
| conceivably | malice | |
| inexplicable | | |
| conjured | | |
| exasperated | | |
| dawdled | | |

## Comprehension Questions

1. What does Ranofer ask that sends Gebu into a rage?  (Chapter 10)_____

_____

_____

2. Why are the people happy that the waters of the Nile are rising again?  (Chapter 10)

_____

_____

3. How does Ranofer discover where Gebu is getting his wealth? (Chapter 10)

_____

_____

4. What is the Ancient's papyrus used for?  (Chapter 10)_____

_____

_____

5. Gebu begins acting differently towards Ranofer.  Why?  (Chapter 11) _____

_____

_____

6. What happens to the golden goblet?  (Chapter 12)_____

_____

_____

7. Why does Ranofer have to follow Gebu?  (Chapter 12) _____

_____

_____

# Secrets

In Chapter 12, Ranofer is very distressed because he knows a secret about Gebu. He wants to tell someone what he knows, but he is afraid of the consequences. Have students describe times in their lives when they had secrets that they were dying to tell. Tell them to explain the situations in which they learned the secrets, what they did once they had the secret information, and what happened when they finally told someone else their secrets.

Discuss the situations as a class and compare them with Ranofer's secret. How are the feelings and consequences the same? How are they different? If your students could give advice to Ranofer based on their own personal experiences, what would that be?

## Chapter Dramas

Check your students' skills at inference by having them dramatize one of the following:

- **Chapter 10**—where Gebu went and what he did the night Ranofer found the golden goblet
- **Chapter 10**—what Gebu and Wenamon discussed during their secret meeting in the stone shop
- **Chapter 11**—the fight between Setma and Gebu at the fish docks
- **Chapter 12**—what Heqet, Ranofer, and the Ancient discussed when they talked about the High Nile Festival

Divide the class into eight groups. Assign each group a scene to reenact. There will be two groups for each scene. Tell students that they will have to use clues from the story to come up with logical dialogues for their scenes.

Have students write their dramatizations and practice them. Have students bring in basic costumes and props for their scenes. If you wish, students can wear large name tags instead of costumes. Have each group perform their drama.

After each performance, discuss how logical their situation appeared to be. Was it based on the story? Could that conversation have actually happened? Also discuss the differences or similarities between groups who performed the same scene. How did each group interpret the situation?

Have students check their dramas for accuracy as they read the rest of the story.

# Design a Golden Goblet

Ranofer finds a golden goblet from a pharaoh's tomb. Have students design and decorate their own goblets, using the etching technique.

## Preparing for the lesson:

1. Gather 9" x 12" (23 cm x 30 cm) sheets of yellow and royal blue construction paper, scratch paper the same size, and thick yellow crayons.

2. Mix white and black tempera paint together to make a silver-gray color. Do not add water. Gather paint containers and thick tempera brushes to apply the paint.

3. Gather etching implements such as scissors, mechanical pencils without lead, or large paper clips bent open.

4. Cover the work areas with large sheets of plastic or butcher paper to catch the paint and etching scrapings.

5. Look through books to gather examples of goblet shapes. Make a sample of your own to show the class as motivation for the project.

## Teaching the lesson:

1. Tell students that they are going to make golden goblets for the pharaoh. The first step is to prepare their sheets of gold. Distribute the yellow construction paper and the yellow crayons. Have students HEAVILY coat the entire page with crayon. It is best to work on one area on the paper until it is heavily coated and then move on to another area. There can be absolutely no construction paper showing through, or else the paint will not etch off.

2. Next, have students paint on a layer of silver tempera paint and let it dry. If the paper is coated properly, the paint will resist and not coat evenly. Repeat this paint and dry process one more time until the page is completely covered with silver paint.

3. While waiting for the paint to dry, show students examples of goblets. Distribute the scratch paper and have students sketch goblet designs. Tell students to make their goblets as tall as possible and to fill their pages. Have them add details to their goblets and decide which parts will be gold and which will be silver.

4. Once their final coats of paint are completely dry, have students place their sketches on top of the painted paper and trace over the lines heavily with their pencils. This will transfer their designs onto the painted surfaces.

5. Distribute the etching utensils. Describe and demonstrate to students the process of etching away the silver paint to reveal gold underneath. Have them etch the outlines of their goblets to show the gold and then etch the other golden parts onto them.

6. Once the goblets are completed, have students cut them out and glue them onto the sheets of royal blue paper. Display the goblets on a bulletin board.

# Vocabulary

| Chapter 13 | Chapter 14 | Chapter 15 | Chapter 16 |
|---|---|---|---|
| crevice | futile | precariously | bewildered |
| consternation | conviction | recklessly | |
| ominous | brandish | insolent | |
| apprehensive | | | |

## Comprehension Questions

1. What is the significance of the broken tree?  (Chapter 13)

   _____

2. Why doesn't Ranofer go to the Festival of the Nile?  (Chapter 13).

   _____

3. Why does Ranofer fall into the tomb?  What does he think the vulture was?  (Chapter 13)

   _____

4. How did Heqet and the Ancient discover where Ranofer had gone?  (Chapter 13)

   _____

5. How is Gebu able to plan a robbery?  (Chapter 13) _____

   _____

6. Describe the tomb and its contents.  (Chapter 14) _____

   _____

7. How does Ranofer figure out the owners of the tomb?  (Chapter 14)

   _____

   _____

8. How is Ranofer able to escape from Gebu in the tomb?  (Chapter 14)

   _____

9. When Ranofer runs into town, how does he finally get into the palace?  (Chapter 15)

   _____

10. Why do you think the dwarf comes to his rescue in the palace?  (Chapter 15)

    _____

11. How does the queen test Ranofer to make sure he is not lying about the tomb?  (Chapter 16)

    _____

12. How is Ranofer rewarded?  Why is this such a surprise to the royal court?  (Chapter 16)

    _____

13. What do you think happened to Wenamon and Gebu once they were caught?  Why?  (Chapter 16)

    _____

# You Write the Climax

The climactic scene from the story happens when Ranofer is discovered in the tomb with Gebu and must escape to get help. As a class, reread this scene and note how exciting and suspenseful the author makes it. Divide the class into groups. Have each group create a climactic scene of their own to replace the one written by the author. Tell the students exactly where to begin their scenes and where their scenes should end.

Allow students plenty of time to rewrite the scene. Then share as a class by reading from the book a few sentences leading up to the scene, by having students read their replacement climaxes, and then by finishing with sentences from the book again to end the scene. How logical and believable were the replacement scenes? How suspenseful were they? Which scenes were the most exciting? Why? Were any of the students' scenes better than the original? Which ones and why?

## Memory Test

When Ranofer told the queen about the tomb, she gave him a memory test to see if he was lying. How observant are your students? Would they have been able to pass the queen's test? Create an overhead transparency of "Memory Test" (page 216) and also reproduce it for students. Tell students they will test their own memories. Distribute a copy face down to students and tell them not to turn the page over until you say "Begin." Tell them they will have two minutes to study and try to remember as much about the picture as they can. Say "Begin" and have them turn over and study their pages. At the end of two minutes say "Stop" and tell students to turn their pages face down. Tell students you will read each question only one time, and they will have one minute to write the answer on the back of the paper.

1. What was the painting of on the west wall? (a fishing scene)
2. What was painted on the chest area of the central mummy? (a vulture)
3. What piece of furniture was sitting against the back (north) wall? (a chair)
4. What was painted on the backrest of this furniture? (a scarab)
5. What two items were propped up against the east wall? (a mummy case and a reed boat)
6. What scene was painted on the north wall? (weighing of the heart judgment scene)
7. What was in the chest sitting at the south end of the tomb? (jewelry and a collar)
8. What was written on the chest? (Precious One)
9. What filled the boxes sitting in the north end of the room? (clothing, toys, and shabtis)
10. What was on the tray between the sarcophagus and the boat along the east wall? (jug and cups)
11. What was on the couch along the west wall? (a mirror and comb)

When you have finished, have students take out correcting pens. Display the transparency and, with the class, answer each question.

9-11 correct—You pass with flying colors and are made head goldsmith for the queen!

6-8 correct—You pass and become an apprentice for Zau the goldsmith.

4-5 correct—Are you sure you were there? Your life will be spared, but you must go back to being a hireling at Rekh's shop.

3 or fewer correct—You must be lying about being in the tomb! You will be punished like a tomb robber, along with the evil ones Gebu and Wenamon!

# Memory Test *(cont.)*

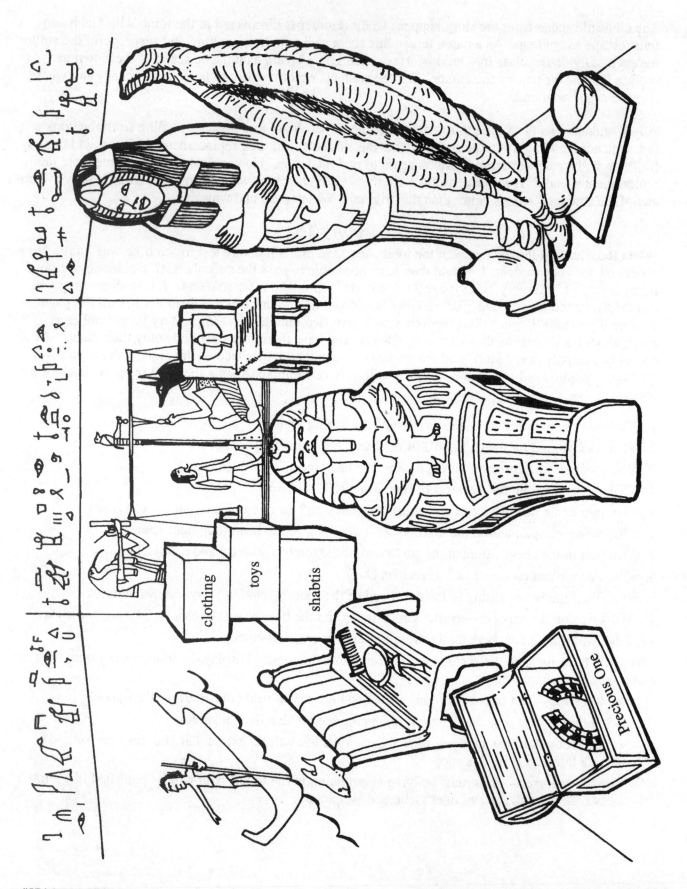

# Make a Story Map

Making a story map will help students review the plot and setting of the book.

## Preparing for the lesson:

1. Gather large sheets of butcher or drawing paper for each student.
2. Provide drawing materials, such as pens, crayons, pencils, and erasers.
3. Reproduce the Story Plot Outline (page 125) for students.

## Teaching the lesson:

1. Distribute the Story Plot Outlines. Allow students to work in groups to complete the outlines with the characters, setting, problems, obstacles, climax, and conclusion.
2. As a class discuss the different elements of the setting, such as the river, vegetation, streets, work areas, the palace, etc. Have students look in their books for descriptions of the setting while you record the various elements on the chalkboard or overhead.
3. Distribute the large sheets of paper. Have students write "Golden Goblet Story Map" at the tops of their papers. Instruct students to draw and label maps of the setting. Do not have students color their maps yet.
4. Once the maps have been drawn, tell students that they are going to turn their maps into story maps by writing the sequence of the story onto their maps. Have students pick a place on the maps to begin the story. Label this location #1 characters. Have students copy onto the map the descriptions of the characters they wrote on the Story Plot Outline.
5. Then have them go to a different location on the maps and label a #2 Setting. Have them copy the setting description at this location. Do the same for #3 Problem and for the different obstacles, climax, and conclusion.
6. Once the story sequence has been written on the maps have students color and outline their maps so that the sequence can be read and followed clearly. Tear the edges to make it look old.
7. Evaluate each map based on portrayal of the setting and also accuracy of the main sequence of the story. Display the maps on a bulletin board.

# Vocabulary Review

Write the word from the box that correctly completes each sentence.

1. The stream of molten gold flowed smoothly from the _____ to make a new gold ingot.

2. "Why can't I be an _____ like Heqet and pay to learn the gold trade?" asked Ranofer.

3. Winking _____ with a sense of revenge and punishment, Gebu made for the stairs, taking the torch with him.

4. The first craftsman yelled to Heqet and Ranofer. His _____ rang out across the courtyard.

5. Ranofer stared at the distant brown figures twisting and _____ against the white wall as if they were punished for robbing the tomb.

6. Ranofer was _____. He could not believe Gebu would sneak out at night without any fear of khefts.

7. Excited and _____ about meeting Heqet for lunch, he tucked an onion into his sash, along with half a bread loaf.

8. Ranofer practiced what he would say to Zau so that he would not come off as being a foolish _____.

9. The Ancient was skeptical and _____ about Ranofer's plan to catch Gebu.

10. The three friends made their way through the papyrus marsh secretly with great _____ so as to follow Wenamon without raising suspicion.

11. Ranofer waited, _____, for Gebu to make the next move, becoming more irritated and annoyed when nothing seemed to happen.

12. The three friends planned to meet the next day. They were disappointed that their spying had led to nothing, but at least they had the Festival to_____ them.

13. In the desert a large vulture flew up from behind a sinister and _____ rock pile, making Ranofer fall into the tomb.

14. Heqet and the Ancient became discouraged while looking for Ranofer in the vast desert. Their search seemed useless and _____.

15. A heavy hand slammed across Ranofer's face. "_____! How disrespectful and bold to speak the name of the queen," roared the gardener upon finding Ranofer.

| | | | |
|---|---|---|---|
| stealth | devise | ceased | incredulous |
| aghast | conjured | crucible | ominous |
| jubilant | imbecile | console | inexplicable |
| insolent | collided | dubious | vindictively |
| dawdled | futile | scant | exasperated |
| bellow | lithe | writhing | apprentice |

# Plot Problems

Answer the following questions, using complete and well-elaborated sentences.

1. What is the main problem of the story? _____
   _____

2. Name at least three obstacles Ranofer has to overcome throughout the story._____
   _____

3. Why do you think Heqet and the Ancient befriended Ranofer?_____
   _____

4. How is life different for Ranofer when living with Gebu instead of his father? Give at least three
   examples. _____
   _____

5. What clues lead Ranofer to believe his brother is stealing from tombs? _____
   _____

6. What scene would be considered the climax of the story?_____
   _____

7. How would the plot of the story be different if it had happened in modern times? Give at least
   three examples. _____
   _____

8. What have you learned about life in Ancient Egypt from reading this book? Name at least two
   things._____
   _____

9. With which character do you identify most? Why?_____
   _____

## Match the following descriptions of the characters to their names:

10. Ibni

11. Heqet

12. Gebu

13. Ranofer

14. Setma

15. Zau

16. Wenamon

17. The Ancient

a. He wanted to become a goldsmith, but his half-brother wouldn't allow it.

b. A boat captain, he plotted to rob the tombs and smuggle the goods.

c. A Babylonian, he stole gold from Rekh's shop, using wineskins.

d. The partner of Gebu who went with him to rob the tomb; he was a mason.

e. He was an apprentice at the gold shop who became Ranofer's best friend.

f. This famous goldsmith inspired Ranofer to change his life.

g. Ranofer's cruel half-brother who was caught robbing the tomb.

h. This friend of Ranofer's cut papyrus along the river banks.

# Answer Key

## Comprehension Questions Chapters 1–3 (page 194)

1. Ranofer cannot actually make things out of gold or stop to watch the craftsman as he shows the other apprentices how to do things. He is only responsible for pouring ingots, sweeping, and making charcoal, so he will never improve his goldmaking skills.

2. Ranofer learns the only reason he is working in the gold shop is to help steal small portions of gold for Gebu.

3. Heqet and the Ancient are Ranofer's friends. He met Heqet at the gold shop and met the Ancient while walking through the papyrus marshes.

4. Gebu beats Ranofer for telling him about the wineskin. (Accept reasonable answers for the second part.)

5. Accept reasonable answers.

6. Making gold leaves. He used the gold wire and blow pipe to fashion 50 leaves by melting the wire and hitting it with a mallet.

7. He beat Ranofer again and threatened to take him out of the gold shop and make him an apprentice at the stonecutter's shop. (Accept any reasonable answers for the second part.)

## Comprehension Questions Chapters 4–6 (page 199)

1. Accept reasonable answers.

2. The wealthier you were, the more elaborate burial you received. All were was mummified and buried with items for their afterlife. Wealthy individuals had rooms full of items and intricate funeral ceremonies.

3. Accept reasonable answers.

4. If the tomb was robbed the person could not enjoy a happy afterlife.

5. Gebu wants to keep his eye on Ranofer and get some use from him. Now that Ibni is no longer stealing gold for Gebu, he has no use for Ranofer in the gold shop. Ranofer decides that he will get his own donkey and become a papyrus cutter like the Ancient. That way he could live on his own.

6. Ranofer is treated like an imbecile at the stonecutter's shop, since he knows nothing about the trade. (Accept reasonable answers for the second part.)

7. The Egyptians believed khefts, or evil spirits, flew around at night and would harm you. They also believed a dead person's spirit or ba could come and visit.

## Comprehension Questions Chapters 7–9 (page 204)

1. Heqet would meet Ranofer for lunch and describe everything that he learned from the gold shop.

2. The spring is harvest time, and all men are required to go work in the fields.

3. Ranofer is excited to learn more about the gold trade. They get in a fight because Ranofer thinks Heqet is showing pity for him because of his food.

4. Zau tells Ranofer that he must reshape his life before he can come to apprentice for him. This lets the reader know that for the rest of the story Ranofer will become braver and try to change his situation with Gebu.

5. Ranofer notices that Gebu has many new things. He decides to spy on him and see what he is doing to get his new wealth.

6. Ranofer is afraid of khefts in the night.

# Answer Key *(cont.)*

## Comprehension Questions Chapters 10–12 (page 211)

1. Ranofer asks about a little room on the blueprints, which makes Gebu very angry.

2. When the Nile rises again, that means they can travel down the river to trade. It also is a sign of renewal in that the river brings fresh silt for their fields.

3. Ranofer finds in his room a golden goblet with the inscriptions of a famous pharaoh.

4. The Ancient's papyrus is used for making boats and other items.

5. Gebu is acting differently toward Ranofer because he is preoccupied with the goblet and how to smuggle it out of town.

6. Gebu takes the goblet to the stonecutter's shop and hides it in the scroll room.

7. Ranofer follows Gebu to find out how he is stealing. If he can get more information, he can go to the authorities about Gebu and get rid of him forever.

## Comprehension Questions Chapters 13–16 (page 214)

1. The broken tree is a marker to help find the tomb.

2. Ranofer follows Gebu and Wenamon to the tomb instead of going to the festival.

3. Ranofer is startled by a big vulture and tripped into the tomb. (Accept any reasonable answer for the second part.)

4. Heqet and the Ancient review things Ranofer had said to them and discover that he must have found out Gebu was stealing from the tomb.

5. Gebu has access to all of the plans about the building of the tomb.

6. The tomb is filled with furniture, coffins, and food offerings.

7. Ranofer is able to read the hieroglyphics to discover the owners of the tomb.

8. Ranofer throws a box of gems at Gebu, making him drop the torch. At the opening he rolls the big rock back into place.

9. Ranofer climbs over the wall to get into the palace.

10. (Accept reasonable answers.)

11. She gives him a memory test by asking him what was located on the north wall of the chamber.

12. Ranofer is offered anything he could ask for. The others are surprised because he asked for such a small reward, showing what a good yet simple person that he is.

13. (Accept reasonable answers.)

## Vocabulary (page 218)

1. crucible, 2. apprentice, 3. vindictively, 4. bellow, 5. writhing, 6. incredulous, 7. jubilant, 8. imbecile, 9. dubious, 10. stealth, 11. exasperated, 12. console, 13. ominous, 14. futile, 15. insolent

## Plot Problems (page 219)

1.–9. (Accept reasonable answers,) 10. c, 11. e, 12. g, 13. a, 14. b, 15. f, 16. d, 17. h

# Technology Bibliography

## Videos

**Ancient Wisdom; Giants for the Gods**—from Arthur C. Clark's Mysterious World, v. 5, Beverly Hills, CA, Pacific Arts Video, 1989, ©1980.

This is a re-evaluation of ancient technology. (60 minutes)

**Egypt, Quest for Eternity**—National Geographic Society and WQED/Pittsburgh Stamford, CT, Vestron Video, 1987, ©1982

Egyptologists travel to the temples of Luxor and Karnak to unravel and interpret the riddle of Egypt's past. (60 minutes)

**The Nile**—French Television

Burbank, CA, Warner Home Video, 1979

This Cousteau Odyssey documents a 10-month saga down the longest river on earth. (116 minutes)

**Egypt, Land of Ancient Wonders**

San Ramon, CA, International Video Network, 1993

Take a tour of Egypt's natural wonders, including historical and cultural sites. (61 minutes)

**Mysteries of the Pyramids**—LBS Pyramids Inc.

Rochester, NY, Eastman Kodak Co., 1988

Look into the secret passageways and chambers of the Great Pyramids of Egypt. (52 minutes)

**Pyramid**—Unicorn Projects and David Macauley

New York, NY, Dorset Video, ©1988

Based on the book *Pyramid* by David Macauley, this program explores the geography, history, archaeology, and mythology of Ancient Egypt as background for the examination of the Egyptian pyramids. (60 minutes)

**Secrets of the Mummy**—FR3 Lyon TV on the Learning Channel

Bethesda, MD, Discovery Channel 1994, ©1987

This program discusses what the study of mummies reveals about the Ancient Egyptians. It also shows an autopsy of a mummy. (46 minutes)

**Egypt: 5000 Years Fascination**—Filmpro Filmund Video-Productions

New York, NY, VPI/AC Video, 1991, ©1985

This Artful Journey Series is designed to give both visitors and art lovers a complete overview of Egypt's past splendors. (60 minutes)

## Compact Discs

**Ancient Egypt, Middle East, and Greece**—World History Series by Queue

IBM396 and Multimedia PC, (MPC) Macintosh

MS-DOS 3.1 + Microsoft Windows 3.0 + Apple HFS

This highly interactive tutorial is designed to teach students the nature and achievements of early civilizations. It includes stunning photographs of architectural remains, as well as vase paintings, sculpture, and artifacts of these cultures.

**The Egyptian Pyramids**—Great Wonders of the World: Manmade (series)

Inter Optica Publishing

Apple Computer, Inc.

Multimedia PC (MPC), Macintosh LC/+Microsoft Windows 3.1/+, Apple HFS 6.0.7/+

This disc contains a multimedia presentation of the great pyramids of Egypt.

# Technology Bibliography *(cont.)*

## Compact Discs *(cont.)*

**The Time Table of History:** Arts and Entertainment

Xiphias

Compton's New Media/Sony Data Discman, Electronic Book

This disc contains over 4,300 stories from the first cave paintings to today's computer-generated graphics.

### Nile: Passage to Egypt—The Discovery Channel

The Discovery Channel 7700 Wisconsin, Suite 700 Bethesda, MD 20814-3579
Windows CD-ROM, 484 SX or higher
Macintosh CD-ROM System 7.0 or better.
This disc includes an introduction to the geography and history of the Nile. It includes the game of *Senet.*

## Software—All Apple II Family and Compatibles

### Crypto Q2uest—MECC

Similar to decoding hieroglyphics, players practice various methods of enciphering and deciphering messages provided by the computer, themselves, or a friend. Players then follow a trail of clues that lead them to the final secret document.

### Wood Car Rally—MECC

Players investigate the effects that five variables will have on the distance a car will travel once it leaves an inclined plane. Students are then challenged to find a set of conditions that will make a car travel a given distance. This is a good program to reinforce the use of simple machines.

### Caravans to Timbuktu—MECC

Players are sent on a mission by a king who provides them with a gift to deliver. To deliver the gift, students must traverse 16th century Africa seeking information and trading along the way. Students will learn about the history, geography, and cultures of the African Continent.

### Time Navigator Around the World—MECC

Players are sent back to a random point in history from 3999 B.C. to the present and must make their way forward in time by choosing which item from various categories is the most recent. Categories include arts and literature, artifacts, headlines, conversations, and people.

## Software—Macintosh

**Wood Car Rally**—MECC (See description for Apple II)

### Miner's Cave—MECC

Players stumble upon carts of jewels abandoned in a cave. However, they must determine which simple machine will work within the given space to lift the load while making maximum use of the amount of force available. The choices for simple machines include pulley, lever, inclined plane, or wheel and axle. Excellent program for experimentation with load, force, and the different benefits of each type of simple machine.

### Sim Earth: The Living Planet—Maxis

This program gives players control over the evolution of a planet from the origin of life to the development of intelligence, civilizations, and interplanetary travel. Players can create their own planet or use one of seven prebuilt planets.

# Bibliography

Crouch, William. *Life in Ancient Egypt*. Derrydale Books, 1990.

Harris, Geraldine. *Ancient Egypt Cultural Atlas for Young People*. Facts on File, 1990.

Koenig, Viviane and Veronique Agerges. *The Ancient Egyptians*. The Millbrook Press, 1992.

Lattimore, Deborah. *Digging Into the Past*. Educational Insights, 1986.

Millard, Anne. *Ancient Egypt*. Warwick Press, 1979.

Morley, Jaqueline, Mark Bergin, and John James. *An Egyptian Pyramid*. Peter Bedrick Books, 1991.

Nicholson, Robert and Claire Watts. *Journey into Civilization, Ancient Egypt*. Chelsea House Publishers, 1994.

Odyk, Pamela. *The Ancient World, The Egyptians*. Silver Burdett Press, 1989.

Payne, Elizabeth. *The Pharaohs of Ancient Egypt*. Random House, 1982.

Purdy, Susan and Cass R. Sandak. *Ancient Egypt, A Civilization Project Book*. Franklin Watts, 1982.

Reeves, Nicholas. *Into the Mummy's Tomb*. Scholastic, 1993.

Wright, Rachel. *Egyptians*. Franklin Watts, 1992.

## Resource and Reference Materials

Allen, Tony. *The Time Traveller Book of Pharaohs and Pyramids*. EDC Publishing, 1992.

Boase, Wendy. *Ancient Egypt*. Gloucester Press, 1978.

Crosher, Judith. *Ancient Egypt*. Viking Penguin, 1993.

Davis, Kenneth C. *Don't Know Much About Geography*. William Morrow and Company, 1992.

Edwards, I.E.S. *Treasures of Tutankhamen*. Ballantine Books, 1978.

Halliburton, Richard. *Book of Marvels*. Bobbs-Merrill Company, Inc., 1960.

Houston, James D. *Writing from the Inside*. Addison-Wesley Publishing Company, Inc., 1973.

Ions, Veronica. *Egyptian Mythology*. Paul Hamlyn, 1968.

Milton, Joyce. *Secrets of the Mummies*. Random House, 1984.

Rosicrucian Egyptian Museum. *The Egyptian Alphabet*. 1990.

Schar, Grant. *Making Mummies*. Rosicrucian Egyptian Museum, 1991.